21·97
$19

D1112697

Caring

'In this finely nuanced book, Peta Bowden develops a picture of caring as the intricate skill and intelligent practice that many feminists have asserted it to be; yet few have demonstrated the point so well. The writing is consistently excellent, the style accessible, as Bowden moves through an impressive range of literature to effect innovative connections across caring practices and the ethical issues they invoke.'

Lorraine Code, *York University, Canada*

In *Caring* Peta Bowden extends and challenges recent debates on feminist ethics. She takes issue with accounts of the ethics of care that focus on alleged basic principles of caring, rather than analysing caring in practice. Caring, Bowden argues, must be understood by 'working through examples'.

Following this approach, Bowden explores four main caring practices: mothering, friendship, nursing and citizenship. Her analysis of the differences and similarities in these practices – their varying degrees of intimacy and reciprocity, formality and informality, vulnerability and choice – reveals the practical complexity of the ethics of care.

Caring recognizes that ethical practices constantly outrun the theories that attempt to explain them, and Bowden's unique approach provides major new insights into the nature of care without resorting to indiscriminate unitary models. It will be essential reading for all those interested in ethics, gender studies, nursing and the caring professions.

Peta Bowden is Lecturer in Philosophy at Murdoch University, Western Australia.

Caring

Gender-sensitive ethics

Peta Bowden

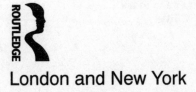

London and New York

First published 1997
by Routledge
11 New Fetter Lane, London EC4P 4EE

Simultaneously published in the USA and Canada
by Routledge
29 West 35th Street, New York, NY 10001

Typeset in Times by
Ponting–Green Publishing Services, Chesham,
Buckinghamshire
Printed and bound in Great Britain by
Clays Ltd, St Ives PLC

British Library Cataloguing in Publication Data
A catalogue record for this book is available from the
British Library

Library of Congress Cataloging in Publication Data
Bowden, Peta
    Caring: Gender-sensitive ethics/
    Peta Bowden.
            p.   cm.
    Includes bibliographical references and index.
    1. Caring.   2. Feminist ethics.   I. Title.
    BJ1475.B68   1996
    177'.7–dc20   96–5488

    ISBN   0–415–13383–1 (hbk)
    ISBN   0–415–13384–X (pbk)

Contents

Acknowledgements

It is a great pleasure to thank the many people who have helped me with this book. I would like to express special thanks to Jim Tully. His continuing intellectual stimulus and inspiration has been the single most important contribution to this work. Thanks are also due to my friends and colleagues, especially to Judith Anketell, Sue Ashford, Natalie Brender, Sandra Gottlieb, Sheila Mason, Iola Sise and Sally Talbot, for their unflagging support, intellectual insight and creative caring. To the women of The Alumnae Society of McGill University I also owe a great debt. Their hard work and their commitment to the advancement of women in higher education resulted in the fellowship that provided most of the financial support for this project.

In the final stages of the project I have also received support from the Australian Research Council Small Grants Scheme and the School of Humanities Research Assistance Fund, Murdoch University. I would like to thank Sally Talbot for her excellent research assistance, for reading every word (several times!) and for her perceptive comments. And I am grateful to Sue Ashford for applying her special critical attentiveness to reading the whole work, and to Gerard Hill for his careful and thoughtful reading of the typescript. In addition, I have benefited from the convivial and encouraging atmosphere at Murdoch University.

Sections of this book have been published elsewhere. Parts of the introduction appeared in 'Theoretical care: feminism, theory and ethics', *The Critical Review*, 1993, no. 33, pp. 129–47; parts of Chapter 4 have been published in 'The ethics of nursing care and "the ethic of care"', *Nursing Inquiry*, 1995, vol. 2, pp. 10–21. I thank the editors and reviewers of these publications for their comments and permission to reprint this material here. I am also grateful to three anonymous reviewers for Routledge and my Routledge editors, Adrian Driscoll, Emma Davis and Michael Leiser, for invaluable suggestions and assistance. Judith Anketell responded to a call from a friend with her artistic exuberance and intelligence.

Most of all, my thanks to Dick Ounsworth. He has discussed ideas with me, listened to my complaints, calmed my anxieties, laboured at the word processor, and given more intellectual and emotional companionship than I ever imagined was possible.

Abbreviations

FAM   L. Blum, *Friendship, Altruism and Morality*, London, Rout-
      ledge & Kegan Paul, 1980.

FNE   P. Benner, *From Novice to Expert: Excellence and Power in
      Clinical Nursing*, Menlo Park, California, Addison-Wesley,
      1984.

FPP   A. Rossiter, *From Private to Public: A Feminist Exploration
      of Early Mothering*, Toronto, The Women's Press, 1986.

MAD   M. Minow, *Making All the Difference: Inclusion, Exclusion
      and American Law*, Ithaca, New York, Cornell University
      Press, 1990.

MF   S. Miller, *Men and Friendship*, Boston, Houghton Mifflin
      Company, 1983.

MT   S. Ruddick, *Maternal Thinking: Toward a Politics of Peace*,
      Boston, Beacon Press, 1989.

NE   Aristotle, *Nicomachean Ethics*, trans. W.D. Ross, Oxford,
      Oxford University Press, 1925.

PC   P. Benner and J. Wrubel, *The Primacy of Caring: Stress
      and Coping in Health and Illness*, Menlo Park, California,
      Addison-Wesley, 1989.

PF   J.G. Raymond, *A Passion for Friends: Toward a Philosophy
      of Female Affection*, Boston, Beacon Press, 1986.

PI   L. Wittgenstein, *Philosophical Investigations*, 2nd edn, trans.
      G.E.M. Anscombe, Oxford, Basil Blackwell, 1958.

Introduction

> We feel as if we had to *penetrate* phenomena: our investigation,
> however, is directed not towards phenomena, but, as one might
> say, towards the '*possibilities*' of phenomena.
>
> – Ludwig Wittgenstein[1]

I

My starting point is the intuition that caring is ethically important.
Caring expresses ethically significant ways in which we matter to
each other, transforming interpersonal relatedness into something
beyond ontological necessity or brute survival. This is a rather
vague perception, I know, and I have deliberately articulated it in
such general terms in part to gain the widest possible acceptance
for it. For the most general purpose of this work is to motivate
comprehensive philosophical interest in the ethical possibilities
of caring.

Vagueness, however, is not meant to ensure an unassailable
truth; it is the starting point for both the substantive and conceptual orientations of this work. For the absence of specificity
immediately raises a host of questions concerning the actual range
and detail of the insight. What goes as caring and what is
understood as its ethical significance are by no means indisputable
in any particular case. For some theorists, for example, caring is
an activity that includes all that we do to sustain the best possible
lives;[2] for others, caring may signify the justification of colonizers
for the subjugation of distant foreigners;[3] for still others, caring
inevitably leads to endless self-sacrifice.[4] These conflicting understandings point to a whole spectrum of issues concerning the
nature of caring, the variety of relationships in which it is

practised, the circumstances, aims and purposes of those relations, and the ways in which differing circumstances affect their ethical significance. It is to these questions that my investigation of the ethical possibilities of caring is addressed.

Interest in the ethics of care is, of course, not new on the contemporary landscape of moral philosophy, especially to those familiar with recent developments in feminist ethics. And this enquiry shares the feminist insight that connects the ethical significance of caring with sensitivity to the morally repugnant biases produced by a tradition that persistently favours interests associated with men at the expense of those characteristically ascribed to women. I depart from the main corpus of feminist work on the ethics of care, however, on the basis of certain methodological concerns. Briefly, my motivating claim is that current analyses of the ethical imports of caring frequently forget the epistemological insights of the practices of care from which they emerge. Caring highlights the ways in which ethical practices outrun the theories that attempt to explain them. My concern is that the very real challenge of caring ethics to the moral reductions produced by conventional ethical theories is frequently lost in accounts that tend to reaffirm caring itself as yet another universal and unitary moral concept.[5] I worry that the radical call to attend to the complex ethical possibilities of interpersonal relationships is subverted by moves to penetrate the essence of care. My aim, then, is to reorient interest in the ethics of care by directing attention to the multiplicity and diversity of its practice in a variety of examples of specific caring relations – namely, mothering, friendship, nursing and citizenship. Thus, this investigation is directed 'not towards phenomena' but, in Wittgenstein's words, 'towards the "*possibilities*" of phenomena'.

The important issue here is my claim that the substantive impact of the project is intimately connected with its epistemological stance. And since I believe that these connections are so frequently overlooked or misunderstood, the remainder of this introduction is largely concerned with tracing their significance. For some readers my emphasis on epistemology may be rather abstruse. Rather than following my explanation of its rationale, they may wish to plunge straight into the treatments of specific practices in Chapters 1 to 4. For other readers, conversant with the development of feminist reflections on caring, the following sketch of the theoretical context of my concerns in this section and in Section II of the Introduction will be well trodden ground.[6] I return to it here, not only for that vast majority of philosophers who are not familiar with this body of work, but also to highlight the significance of the epistemological challenges that my enquiry seeks to express.

At its core my interest in the ethics of caring is shaped in a fundamental way by a global concern for the distortions of grand theory-making in moral philosophy. The difficulties relate to deformations in understanding that emerge from moral theories that self-confidently presume their own universality and impartiality. While it is unjust and cavalier to compress an enormous range of radically different views of morality into a single orientation, this outlook may be seen in strikingly explicit terms in Henry Sidgwick's *The Methods of Ethics*.[7] The determinate goal of *The Methods* is to systematize moral understanding under precise, unified, comprehensive and universal ideals that would rid judgements of the uncertainties and discrepancies inherent in actual circumstances, personal aspirations and desires, and pragmatic considerations. In such methodologies, attention to the messy contingencies of concrete situations is set aside in favour of the theoretical project of organizing moral knowledge under general principles and rules of conduct that exhibit the exactness and formality of mathematics. Unique and definitive answers to moral questions can then be provided by subsuming particular cases under the relevant principles. The point is that these methodological ambitions result in a notion of moral understanding that assumes that universal and impartial ethical codes in themselves give answers to particular, concrete questions of morality; and that the rightness or wrongness of specific judgements is entailed in their general rules and principles.[8]

The alternative approach that shapes my investigation develops from two main lines of reaction to this tradition. The first relates to the reductive tendencies of 'grand theory' according to which the dynamic complexity and diversity of specific situations, and the particular needs, desires, intellectual and emotional habits of the persons participating in them, are theorized in common terms. In contrast, I emphasize the ethical irreducibility of specific situations. According to the view I endorse, no single theory can be created to subsume all instances, no moral concept can catch the essence of all of its uses, and no moral judgement can be expected to resolve a particular conflict without leaving further ethically significant aspects in its train. Instead, understanding is

directed towards consideration of the particularity of concrete
situations, and their complex interconnections in the fabric of their
unique participants' lives. Ethics is recognized as constitutively
contextual and based in the actual experiences of actual persons:
it is a continuous process of mutual responses and adjustments
that recognizes the inherent relationship between the practical
details of that process of mutual response and its ethical possibilities.

The second, intersecting line of concern relates to the alleged
objectivity of principled thinking. Here difficulties stem, not from
the inadequacy of universalizing theories to catch the plenitude
of moral life in their codes, but from their impartialist pretensions.
The focus of discontent is the assumption that moral philosophy
attains truths whose veracity is unbiased by the specific cultural
and socio-historical conditions that shape their authors' interests.
Many theorists have argued persuasively that, regardless of the
form of their expression,[9] such assumptions rely on notions of
philosophical purity and of the conceptual coherence of the
practical world they represent – notions that conceal the partiality
of their motivating structures and purposes. As Bernard Williams
has remarked, although ethical ideals can be seen as elaborations
of pre-cultural conditions, 'a claim to the effect that a particular
conception lies within our actual social space is basically a social
claim, not a conceptual one'. Pointing to the inevitable distance
between theoretical coherence and practical moral life, he continues: 'there is no necessary expectation that the world of ideas
and practices in which we find ourselves should conceptually
hang together, form one homogeneous ethical whole'.[10] Indeed,
the abysmal record of *a priori* reflection in the search for universals
that underlie the variety of human ethical practices seems warrant
enough for dismissing the impartialist claims of grand theory.

The unmasking of the illusion of atemporal, impartial moral
truth reveals how deeply moral philosophy is intricated in other,
more empirically oriented fields like psychology, sociology,
anthropology, linguistics, history and politics. Given these constitutive connections between ethical theories and studies of the
social contexts in which they arise, it is clear that progress in
thinking about ethical issues requires serious consideration of
what is entailed psychologically, socially and politically in living
a decent life in the modern world.[11] In addition to finely
honed analytical skills, successful moral philosophy demands

attentiveness to the cultural conditions in which that philosophy is envisaged. This approach to ethical understanding is integral to the chapters that follow; the investigation they chart aims to contribute to its vindication.

More importantly, however, this orientation underpins my central concern with gender sensitivity. For, as feminist philosophers have repeatedly shown, one of the most fundamental social processes regularly ignored by impartialist theories is the gendered ascription of distinctive social roles and concerns to different groups.[12] Recognition that ethical understanding involves attentiveness to the social conditions of life, therefore demands sensitivity to the ways in which gender impacts on the possibilities of values, and to the kinds of gendered experiences, interests, processes, needs and desires that conceptions of values characteristically include and exclude from their compass.[13] Currently the dominant tradition is focused primarily on the obligations owed universally and impartially in the kinds of relations that are typically associated with men. Given this focus, gender sensitivity requires an equal stress on the ethical implications of the special and 'partial' relations in which women are characteristically involved.

Here, not surprisingly, content and form – my substantive intuition and the methodological commitments of its investigation – converge. For personal practices of caring – the subject of this study – exemplify precisely the kinds of relations that are conventionally omitted from the canon of moral philosophy, as well as the kinds of ethical experience that are central to many women's lives. This connection, of course, is the basis for contemporary feminist reflection on the nature and ethical implications of caring.

I think it is important, however, not to infer that inattention to caring in the tradition is simply or necessarily the result of gender insensitivity. There are other important and interconnected reasons why caring may have been overlooked, which also contribute significantly to the motivation for this project. In particular, these include the reasons suggested by Wittgenstein when he observes that we often miss 'the aspects of things that are most important for us ... because of their simplicity and familiarity' (PI 129). The very common and everyday nature of our involvement in caring relations – from the deep intimacies of family relations to the innumerable, publicly exchanged gestures and words of personal significance that craft institutions and communities – produces an aura of invisibility. (The same insight might be applicable to gender bias as well.) As a consequence, the important ethical possibilities of practices of care tend largely to be taken for granted, or left out of explicit moral consideration or assimilated to more obvious concerns. Or when they are noticed, as in the case of health care, for example, these possibilities are reduced to their purely instrumental dimensions. Thus it is also with a view to bringing the 'ethics of everyday life' into light that this project has unfolded.[14]

Most immediately, however, this project takes its shape in relation to recent feminist discussions of caring relations, the exclusion of these relations from traditional theories, the links between this exclusion and gender bias, as well as the ethical significance of practices of care. Before going further, then, I want to clarify and elaborate the specific problematic within which my study is located, by reviewing the main contours of these discussions of the 'ethic of care'.

II

Philosophical reflection on the ethical significance of caring relations became popular following Carol Gilligan's research in moral psychology in the early 1980s.[15] In her studies of persons' understandings of their moral agency and the nature of certain moral dilemmas, Gilligan identified what she called a 'voice of care' as characteristic of many women's thinking about morality, in contrast to a 'justice' voice more typical of the responses she received from men. The caring perspective is distinguished by a concern for care, responsiveness and taking responsibility in interpersonal relationships, and by a context-sensitive mode of deliberation that resists abstract formulations of moral problems. According to the justice perspective, emphasis is placed on rights, duties and general obligations, while moral reasoning is marked by schematic understandings of moral problems that allow previously ordered rules and principles to be applied to particular moral cases.

Detecting commonalities between the justice perspective and the dominant conventions of moral theory, many feminist philosophers see Gilligan's work as providing support for challenges to those conventions. For despite controversies over the adequacy of her evidence for gender-related differences in ethical thought,[16]

Gilligan's identification of a significant, but overlooked, female voice has resonated strongly with critiques of traditional accounts of moral life based on the failure of those accounts to take women's ethical experience into consideration. As a result, many feminists have looked to the possibilities of a revalued 'ethic of care' as a ground for more inclusive moral theories.

Some discussions have taken up the project of revaluing and elaborating the nature and implications of care as an ethical concept.[17] Others have pursued in more detail the idea that the different ethical interests of women and men are created by the responsibilities of the different kinds of relationships in which they typically engage.[18] Many writers have also explored the connections between the justice and care perspectives in moral theory.[19] Still others take Gilligan's problematization of 'justice' models of moral theory as the starting point for recognition of the enormous complexity of moral experience.[20]

From the perspective of the canonical tradition, these discussions are fraught with problems. The strong connections between the 'ethic of care' and personal or informal relations have brought allegations that the ethical possibilities of caring are limited by their inapplicability in the public domain of impersonal relations. Following the traditional, and definitive, split that is presumed to divide public and private values, moral theorists have argued that since the 'ethic of care' is constitutively based in private relationships, it is incapable of translation into the impersonal values that are crucial to public relations. While caring may provide an inspiring ethical ground for personal practices, it is held to fail to fulfil the most fundamental requirements of a universalizable moral theory.[21]

More radical proponents of the public/private split have claimed that the concerns arising in personal relations, though they may be legitimate in terms of personal integrity, are not properly moral concerns at all; and thus, that caring practices have value only with respect to subjective desires and needs.[22] Other critics of the 'ethic of care' claim that its moral legitimacy is somehow secondary, parasitic, or inferior to impartialist moral theories. It is argued that caring considerations are fully encompassed within 'justice' theories; that personal attachments are supererogatory; that the development of care is psychologically dependent on the sense of justice; that, in cases of conflict, justice trumps care; that the validity of caring concerns rests ultimately on impartialist affirmations.[23]

Feminist theorists, too, have voiced considerable disquiet with endorsements of the care perspective, issuing strong warnings about the 'dangers of moral reclamation'.[24] It is observed that celebrations of the 'ethic of care' as the basis of women's moral agency fail to take into account the oppressive conditions in which many women's practices of caring occur. Feminists stress the damage that female carers have suffered from the relations of domination and exploitation in which their caring has been practised, and argue that the feminine values of care are little more than the symptoms of subordination and dependency, weak ego boundaries, and an inability to act autonomously. Women's caring is seen as a coerced practice on which their survival depends, and the values and perspectives it generates are seen as malformed commitments reminiscent of Nietzsche's slave moral-ity. Attentiveness, responsiveness and sensitivity to the needs of others are held to be either malformed techniques of the power-less, or masks for the deceit, cunning and manipulation that are the only defences of the socially vulnerable.[25] These critics note the typical lack of reciprocity in women's practices of care, the limited sets of relations in which caring is normally expected, and the ways in which practices of care may undermine integrity and ethical agency. The challenge directed to care theorists is that their ethic fails to confront the morality of gender inequality itself and, in fact, perpetuates the reign of the dominant by encouraging self-sacrifice and servility in the guise of care.

A second cluster of critiques points to problems with the 'naturalizing' tendencies of the ethic. Coloured by links to the biological dimensions of mothering, caring comes to be perceived as an innate characteristic of women and therefore a natural determinant of women's social possibilities and roles.[26] Correlat-ively, the absence of caring attributes is used to castigate and denigrate women. At the heart of these reproaches is a reduction-ist, or, in postmodern terms, an essentialist allegation. The com-plaint is that celebrations of caring reduce and simplify the range of women's moral possibilities to those displayed in practices of care, and further, that the analysis of caring itself tends to be reduced to romantic stereotypes of mothering – usually those emanating from Western, white, middle-class, domestic relations. As a result, the enormous diversity of women's ethical experiences, and the wide range of caring practices, tend to become ossified in abstracted and prejudiced models of femininity and care.

This set of criticisms supports those already mentioned from both the canonical and the feminist camps. For the stereotypical associations between the 'ethic of care' and mothering tie its values to the realm of domestic practices, limiting its range and reinforcing the traditional split between public and private values, and between men's and women's ethical possibilities. On this basis, the ethic is impotent in face of gendered, social inequalities. Further, the tendency to see the perspectives and concerns arising from maternal and other practices of caring simply in a positive light glosses the dark side of these practices: the frustrating, demeaning and isolating dimensions of their routines. 'Care' has a lengthy history in the (English-speaking) West as a burden, a bed of trouble, anxiety, suffering and pain;[27] care ethicists ignore this history, and the dismal actuality of many contemporary practices of caring, at great risk.

Thus, while the 'ethic of care' holds some promise of providing a gender-sensitive corrective to conventional moral theories, its articulation raises serious difficulties. The pressing need to recognize insights gained from the important ethical practices typically associated with women is severely impeded by the inability to conceptualize adequately their ethical possibilities and limitations. It is evident from these challenges that, whether the values and priorities expressed in practices of care are either learnt or innate, they cannot be appealed to in any simple way as a worthy source of an alternative ethics. The result within feminist theory is a crucial dilemma. Attempts to develop a conception of ethical understanding that is sensitive to the concerns of gender are caught between the opposing dangers of including the perspectives and values of caring practices identified with women, and of omitting to do so.

In many ways this impasse intersects and overlaps with the contemporary philosophical debates over the apparently competing demands of modernism and postmodernism.[28] From one perspective, recognition of the rich potential of women's experiences for bringing balance and full responsiveness to the ethical possibilities of human life seems to be continuous with postmodern understandings of the significance of human

diversity *vis-à-vis* the 'totalizing' forces of modernism. The substantive concerns of the 'ethic of care' with relationships, sensitivity to others, and responsibility for taking care, coupled with
engaged attentiveness to the context and concrete particulars of
situations, coincide with many postmodern themes. Postmodern
disenchantment with the universalizations and exclusions of
'master discourses' has produced a focus on the particular and the
local – on narrative and contexual accounts – that encourages
respect for the differences between persons and sensitivity to the
complexity of our interconnections.

Despite this overlap in emphases, however, it is largely through
the influence of postmodern themes that many of the difficulties
with the 'ethic of care' have arisen. While care theorists may enlist
postmodern insights to strengthen their cases against the abstract,
universal values of modernist moral theories, talk about caring
itself readily slips into generalizations that are abstract and distant
from the lives of the very different practitioners of caring values
and the range of practices in which the values of caring are
embedded.[29] When caring is elaborated in contrast to traditional
theoretical concepts like justice, the 'ethic of care' becomes en-
tangled in the concerns of that tradition. Attempts to articulate the
ethical aspects and meaning of care tend to be understood – at
least implicitly – within the conventional forms of moral reasoning. As a result, the 'ethic of care' takes on the dimensions of a
unified theory that can be applied across diverse and sometimes
unrelated relations – in some cases even assuming a foundational
status.[30]

Where analyses of caring are tied directly to particular practices,
for example, mothering or friendship, these specific expressions
of care tend to be raised to the status of paradigms.[31] The
particularity of their contexts and the diversity of their ends is then
sometimes homogenized into a regulating ideal for widely differing practices and relationships. As many theorists have noted, care
ethicists have been largely inattentive to differences between
women, the ways in which culture, race, class, sexual orientation
and so on, constitutively shape the practices in which they engage,
and the different interests, values and attitudes they create.
Invoked uncritically in the name of a universal 'woman', the ethic
conceals or distorts the multiplicity of women's perspectives.
Women of diverse racial ethnic groups, for example, have been
particularly critical of the ways in which the values of caring

relations are universalized without attentiveness to the very different experiences of caring and relations of intimacy that emerge from different social locations.[32]

Seen in this light, attempts to identify women's values or to produce a feminist ethics fail to resist the universalizing and exclusionary habits of modernism. Moves towards the inclusion in moral theory of values informed by intimate life practices seem only to create new exclusions. From the other side, however, both respect for the complexity and ambiguity of practices of care – their dark sides and their light sides – and attentiveness to the constitutive function of their different contexts and purposes, as well as to the personal biographies of their participants, appear to pose fatal limitations and insoluble problems for the 'ethic of care'. The identification of links between caring relations and conditions of social vulnerability, economic dependence and servitude, together with nuanced understandings of how engagement in caring frequently has debilitating effects on moral character, has often resulted in blanket dismissals of its ethical possibilities. Instead of reading these dimensions of care as further, caring specifications of the complexity and variety of the concrete situations of moral life, theorists have seen them as deadly flaws that signal the inevitable demise of care theories in ethics. In other words, conceptualizations of caring are construed simply as (inadequate) alternatives in the grand theory tradition.

Criticisms of the 'ethic of care' are further reinforced by the demands of postmodern approaches for detailed sensitivity to the distinctiveness of concrete particulars. The perception that our identities and self-understandings are in continuous flux, in virtue of the way we are embedded in a dynamic and changing context of relations, leads to difficulties in making statements in the name of any individual, let alone women, or carers, as a group.[33] From this perspective it would seem that serious, ethically minded care ethicists are doomed to endless and futile descriptions of incommensurable particulars.

My aim in this work is to try to clear a way through this impasse. While recognizing both the need for gender-sensitive, ethical understanding of care, and the plurality of possibilities expressed by different forms of caring in different persons' lives, I want to show that the theoretical orientations that tend to see these two concerns in opposition to each other, misunderstand the connections between practical moral life and its theoretical discourses.

III

My theoretical approach to the process of conceptual clarification develops from certain Wittgensteinian insights concerning the active, practical nature of discursive understanding. It is best explained by returning once more to the specific problematic that poses concern for gender sensitivity in the ethics of care, in opposition to recognition of the plurality of possibilities expressed in differently located practices of care. Substantive discussions of the ethical nature of caring practices suggest that caring relations vary enormously in their range and application, and that the values of care are intimately connected with the different and specific practical contexts in which those relations occur. By these lights, attempts to theorize care within a set of definitive concepts and precepts, will always overlook important aspects of this dynamic family of ethical practices. Alternatively, the turn to endless deconstructions of the identities, needs, experiences and ethical perspectives of women, for example, fails to recognize that each description is itself necessarily drawn from a particular context, and, as a consequence, manifests a particular interest.

Following Wittgenstein, these two sides of the conceptualization problem both fall into the same sort of mistake about the relation of words and concepts to the objects or practices they describe. A major source of illusion in these conventional uses of concepts is the failure to understand that it is impossible to 'command a clear view' of their use (PI 122). In the desire to understand, language users are misled by their grammar into thinking that their concepts can catch the essences of things, that successive refinements and particularizations of expressions move towards complete exactness and clarity (PI 91–2). But, on the contrary, Wittgenstein claims, concepts have 'blurred edges': they do not give a precise or complete picture of their references; nor do they pin down what is common or essential to every example for which they are used, or provide comprehensive rules or decisive judgements for their use (PI 71–96).

Wittgenstein illustrates this idea in a discussion of the use of the word 'game'. Through a succession of questions and answers concerning its meaning, he shows that 'game' can be explained by giving examples of particular ways it is used, not by defining its boundaries or by giving a complete analysis of its function. Understanding the concept is, thus, a practical capacity of knowing how to go on using it – of knowing the salience of the uses given in the explanatory examples – when other examples are encountered. Wittgenstein summarizes this process of explaining to someone what a game is in the following way:

> One gives examples and intends them to be taken in a particular way. I do not, however, mean by this that he [*sic passim*] is supposed to see in those examples that common thing that I – for some reason – was unable to express; but that he is now able to employ those examples in a particular way. Here giving examples is not an indirect means of explaining – in default of a better. For any general definition can be misunderstood too. The point is that this is how we play the game. (I mean the language-game with the word 'game'.) (PI 71)

In this description of showing the meaning of a concept, the oppositional 'dilemmas' of the conceptualization problem with caring can be seen to set out the inherent patterns of explanations of practical life.

On the one hand, concepts are incapable of expressing the 'common thing' in the practices they represent. But on the other hand, it is their very partiality – the fact that they are intended to be taken 'in a particular way' – that enables their users to draw attention to particular aspects of things: to throw light on the specific dimensions that are relevant for being taken that 'particular way' in the face of the multiple possibilities for their interpretation. When the perspectival character of theories or descriptions is recognized in this way, it is possible to see that conceptual explanation is a matter of assembling particular exemplars that direct interest in particular ways. Though the limitations of contextuality may seem to signal the demise of any theoretical ambitions, seen from this perspective they provide the means of investigating the possibilities of practical life.[34]

Clarity of understanding, or 'perspicuity' as Wittgenstein describes it – in order to distinguish his perspective from the more conventional claims about the powers of understanding – is produced by a discerning juxtaposition of different 'objects of comparison' that enables appropriate connections to be made among them (PI 122). A survey of different examples can guide understanding by pointing to patterns of similarities and dissimilarities among them that bring a certain dimension into focus. This particular aspect, or more precisely, the 'perspicuous representation' that brings it into view, can then be further illuminated through the presentation of another survey that draws attention to another dimension. For it is evident that no attempt to understand the nature of things can achieve a complete 'bird's-eye' view; even Wittgenstein's own understanding, of the relationship between concepts and life practices, is produced under a specific interest (though perhaps one as wide as a whole way of life). In short, as Gordon Baker has remarked, the method of understanding which Wittgenstein advocates is 'nothing more (and nothing less!) than different possible ways of looking at things'.[35]

Standard objections to this process complain of its apparent indifference to the world, or, as Wittgenstein himself noted, that 'it leaves everything as it is' (PI 124). But these dismissive responses themselves fail to understand the internal connection between criticism – or change – and understanding, that Wittgenstein's approach demonstrates. For they imply that critical potential, or the ability to make a difference to the world, must come from having a perspective that lies outside the world. Wittgenstein's understanding of his own, and all philosophical work, as firmly located within the landscape of possibilities, assembling 'reminders' that show up particular purposes (PI 127), reveals the deceptive nature of these God-like aspirations. The critical potential of understanding, familiarly described as its therapeutic possibility (PI 133), is found in its capacities for illuminating the particular interests that direct different ways of looking at the world, and for recognizing its own purposes.[36]

Seen in this light, Wittgenstein's suggestions are revolutionary. From the one side they dispel the claims of the many generalizing and reductionist forms of conceptual understanding that are deeply embedded in human thinking and ways of living.[37] Wittgenstein's suggestions bring into view the particularistic and concrete bases of understanding that have been concealed by these conventional aspirations towards truth. The seductive but illusionary hold of these discourses is loosened, opening up possibilities of interrogating practices that authorize (in the name of objectivity and impartiality) the universalization of particular ways of looking at the world. Accordingly, substantive claims about the ethical possibilities or disabilities of caring are rendered suspect by the recognition that understanding of them demands attention to the particular context of concerns within which they are expressed.

From the other side, however, Wittgenstein's elimination of some forms of theorizing by no means implies that understanding is prey to limitless manipulations of examples. The assembling of examples is itself, of course, constrained by the range of particular purposes the philosopher/assembler shares with those persons she or he would 'remind' of any number of them. A survey of 'objects of comparison' can only produce understanding when it brings to light patterns or connections that reveal dimensions of meaning hitherto hidden or dormant in the practices of those who would understand.[38] A survey of different relations of care can only produce understanding of caring if it illuminates aspects of caring that already lie implicit within the range of those seeking understanding.

By adopting this Wittgensteinian approach to exploration of the ethics of care, the epistemological problematic is modified in such a way that the persuasive but illusory power of conventional modes of thought and authority, in reflection on – and in the practice of – ethics, may be stripped away. To this end my enquiry will proceed, as mentioned earlier, by surveying the possibilities and limitations of four examples of caring relations: mothering, friendship, nursing and citizenship. Each chapter takes up one of these sets of practices in a relatively independent way, drawing attention to the particularity of its contextual setting and the specific kinds of relational concerns that that setting brings to bear on the form of caring expressed. Within each chapter I juxtapose different writers' perspectives on the set of practices under consideration, thereby following a process that repeats the 'survey' method that connects the separate chapters.

Instead of moving at length on a single and high level of generality, the investigation consists in a series of intensive analyses of fairly specific practices in a variety of special areas of human relationship. The range of different practices and the array of different descriptions I have used, however, are not simply arbitrary; nor are their analyses neutral or indifferent. They are selected for their central significance in the range of forms that caring among persons can take, for the diversity of priorities, commitment, attitudes and beliefs they display, as well as the way these differences interweave and overlap. My accounts of them are intended to point to the complex of ethical possibilities sustained in the ways we matter to each other as caring persons. In addition, these particular practices are especially chosen to show up issues of gender sensitivity in sharp relief. My larger theses thus acquire their meaning from the process of moving back and forth through the intersecting and overlapping terrains of the landscape of different, and differently perceived, caring practices. Though these themes emerge from particular substantive issues that have to a large extent been studied for their own sake, they derive their coherence from the mutually reinforcing and amplifying character of the criss-crossing discussions of particular practices.

Of course, by taking up this particular approach in this unique context I do not wish to imply that it provides answers to all the problems of conceptual understanding, or that principled thinking has no role in ethics. It is clear that in some contexts relatively abstract analyses may be entirely appropriate; in others, singular descriptions may be more illuminating. My approach develops out of the specific context of my central concern with the inadequacy of grand theory-making when it attempts to explicate practical life.

At its most general level, then, my investigation aims to challenge exclusionary tendencies in both traditional and feminist ethics. In the first instance, by drawing attention to a domain of practices characteristically associated with women, my project highlights the ways in which issues of gender are deeply implicated in understandings of the values of caring. The significance of, and need for, gender sensitivity in ethics is thereby brought into full view. Second, through the use of its survey approach, my investigation disarms positions that work with pre-articulated, foundational or universalist understandings of ethical concepts, including those that tend towards the naturalization of caring as a distinctive, and/or morally superior, women's ethical orientation. My explorations of particular practices emphasize the socio-historical location of the participants and the unique contexts in which they occur with the purpose of demonstrating the practical nature of ethical caring.

The ethical possibilities of care emerge as constitutively shaped by the practices in which they are embedded; as intricately connected with the possibilities of other ethical concepts, such as responsiveness, self-understanding, reciprocity, trust, respect, openness and vulnerability; as inherently conflicted; and as always open to further discussion and interpretation. The investigation also directs attention to ways in which ethically valuable forms of caring may be differentiated from those that entrench relations of oppression. Finally, the discussion of citizenship in Chapter 4 extends understanding of the significance of caring beyond the familiar ground of close, personal relationships, into a realm of more attenuated and formalized practices. In contrast with the emphasis on the differences and specificity of caring relations in the first three chapters, this fourth chapter highlights commonalities among interpersonal relations in order to imagine new ethical possibilities for caring.[39]

But despite these purposes, I do not argue for any definitive or comprehensive conclusions. The results of this work are not more than the guidance that my assembly of examples provides for readers' own understandings of the ethical possibilities of care. Nowhere do I presume to define 'caring' or any of its grammatical variations; I have not attempted to set out a precise formulation or an elaborate analysis of what caring is or what the word 'caring' means. This resolve, of course, stems from my original intuition of the significance of caring in what matters in relations among persons, in the 'form of life' which I have to trust that I share with the reader. From this perspective, setting out what caring means is a matter of extending and bringing to light new aspects of pre-existing, though perhaps dimly perceived, understandings by means of the survey I have outlined above.

IV

It remains, finally, for me to mention the more explicit conditions that limit this work. Clearly I make no claims to offer a whole ethics, nor even a comprehensive survey of ethical practices of care. Inherent in the conception of this project is my consciousness of its partiality, that it presents the particular perspective of my own purposes. Only a small selection of the vast range of caring relations are studied, and they are presented in very specific ways. Although I have tried to find a balance of emphases, these different studies have been assembled and arranged according to the aspects that I have considered to be most important. For instance, the easy categorizations I adopt for distinguishing my

four particular sets of caring practices raise questions in relation
to my own resistance to categorical understandings of care itself.
It may well be asked how the multitude of different relationships
that we call mothering, or friendship, for example, can be usefully
collapsed in this way. Indeed, from some perspectives this failure
to distinguish the variety of relational possibilities within each set
is an invalidating flaw.[40] The limits on specificity I have imposed
here are aimed at loosening the hold of perspectives that endorse
a static, determinist view of the ethical possibilities of caring. At
the same time the array of caring relations I present seeks to carry
the ethical claims of the enormous complex of 'brute' practices
from which it abstracts beyond the uniqueness of their historical
contingency and toward a more ambitious understanding. These
are delicate tensions, readily stretched or weakened by inattention
to significant detail or over-scrupulous zeal for the minutiae of
particulars. How the current investigation measures up depends
ultimately on its resonance with the readers' own perceptions.

Given the heuristic nature of progress in understanding, however, it is clear that the survey would be enhanced by its extension
to other sets of practices: for example, relations between same-sex
and heterosexual intimates, relations in different 'caring professions', educational relations, or even, as one commentator has
suggested, relations between jailers and their prisoners. And no
doubt further insight would be gained from surveying examples
of self-reflexive practices of care, and caring relations with non-
human entities, as well.

A second limit related to my particular interests results in an
emphasis on the positive possibilities of women's involvement in
practices of care. While cognizant of the damage many women
incur from the oppressive relations in which their caring is
expressed, it seems wrongheaded to reject out of hand the responses and skills learnt in these relations. It is not oppression, *per
se*, that produces the values attached to caring but the personal
responses to it; and there is nothing to say that these values could
not have been learned from other, non-oppressive experiences.[41]
There is also nothing to suggest that responses developed within
relations of domination and subordination are intrinsically flawed,
or that their practice necessarily sustains or encourages oppression. Condemnation of caring runs the danger of silencing all
those who recognize its ethical possibilities, and risks capitulating
to dominant models of ethics that characteristically exclude

consideration of women's ethical lives. On the other hand, romantic idealization is also a danger. My intent is to promote recognition of the skills, knowledge and values manifest in caring relations, of the ways in which the women involved in those relations can function ethically in the world, as thinking and feeling beings, and of how social structures may constrain these possibilities.

I am acutely aware, also, that my response to ethical enquiry in the interest of gender sensitivity is just one context for reflection on caring, and that it thereby solicits further responses as part of the continuing process of reflection. The work of Rupert Ross on the ethical orientation of traditional Cree and Ojibway peoples, for example, illustrates another interest, cultural sensitivity, and with it a strikingly different expression of care. Ross describes the 'fundamentally different' ethic of care demonstrated in the characteristic stance of non-interference that is adopted by traditional peoples, and maintained even when intimates fall into self-destructive behaviour. Care is demonstrated, he says, 'by conferring virtually absolute freedom on everyone and, when damaging events do occur, by doing whatever is possible to put those events behind them, to let bygones be bygones and to restore essential harmony'.[42] Ross's study suggests that a richer investigation of caring would also address its possibilities from the perspective of its cultural variability.

Even within my more general purpose, however, the project displays specific aspects of my own social location and interests. The choice of voices and themes is heavily conditioned by my particular and privileged white, middle-class, female view of the world; by the experience and resources accessible to me in that location. But, once again, it is in the very nature of this enquiry and the ethos it embraces that this perspective, and these themes, do not make any universal claims for their relevance. On the contrary, it is my aim merely to set out the beginnings of an heuristic process – a way of going on that will encourage others to continue the investigation under other, differently significant, aspects. The experiences of underprivileged women, 'women of colour', Third World women and the women of indigenous peoples, will provide opportunities for further rethinking and enrichment of the understanding of the possibilities of caring begun here. And no doubt there are other important dimensions of caring relations, like their economic context, for example, that intersect with the dimension of gender sensitivity on which I focus.

The point is not that the problem-specific understanding I attempt to achieve can necessarily be expanded by simply adding a survey that is ordered under different aspects, like race or class; nor that a single representation of examples of caring could make several aspects of caring simultaneously visible. The Wittgensteinian approach to understanding I use here does not presume that any one assembly of examples could simultaneously dissolve all the problems that arise from consideration of the different aspects involved in ethical practices of care. Instead, it consistently advocates looking at caring from different angles, not trying to catch all the 'facts' of the matter in a single statement.[43] My aim is that the present investigation will suggest other significant aspects for looking at the ethical possibilities of caring.

Perhaps this is a naive intent, flawed by the inability to understand just how different different perspectives can be: how some voices can never be heard, can never overcome, or may never want to overcome, the obstacles to joining the process of reflection. Perhaps by my omissions, I am perpetuating the same kind of ideological entailments that I challenge. My failure to consider gender-sensitive caring under the different aspects of race and class, for example, will no doubt raise the ire of many theorists who will feel excluded, once more, by the restricted focus of this account. These are complicated and troubling questions which cannot be resolved through any single enquiry, or any single ordering of perspectives. This investigation is conceived to speak to the concerns of those with whom I share a 'form of life', but it is my self-conscious aim to present an orientation that will provide openings for the recognition of perspectives that lie beyond this limitation.

Chapter 1

Mothering

I

Consideration of relationships between mothers and their children has been sadly missing from the traditional philosophical repertoire of ethical concerns. For those interested in the ethical potential of caring, however, mothering has been the source of continuous reflection and analysis. Maternal relationships are of fundamental importance in the present context for several reasons. First, as the very first human relationship that most persons experience, the mothering connection provides a privileged example of the possibilities of human connectedness. It has a pre-eminent role in the creation of new persons, in shaping their language and culture, and developing their morality, as well as providing a stock of memories of caring on which they can draw in their ethical practices.[1] In terms of this reproductive and creative potential, mothering is the most fundamental of caring relations.

Second, and intimately connected with this notion of primacy, there is the perception that mothering relationships express, at least symbolically, a way of mattering to another that represents something of an archetype for caring. Seen as the functionally necessary and natural realm of affection and love, enduring and unconditional openness, and responsiveness to the particular material, emotional and social needs of another person, mothering frequently carries the full weight of ideological constructions of caring. The very nature of caring seems to be produced in the connection between the apparently ultimate vulnerability of early childhood and the potentially perfect responsiveness of mothers. Nel Noddings, for example, spells out what she means by caring through repeated reference to the ways mothers care for their children.[2] Similarly, Virginia Held uses mothering relations as the central model for her ethics of care.[3] The present investigation, in its move towards examining the variety of caring relations, questions the power of these constructions and thereby seeks to loosen the ties of their claims.

Third, mothering relationships are of direct interest to the larger project of this enquiry into the ethical import of caring because of their explicit 'bio-metaphysical' idiosyncrasy with respect to conventional ethical claims.[4] For the peculiar quality of selfhood that characterizes the relationship of mothers to their children – the 'binary–unity' of self so aptly described by Kathryn Allen Rabuzzi[5] – exposes the absurdity of the universal claims of more traditional moral philosophies based on codifications of the utility or the rights of individuals. In contrast to the singular and autonomous selves of that tradition,[6] the gradual development of first bodily and later social individuation of children with respect to their mothers suggests the notion of selves that are simultaneously two and one, mother and child in varying degrees of relationship to each other. The complexity of this dynamic process of relatedness undermines the universality of many established understandings of personal possibilities. Hence, conceptions that set ideas of dependency and interdependency in opposition to those of autonomy and independence, or juxtapose courses of creativity and transformation against those of replication and transmission become patently inadequate.[7]

Mothers commonly describe the bewildering experience of their relationships to their children in terms that confound classic individualism: an extension of self that is not yet self, a sense of being in two places, or being two persons, at the same time, or of not knowing whether one is mother or child.[8] In addition, these blendings and dispersions of self are marked by continuous change through time as the relationship moves through different expressions of dependency and attachment. Thus mothering relations present a direct challenge to the structural forms of conventional moral theory and provide a powerful demonstration of the need for elaboration of the complexity of the moral domain.

For gender-sensitive ethical enquiry, mothering is also of particular importance. And in this respect, since Simone de Beauvoir's ovarian work, debunking the mystique surrounding women's 'natural calling', mothering has been the subject of widespread

examination by theorists interested in problems of gender bias.[9]
The issue arises through women's central physiological role in the
bearing of children and our profound social implication in child-
rearing. In this interplay between the biological and the social,
the relationship of women to mothering is doubly inscribed: not
only are women actually involved in mothering practices, but the
possibility of mothering is a central constitutive of women's
identities.

Whether we are actual mothers or not, the possibilities of our
lives are inevitably touched by the deep cultural and biological
relations that characteristically conspire to connect us, at least
indirectly, with mothering practices. Though these connections
may elicit a wide range of responses, from ecstatic identification,
unreflective acceptance, questioning uncertainty to open hostility,
it remains an unavoidable – if unconscious – frame of reference
for women's lives. Mothering is a realm of potentiality to which
all women are in some way accountable. This is not to say that our
lives are exclusively dominated by maternal concerns or our
relationship to mothering; rather, the powerful association between the womanly and the maternal tends characteristically to
demand a response. Thus it is that this gender-identifying activity
and its specific demands on women's lives have been and remain
a key subject for enquiries committed to exploring themes related
to gender sensitivity.

Recent feminist investigations of mothering raise two main
types of ethical concerns. In the first instance, following de
Beauvoir's lead, theorists have questioned the 'external' context
of values within which mothering relations are enacted. Feminists
have examined the ways in which social, economic and political
structures tend to reduce and constrain – or enlarge – the domain
of mothering practices. Attention is thus focused on the ways in
which women's association with mothering has worked against
or for us, constraining or enhancing our social and personal
possibilities. Recognition of the role of socio-political forces in
structuring the boundaries and expectations of maternal relationships has directed attention towards the needs and ethical
possibilities of those participating in, or identified by, association
with mothering, and towards questions about how alternative
structures might nurture those needs. Concern for the personal
well-being of mothers and their children, as well as the ways in
which mothering practices standardly orchestrate concepts of –

and possibilities for – women in general, becomes the central theme.

The second type of concern is connected with consideration of the distinctive values that emerge within mothering practices themselves: the kinds of virtues enacted in mothering relations, the ethical priorities and commitments they express, the possibilities and limitations of the values attached to those virtues. Attention is directed towards understanding the ethical import of a domain of human interaction that has been largely overlooked or diminished in favour of philosophical reflection on less personal and solicitous exchanges. While mothering relationships undoubtedly constitute a profoundly significant sphere of human interaction, the claim is that – typically – deliberation has been focused on the values inculcated in children, rather than the 'internal' values that mothering practices themselves display. As Sara Ruddick explains, 'maternal thinking' has tended to be 'thinking *about* mothers and children by experts who hoped to be heard by mothers rather than to hear what mothers had to say'.[10] The gender specificity that characterizes the realm of maternal relationships provides an additional impetus to these concerns because the central role of mothering in understandings of gender identity casts it as a source of a distinctive 'women's morality' and consequently as the key either to women's empowerment or to our subordination.

These complexly intertwined aspects of mothering make the understanding of maternal caring relations of central importance to understanding the ethics of caring itself, though not, I claim, of paradigmatic importance. In the following discussion I shall set out for view two different descriptions of maternal care, those of philosopher Sara Ruddick and sociologist Amy Rossiter. By consideration of the insights and necessary oversights of this very limited sample of uses of 'mothering', my aim is to make a beginning in the process of understanding this important example in the range of ethical practices we call caring.

II

Sara Ruddick's landmark work on the concept of 'maternal thinking'[11] is one of the most comprehensive discussions of the practices and ethical possibilities of the caring exemplified by mothering relationships. Ruddick attempts to 'identify some of the specific metaphysical attitudes, cognitive capacities, and conceptions of virtue ... that are called forth by the demands of children' (MT 61), with the aim of 'honouring' ideals of reason that are shaped by responsibility and love rather than by emotional detachment, objectivity and impersonality. Her claim is that the practices arising from mothers' responses to 'the promise of birth' have the potential to generate and sustain a set of priorities, attitudes, virtues and beliefs that inform an ethics of care and a politics of peace. Her project of giving voice to the ethical import of mothers' commitments is thus also a critique of the philosophical tradition that pursues a transparent distinction between reason and emotion, a calculus of ethical decisionism, and, more specifically, the reckonings of 'just wars'.

The universal claims concerning non-violence and peace that Ruddick draws from her analysis of maternal thinking are problematic for the present investigation. But despite my intent of undoing precisely these kinds of universalist pretensions I want to sidestep this problem for the moment to consider Ruddick's analysis at the level of its relevance to mothering relations themselves. My immediate concern is not to challenge her universalist move directly, but to investigate the distinctive kinds of caring that mothering relations may exhibit and the ways they contribute to understanding the concept of care. By pointing to the range and complexity of ethical concerns involved in different practices of caring in this way, my aim is to show that they defy the types of universalizations that Ruddick makes. It is, therefore, Ruddick's description of the particular characteristics of mothering relations, and not her general prescriptions, that are of interest.

'To be a "mother"', says Ruddick, 'is to take upon oneself the responsibility of child care, making its work a regular and substantial part of one's working life' (MT 17). With this brief announcement she signals her perception of the central moral dynamic of mothering: the non-contingent, but unenforceable, 'adoption' of obligations for the well-being of a child. With this relatively conventional, largely instrumental understanding of maternal care she sets about unpacking its intertwined emotional, cognitive and ethical significance through a consideration of the specific activities generated by its responsibilities.

Maternal practices are a response, she asserts, to three kinds of 'demands'. Two of these issue from children themselves: the calls for preservation of their lives and the fostering of their growth.

The third requirement is exacted by the socio-political group in which mothers are integrated: the demand that children be raised in a manner acceptable to the values of the group. To be a mother, according to Ruddick, is to be committed to meeting these constituents of maternal work through the activities of preservative love, nurture and training (MT 17).

Although she recognizes that the demands – and the practices these demands solicit – are historically and culturally specific, and that 'conceptions of "maternal thinking" are as various as the practices of mothering from which they derive' (MT 52), Ruddick maintains that there is sufficient commonality in the expectations of mothers to justify the universal relevance of her claims. And although she also says that she recognizes that her orientation is a product of her socialization in a tradition that affirms cross-cultural generalizations of needs and desires, her assertion that maternal practices are organized to meet 'a demand intrinsic to the promise of birth' stands steadfast against these disclaimers. Consequently, as she lays out the implications for mothers of their children's requirements for 'preservation', 'growth' and 'social acceptability', Ruddick articulates the guiding conception of achievement under which the 'struggle' of mothering relationships occurs for all mothers.

Preservative love – the continual response to children's demand for protection and preservation – is a passionate work of securing the safety of the extremely vulnerable child within a largely uncontrollable and dangerous environment (MT 65–81). For many mothers this activity begins with their recognition of the 'dangers' that they themselves present to their children. Sometimes this recognition may come from a perception of the intense dependency of their children on them. In this case a mother's absence, sickness or death is seen as a threat to her child. Sometimes the perceived risk may stem from a mother's sense of her own emotional, material and intellectual inadequacies. These dimensions of vulnerability require mothers to be attentive to their own well-being, as well as open to the possibilities of experiential learning, the capacity to modify and refine their skills through the accumulation of experiences of responding to their children.

The environment at large also presents extensive dangers to children, in view of their unfamiliarity with it and their inability to cope with their survival needs.[12] Following Ruddick, mothers maintain the balance of control in the face of these perpetual risks through a characteristic protectiveness that Ruddick calls 'holding'. She describes it, rather cryptically, as a relational stance to another that minimizes risks and reconciles differences rather than sharply accentuating them, and goes on to explain that 'holding is a way of seeing with an eye toward maintaining the minimal harmony, material resources, and skills necessary for sustaining a child in safety' (MT 78–9). The term 'holding' originates in psychology where it is used to describe the transitional zone between the early, 'total' identification of infants with their mothers and their separation in maturity. Accordingly it denotes a 'space' in which children may play, create and fantasize in the unobtrusive but reassuring presence of their mothers. The children's own world is both validated and suffused with the mother's protection. 'Holding' thus provides the child with a feeling of safety without domination or confinement, a sense of security that is open to possibility.[13]

Ruddick explains that 'holding' is bound up with the two enabling virtues of humility and cheerfulness, both of which draw on a profound sense of one's limits and expectations in an uncontrollable world. Humility expresses the optimal mean between the extremes of abandonment of control and domination; cheerfulness expresses the mean between the denial of limits and passive submission. Identification of these virtues is, for Ruddick, the acknowledgement of the struggle that mothering entails. Humility and cheerfulness are but ideals – constantly under threat from the exhausting, thankless and uncertain nature of protecting vulnerable and unpredictable persons in a world that is beyond their mothers' control. Mothering practices are therefore frequently marked by an intermixture of emotions like love, hate, fear, sorrow, impatience, resentment and despair, provoking the ambivalence that Jane Lazarre has claimed is 'the only thing which seems . . . to be eternal and natural in motherhood'.[14]

Maternal care is constituted in multiple levels of vulnerability. Infants and children are vulnerable to their physical and social environments; mothers, too, are vulnerable to an unpredictable and uncontrollable world. In such contexts of uncertainty and lack of control, moral codes and principles may be seen as attempts to impose order and control over a world that outruns human limits. From this perspective, Ruddick's virtues may appear to endorse 'codes' of submissiveness, receptivity and empathy, that some feminist theorists claim men impose on women's unruliness. In her work *Lesbian Ethics*, Sara Hoagland, for example, reminds lesbians of the limiting and oppressive underside of these feminine ideals and directs them to the enabling possibilities of creative choice within conditions of uncertainty.[15] While Ruddick's cheerfulness and humility may be interpreted in this way, they are by no means necessarily or best understood as the destructive underside of masculine morality. We can see that she envisages them – like Hoagland's 'creative choice' – as leading to the range of ethical possibilities that lie between the twin dangers of overweening control and unquestioning submission. And like Hoagland, she notes the practical difficulties and ambivalence they entail.

The key attitude that Ruddick associates with the second sphere of maternal activity, nurture of children's growth, is a 'welcoming response to change' (MT 89). Her point is to underline the dynamic character of mothering relations. Thus, in attending to the specificity and minutiae of children's needs, mothers appreciate that change and growth are built into those needs. 'Rapid conversions, shifts of interests, new loves and sudden hates are part of childhood life, however unsettling they may be for a mother who may wish to count on yesterday's friendship or passionate ambition' (MT 89). As a result, mothers' acceptance of these changes, and welcoming of them by means of their own willingness to change and develop themselves with and through their children's shifts and turns, are crucial to maternal nurture. And, since 'welcoming responsiveness to change' involves uncertainty, once again it is evident that the ethical possibilities of caring are bound up with the delicate balancing of vulnerability and submission, abandonment and domination.

Ruddick explains that sensitivity to change entails an holistic appreciation of the separate personhood of the child making her or his own sense of the world, rather than consisting of piecemeal responses to specific changes as if they were episodic and fragmented. Such sensitivity involves receptiveness to children's sudden changes as being coherently structured by a complex of 'interdependent perceptions, feelings, and fantasies and by multiple, potentially unifying acts of responding and interpreting' (MT 92). For although mothering relationships are constituted in and through the intense dependency of children, they are also premised on acknowledgement of children's capacities to forge their own distinctive identities and to establish their own integrity with their own values.

The problem of recognizing and accepting the otherness of other persons is an important aspect of caring relations. Ruddick's description of the cognitive dimensions of recognition and acceptance draws on the terms of concrete and contextual attentiveness made familiar by Carol Gilligan's work in moral psychology. In particular, Ruddick sketches the contours of a style of thinking that is open-ended, that relishes complexity, tolerates ambiguity, and multiplies options, rather than pursuing stable and simplified formulations of the nature of situations and persons. The rapid changes, irregularity and unpredictability of children's emotions and actions, these provide some of the most powerful and immediate evidence for the relevance of this cognitive ethos; the relational practice of responding ethically to children encourages and teaches it.

In an insightful passage, Ruddick suggests how this ethical attentiveness may be developed through a variety of conversational practices (MT 97–102). She points to practices in which mothers' capacities for concrete ways of knowing are refined by articulating their maternal experiences, alternately through storytelling, gossip and focused conversations. Several theorists have discussed the various ways in which verbal communication can be a moral resource and we will see in Chapter 2 how it becomes a vital practice for ethical understanding and mutuality between friends. Storytelling and conversations offer the opportunity to elaborate observations, rehearse judgements, establish continuities and connections, and provoke innovative transformations.[16]

But Ruddick shows that in the particular case of small children, where possibilities for response are limited, storytelling can provide these children with a continuing sense of the uniqueness of their own lives in their inextricable relationships with others, and the ability to see their own creative possibilities:

> Through good stories, mothers and children connect their understandings of a shared experience. They come to know and, to a degree, accept each other through stories of the fear, love, anxiety, pride and shame they shared or provoked. Children are shaped by . . . the stories they are first told. But it is also true that storytelling at its best enables children to adapt, edit and invent life stories of their own. (MT 98)

'Good stories' – told with realism, compassion and delight – establish trust, sensitivity to the complexities of human difficulties, and shared joy in others' lives. They enable mothers to expand and test their understanding of the coherence and otherness of their children's lives, and they arm children with tangible evidence of their mother's loving care and a sense of their own independent worth.

The characteristic intimacy and interdependence in mothering relations add dynamic layers to the understandings that mothers and children have of each other. For there is a very real sense in which children are not 'other' to their mothers: the boundaries between self and other, mother and child, child and mother, frequently seem to dissolve in the activities of protecting and nurturing. For example, mothers often feel their children's pain and joy as their own and children often identify their own security with their mother's protectiveness. Ruddick's discussion, however, plays down this sense of merging identities which is so typical of birthing and mothering. She is wary of the spectre of self-loss that seems to inhere in conventional conceptualizations of experiences of merger and harmony, and also of the characteristic feeling of selflessness experienced by many women as a result of their mothering practices. Ruddick highlights a strong concept of the individuation of mothers and of their children – even in the case of those most plausible contenders for merging selves: pregnancy, birthgiving and suckling. In what appears like an attempt to rule out the dangers of merger by definition, she claims that a 'birthing woman is bound within herself through unshareable pain and overwhelming sensation ... Birth is singular, in outcome as well as process. In being birthed an infant is becoming one and singular. To breathe, an infant must breathe alone.' The momentary entanglement of birthgiver and emerging infant is a singular experience between the 'separateness to come' foreshadowed by pregnancy and the 'union past' recalled by nursing (MT 210).

This distinct division between pregnancy, birthing and mothering, and the failure to acknowledge the feelings of union they have with their children, may, however, be troubling for many mothers. It seems to deny a continuity of experience that is qualitatively significant for their understanding of their relationships with their children. By refuting the idea of any necessary connection between mothering practices, pregnancy and birthing, Ruddick's stance enables her to present mothering and the ethics it may sustain as a non-gendered possibility (MT 49–51). On the other hand, it reflects a strongly individualist – an either/or – framework that seems to be at odds with many mothers' experiences. I have already noted that many mothers express the feeling that they and their children function as a unit – at different times and to differing degrees, sensing that they are sharing their bodies, their emotions and their rational functions. For many mothers, the rich and complex phenomenon of unity and separation that is characteristic of their relationships with their children qualitatively affects the ethical possibilities of their caring.[17]

For example, in her essay 'The maternal instinct', Caroline Whitbeck elaborates this theme, claiming that the experiences of pregnancy, labour, childbirth, nursing and postpartum recovery, strongly influence women's attachment to their children and thus their ability for caring.[18] She suggests that the value of attachment and responsiveness is enhanced when the process of identifying with the baby is fostered by the reproductive experiences of carrying a foetus. Experiencing the helplessness of labour and the weakness of the postpartum period, adjusting the rhythm and substance of one's meals to accommodate the foetus or infant, feeling the sympathetic let-down response while feeding the baby, and so on, all contribute to a bonding with the child that is crucial to ethical maternal practice. Indeed, the social and psychic mediations of this biological attachment are so powerful that the study of differential identifications according to gender has spawned the entire field of psychoanalytic feminism and its influential insights into the centrality of interpersonal attachment in women's lives.[19]

A framework that denies the significance of these experiences, by imposing a series of abstract distinctions, demands sensitive consideration of the problems its generalizations can produce for women and mothers. At its most directly pragmatic level, Ruddick's schema may play into the social institutionalization of a singular lack of public recognition of the special needs of pregnant women, or nursing infants and their mothers. In addition, her determination to maintain gender neutrality also misses the particular ethical significance of the preferential attachment between birthing women and their babies. And while she may wish to sidestep the causal links characteristically made between the values associated with that (preferential) attachment and the structural disempowerment of women, her vision of mothering by those of either gender, as we shall see below, tends to over-look the profound social mediations of specifically women's mothering.

There is another sense in which children seem not to be 'others' with respect to their mothers. Daily nurturing activities which rely on acknowledging rather than ignoring children's dependency on their mothers, produce modifications to the nature of children's 'otherness'. The conventional expectation that mothers will directly affect and influence their children deepens and compli-cates acceptance and understanding of difference in mothering relations. Thus, in the continuous cycles of dependency and separation, and their changing levels, maternal care balances the tensions between the creative movement away from focal identi-fications, the transformative education of responsiveness to one's own world in that of another, and that engaged understanding of difference that comes of travelling into another's world.

In her discussion of training, the third realm of mothering activity, Ruddick tracks this difficult balance, between the intersecting axes of mothers' and children's authority over their own choices and identities, in relation to the dimension of educative control. As she outlines the challenges for and limitations on mothers' empower-ment with respect to their children, we can recognize the strength of the structural and personal constraints through which this relationship is constituted. Ruddick talks about the confusing expectation that mothers will 'pass on' values that are often steeped in uncertainty, and which are ambiguous and variable in their lack of definition. She discusses mothers' own self-doubt and lack of experience, the psychic complications and stress of insist-ent and exhausting demands, and the intensity of their emotional involvement. Mothers must also cope with the recalcitrance of their children in accepting their guidance and authority, the control that children exert on their mothers through their deep dependencies, and the force of social expectations.

Many writers have discussed the pressures and guilt of mother-hood in the continual struggle to comply with perceptions of the 'good mother' in the face of fatigue, self-doubt and overwhelming emotions. Jane Lazarre, for example, talks of the sacrifice of self-knowledge to established visions of motherhood, and of how seductively easy it is for mothers to give up everything for their children.[20] Jessie Bernard has portrayed the dilemma of being trapped between public demands and an unmanageable child:

> Reared to please others ... the mother now finds herself responsible for the behaviour of another human being who does not yet have her discipline, who often does things that annoy and irritate others ... The child nullifies her own compliant efforts. She is held accountable for whatever the child does and the world glares at her.[21]

Patricia Hill Collins suggests an alternative, survival-threatening conception of this tension for racial ethnic mothers who must 'foster a meaningful racial identity in children within a society that denigrates people of colour'.[22] The temptations to acquiesce in external pronouncements may be strong. Ruddick describes the way that mothers frequently slip into 'inauthenticity', abdicating their maternal authority under the fearsome 'gaze' of others. 'When she thinks inauthentically a mother valorizes the judgment of dominant authorities, letting them identify virtues, and appropriate her children for tasks of their devising' (MT 113). Other mothers may resort to direct abuse, either to bring their children into line with external authorities, or to compensate for their own anger and sense of powerlessness.[23] These failures to follow one's own perceptions and values may breed self-disrespect and habits of unreflective submission in both mothers and their children. Frequently, maternal abdications of authority mean imposing unreflected prescriptions that demand children's blind obedience and suppress their creative interpretations, while confirming mothers' self-denial and compliance.

Ruddick's point in describing these temptations and difficulties is to underline the idea that mothers' integrity and confidence in their own reflectively appropriated values – what she calls their 'conscientiousness' – is crucial to the caring training of children (MT 116–19). Caring for children requires attentiveness to self-care, self-understanding and self-formation. But the work of maternal training also typically requires a responsiveness to some kind of external social authority. The difficulty of maintaining a balance between the imposition of externally based norms, and the nurturing of children's growth towards self-established authority over their own definitions is intimately connected with mothers' own sense of empowerment and integrity with respect to social values, according to Ruddick. Mothers who are in tune with their own judgements in relation to dominant values foster their children's responsiveness to those judgements through trust rather than domination.

To a large extent of course children have to trust their mothers, at least when they are infants. Trust is their protection against vulnerability, and the tenderness with which their mothers attend to their 'objective' needs promotes a climate in which trust is unequivocal. This climate, Ruddick suggests, also critically depends on mothers' own trust and confidence in their own ability to reflect on, affirm, or challenge authority, and it depends as well on their trust in their children's receptiveness to their judgements. Mothers' own trust in themselves and their children breeds trusting responses, encouraging in those children the kind of confidence that eventually enables them to take responsibility for their own values.

A large part of this reflexive trust is, however, also bound up with a caring capacity to respond sensitively to alternative conceptions of values. While guidance and intervention are key dimensions of mothering relations, the integrity and confidence with which they are expressed involve the ability to appreciate differences without feeling threatened, defensive or overwhelmed. This can be an expansive process of self-questioning, learning to appreciate new perspectives and to see the power of one's prejudices – the kind of going out to another person that returns in 'invigorating' self-knowledge. Christine Gudorf, a white, middle-class American, who adopted two medically handicapped children from racial and ethnic minorities, describes this process of self-enrichment in a way that challenges perceptions of her mothering as a uni-directional labour of protection and intervention. 'The children have given us not only themselves, but ourselves', she says.[24] Their different origins inspired new interests in foreign travel and languages, and new connections with minority interest groups. The children also enabled the development of new perspectives on the American health care system, education and social work, the cracks in the system and the many children who fall through them. As a consequence she says, 'our children have given us new communities, new loyalties, new insight – new identities'.[25]

Gudorf's aim in this essay, however, is not so much to demonstrate the complex intrication of caring attentiveness to difference with 'training' and tending to children's objective needs, but to undermine conceptions of maternal caring as a self-sacrificing practice of love. Obviously, caring for children demands sacrifices: the ethical significance of this care, Gudorf suggests however, lies not in the sacrifices but in the way that loving sacrifice supports the potential for reciprocity and mutuality. The potential enhancement of mothers is intrinsic to the ethicality of their relationships with their children.[26] This is a troubled question for many feminist theorists. Descriptions of potential reciprocity, or of reciprocity as the apparently one-sided responsiveness of an infant's delighted wriggling (as Nel Noddings has argued),[27] sound dangerously close to ethical exhortations to engage in exploitative nurture. Feminists are rightly aware of the way women are often trapped by social arrangements that enforce their provision of care for those who do not themselves respect women's own needs and desires.[28] Gudorf confirms the point that reciprocity is essential to ethical caring but recognizes that the quality of reciprocity is particular to the specific relationship. Reciprocity between mothers and their children has a different content than reciprocity between adults, whether as women and men, or as citizens and the state.[29]

Ruddick's own claim for reciprocity in the form of 'invigorating self-questioning' is supported by an insight from Audre Lorde. Under the impulse to condemn her son for 'cowardice' when he had run away from a fight, Lorde describes how the incident inspired a re-evaluation of her sense of bravery and courage:

> My son get beaten up? I was about to demand that he buy that first lesson in the corruption of power, that might makes right. I could hear myself beginning the age-old distortion and misinformation about what strength and bravery really were.[30]

From the perspective of training, Ruddick's analysis suggests that the possibility of (future) reciprocal gains is complicated by mothers' present involvement in their children's socialization. Her point may be illustrated by extrapolating from the event Lorde recounts.

Lorde's mothering brings a renewal of values, but the dimension of immediate if diminishing responsibility for her son's choices with which her caring is infused requires additional layers of understanding and judgement. Acknowledgement of differences, even where this facilitates self-understanding, is interwoven with the direct demand to discriminate among these differences, to set limits, and to foster particular kinds of attitudes, beliefs and values in the child. Thus while Lorde is able to reassess her own concept of strength in the light of her son's flight she is also importantly responsible for his survival. This requires judgements about the limits of 'flight' as they shade into self-destructive denial and the origins of 'might' in healthy self-assertion, and assessments of Lorde's own limits in making those judgements. The reassurance and acceptance of his values that her understanding conveys are tempered by her responsibility in guiding his recognition of their possibilities and constraints together with the restrictions inherent in her personal capacity for understanding.

Further, this complex of limits and possibilities is played out in a prodigious movement towards increasing symmetry and eventual reversal in old age. The dependency of early childhood, with its heavy demands for training, is swiftly transformed in developing self-reliance and interdependency. Mothers' trust in their own judgements and children's trust in their mothers' trustworthiness are deepened and transformed over time by their reciprocal enablement of mothers' trust in their children's trustworthiness and responsibility for reflective judgement. For Ruddick, the establishment and maintenance of the 'proper trust' that develops reciprocity is always difficult, and always incomplete. Identification of its possibilities names the ongoing struggle of mothering relations (MT 117).

To the tapestry of virtues and priorities, cognitive attitudes and practices, beliefs and commitments that guide this struggle, Ruddick adds a further 'discipline' that she claims 'knits together maternal thinking' (MT 119). Through 'attentive love', mothers learn to identify the 'proper trust' that straddles the overlapping conflicts and conjunctions between socialization requirements, maternal authenticity and the dynamics of children's own growing authority over their choices. Ruddick draws on the work of Simone Weil and Iris Murdoch to sketch her understanding of this concept in which the attentiveness that is so crucial to the recognition of the reality of others is strengthened with love. Although it may have the potential to slide into damaging self-sacrifice and denial, attention that is informed with love overcomes those intrusions of self-assertion and defensiveness – domination, projection, anxiety and guilt – that threaten mothers' capacities to understand their children. Her brief description reminds us that the loving quality of the attachment and the tenderness that inspires it, together provide both the crucial motivation and the perspective for mothering. For Ruddick, the insights of 'the patient eye of love'[31] offer mothers possibilities for understanding and action in the ambivalence of their mothering relationships. Thus 'clear-sighted attachment, loving clear-sightedness, is the aim, guiding principle and corrective of maternal thinking' (MT 123).

Ruddick's analysis of mothering practices shows us a realm of human interaction that persuasively challenges conventional conceptions of ethical exchanges, as contracts or utilitarian calculations.[32] In her detailed exploration of the specifics of maternal relationships she sets out the dynamics of a connection that is constitutively created in the rich conjunction of intense intimacy, heady emotion, extreme dependency and vital responsibility. Shaped by the force of the remarkable change and growth of infant children to their maturity, ethical maternal care is characterized by passionate and continuous involvement with radical (if decreasing) inequalities and with vulnerability, which are carried along by trust in the potential for mutuality, together with support for strengths and tenderness with weaknesses. These distinctive dynamics admit particular ethical possibilities and constraints. Reciprocity and respect for 'otherness', for example, are held in place by the unique quality and continuity of intimacy and attachment to a particular 'other', as well as by the extensive range of dependencies and the life-shaping responsibilities they generate for relationships that affirm the value of commitment to a life dynamically extending itself.

III

This picture is explicitly based in Ruddick's knowledge and experience of the set of emotionally privileged, white, middle-class mothering practices. Within this culturally and historically specific setting, her detailed analysis throws considerable light on the ethical potential of these particular caring relationships. Claiming a universal dimension to this parochial setting, Ruddick moves on to elaborate the possibilities of a connection between the values inherent in these twentieth-century, Western mothers' responsibilities to their particular children and a generalized commitment to non-violent, life-affirming values. A double abstraction is involved in this move. First she shifts from her specific landscape to mothering practices in general, and then she moves from the mothering of particular children to the model of a generalized mothering perspective towards all life.

The identification of patterns of values and virtues, of commonalities and universals in differing particulars, is the creative work of normative philosophy.[33] Ruddick's immense contribution to this field is her focus on the much neglected and ethically unique practices of mothering. But, as with all generalizations, such work necessarily overlooks other aspects of the particulars it subsumes. In Ruddick's case her abstractions are accompanied by a tendency to underplay the constitutive significance of economic and social conditions in the production of ethical practices. While she clearly endorses a view that sees ethical values embedded in the human practices that distinguish them, her universalist approach imposes a regime that has the effect of severing those practices from important aspects of the socio-cultural field in which they arise. Eschewing explicit discussion of the particular historical conditions and social interconnections of the mothering practices she describes, Ruddick lifts out the apparently essential attitudes and commitments she detects in them to celebrate the possibility of a universal mothering ethos. The effect of this detachment is to isolate the mother–child dyad from some of the significant political, social and psychic relations in which it is integrated, and consequently to overlook important aspects of the caring practices and values enacted in the mothering relationships she describes.

Three central problems can be identified. The first relates to the ways in which mothering tends to be idealized, the second to the individualist assumptions it invokes and the third to the essentializing of the mother–child relation in the mother's life. With respect to the first, Ruddick tends to describe mothering relations largely as if they are isolated demand–response relations, sufficient to themselves in terms of their virtues and their failings. This isolation has the effect of reducing her explanation of the struggles and achievements of mothering to a matter of the internal dynamics of the relationships themselves. Mothers become individually and completely responsible for the care and shaping of their children, and from the other side, children's demands become determinants of mothers' responses. As a result, the virtues of mothering lend themselves to idealization; practices that differ from these ideals are seen as perversions and as cause for condemnation.[34] The success or failure of the relationship is gauged in terms of a quest for individual perfection and the elimination of personal flaws. Even as Ruddick repeatedly insists that her account identifies the everyday struggles of actual mothers' lives, and she explicitly denounces idealized conceptions of good mothers (MT 29–32), she readily promotes mothers' 'preservative love' as a governing ideal for non-violence and she is severely critical of mothers' failures to meet her ideal of authenticity.

While she hedges her virtues with sympathetic remarks concerning the difficulties mothers confront in the face of 'children's unpredictable and independent wills, mother's feelings and the world's obstacles' (MT 110) – including, for example, the 'self-contempt and self-loss [that] are understandable, predictable responses to demoralizing, frightening social and psychological violences perpetrated against women and, for many women, against people of their race or culture' (MT 114) – these obstacles appear as if they are inevitable and contingent. Their inexorable structural components remain veiled. Mothering is a continuous struggle; caring requires 'superordinate efforts against great odds' (MT 71). But the historical, social, economic and psychic orders that construct those 'great odds' are unexamined. We are left with a conception of maternal achievement in which individual mothers bear the full weight of responsibility for its outcomes, both positive and negative.

The ground between heroism and victimism is not easy to divide, and Ruddick's approach discourages defeatism. At the same time it risks producing fantasies of perfectability and a recurrent tendency towards blame.[35] Such a risk is highly problematic from the perspective of gender sensitivity. Although ideals may convey a message of striving and optimism, for persons who do not have a strong sense of their own integrity, the result is that self-knowledge and esteem become difficult because the ideals tend to overwhelm and demean their actual selves. The problem is especially dangerous for those who, like many women, have had little opportunity for self-development, and who have been socialized to identify themselves in terms of others' needs. In these cases, socially constructed ideals provide excellent means for controlling persons who can be persuaded to live up to them.[36] Mothers, as Ruddick herself remarks, have been the objects of a constant barrage of this kind of 'persuasion' that undermines their self-respect and limits their possibilities (MT 31). Ruddick's failure to unpack the elements of this oppression, or to investigate the strong interdependence between the values internal to the mothering dyad and those 'external' values relating to mothers' own self-development, suggest inadequate attention to the structural power of ideals.

While it champions the ethical empowerment of mothers, Ruddick's work also allows potentially dangerous 'individualist' themes to emerge. The problem here arises through the way in which these themes may tend to reinforce the damaging social institutions within which maternal care is enacted. Emphasis on the individual capacities and responses of mothers – without recognition of the intrinsic interrelatedness between individuals, and between individuals and social structures – diverts attention from the significance of these connections in shaping mothering relations. One strand of Ruddick's 'individualism' is evident as she distances herself from the notion that the unique biological base of many mothering relations may give rise to ethical possibilities that belie more conventional claims associated with ontologies of individual identity and autonomy. Her construction of an ideal of gender neutrality in the face of the actuality of almost exclusive female involvement supports this stance.

Other strands emerge from the more generalized abstraction from the socio-political context in which that predominantly female mothering occurs. The re-evaluation of mothers' caring in terms of 'maternal thinking' tends towards conceptualization of that 'thinking' as the relatively transparent, unobstructed choice of self-sufficient persons. Ruddick expresses great sympathy for the difficulties mothers encounter, and her discussion is mixed with comments about their youth, their powerlessness, their emotional conflicts, their isolation and silencing. Yet her presentation of the possibilities for virtuous caring negates the full import of these problems. Insufficient attention to the socio-political conditions within which mothering occurs seems either to naturalize its difficulties, or to assimilate them to the operation of mothers' 'free' choices. Ironically this lack of concern is nowhere more obvious than in Ruddick's discussion of the problem of training – the sphere of maternal activity in which she explicitly invokes social impacts. Coping with the demand for 'socially acceptable' children becomes a responsibility for individual mothers quite independent of the social structures that exert that demand.

It appears that in a 'politically decent and minimally prosperous society', mothers should be able to continue the struggle towards responding appropriately to their children's needs. Thus success in handling the untoward dimensions of mothering – its oppress-ive social construction, characteristic ambivalence and psychic stresses – is understood as a matter of individual virtue rather than a social concern.[37] Ruddick's description of the central maternal virtue of cheerfulness, for instance, illustrates this theme. 'Cheer-fulness', she claims, is 'to welcome a future despite conditions of one's self, one's children, one's society, and nature that may be reasons for despair.' Accordingly:

> ordinary mothers school themselves to look realistically at their children and the dangers that confront them, cheerfully control-ling as best they can what is never fully controlled, creating around them . . . small ceremonies of loving so that the day's disasters can give way to the next morning's new beginnings. (MT 74)

Apart from the burden the requirement of cheerfulness places on individual mothers, Ruddick overlooks the way this priority may be damaging to them and fails to recognize the possibility that the capacity 'to look realistically' may, from the mother's per-spective, be a destructive expression of self-denying resignation and acceptance.

Ruddick's ameliorating acknowledgements that 'any man or woman's mothering depends upon partners, friends and helpers', and that cultures 'fail to the degree that they leave mothers who must protect their children without protection' (MT 211), do not succeed in dispelling this expectation of self-sufficient 'virtue'. For these acknowledgements remain at the level of surface ob-servations of external connections and are insensitive to the profound constitutive power of relational practices. They neglect to address the ways in which ordinary mothers' possibilities for self-schooling are locked into social constructions of motherhood and childhood as in, for example, the 'vicious lie that if a woman is really a woman, she will bear children gracefully; if she is ultimately feminine, she will unconsciously know how to be a good mother'.[38]

Lorraine Code has suggested that although attempts to revalue

maternal caring appear to repudiate understandings of persons
as autonomous individuals, the failure to accommodate the historically contingent nature of the self of the nurturer, and the
multiplicity of her needs and desires, posits an unproblematic
unity and 'single-mindedness on the part of maternal caregivers'.
It appears 'as though "maternal thinking" might, in fact, amount
to an attempt to replace one unified individual/agent with another, who differs mainly in being collectively or altruistically,
rather than individualistically oriented'.[39] Ruddick's account of
mothering seems to support this analysis, for it gives the impres-
sion that mothers can and do choose to be fully independent and
complete child-carers, capable of detecting temptations, identifying denials, warding off the distortions and inhibitions that
impede their caring. Paradoxically, these claims tend to support
dominant conceptions of individualist moralities that deny the
structural dimensions of ethical possibilities. In particular, for
mothering, this suppression of structural contradictions and ambiguities serves to reinforce social conditions that are oppressive to
mothers.

The difficulties of idealization and individualism are intertwined with, and partly produced through, what I want to call an
'essentializing' tendency. Here, contrary to more conventional
understandings of this term, I do not mean that mothering persons
or women are seen to be innately maternal. I am referring to the
way in which Ruddick seems to identify mothers solely with their
roles as nurturers of their children's growing sense of self, and
children with their insistent and insatiable demands for care. To
be sure, any account of mothering relations must necessarily be
preoccupied with these roles, but the tendency to see mothering
in terms of meeting children's needs loses sight of the perspectives
of the full selves who are experiencing the interaction.[40] Instead
of seeing mothering as one vital aspect of a mother's life, Ruddick
describes the relation as if it were the essence of that life – as a
mother's 'identity' in the sense of the whole horizon of her ethical
life, rather than a single, albeit singularly important aspect of it.[41]
When responding to a child is seen as the whole of a person's life
in this way, other significant social relations that may create
and constrain that response are frequently neutralized. Thus while
Ruddick's account moves our understanding forward from object-
ivizing and contradictory cultural scripts for child-care towards
an appreciation of the complexity of the ethical values mothering

relations may generate, it is simultaneously limited by that very focus.

Ruddick's description of mothering persons effectively reduces to a focus on the welfare of the child – responding, giving, protecting, empathizing, accepting, attending. Mothers as persons in their own right, with their own needs and desires within and apart from their maternal roles, seem to be invisible in her analysis. Although she is versed in contemporary feminist insights concerning the oppressive effects of maternal self-sacrifice for women, and unequivocally warns and chastises mothers about the dangers of self-loss, she is silent about the ways in which mothers' integrity, authenticity, and sense of self are developed and maintained. While she applauds those writers who distinguish the oppressive institutions of mothering from the experience itself, her suggestion that 'respectful listening' to mothers' voices will provide the key to their liberation falls far short of explaining how this liberation might occur (MT 39–40).

From the other side, infancy and childhood reduce, in the main, to the exertion of 'demands' on mothers. Passing references to children becoming 'co-operative partners in their own well-being', their 'high-spirited resilience' and their 'hospitality to goodness', hint at an interactive concept of development. And, as noted, Ruddick's account of 'proper trust' presages a movement towards reciprocity. But her central emphasis on mothers' responses to children's 'demands' defuses the force of these acknowledgements of children's active intentional capacities. Child development appears to involve a movement from total dependency through the education of unruly natures and impulses into the social virtues and 'proper trust' to which they are hospitable. Children appear largely as fragile and 'passive reactor[s] to drives or environmental pressures'.[42]

The point is that Ruddick's concern with mothering in virtual seclusion from the complex patterns of social relations that structure the consciousnesses of their participants and the nature of their practices, severely constrains understanding of the ethical possibilities of these relationships. She focuses on struggles between adversaries and recalcitrant forces rather than on intrinsic relational capacities of mothers and their children, and names ideals of care rather than exploring the ways in which historical conditions structure mothers' ethical possibilities. Obviously, mothering relations involve elements of struggle and conflict as well as commitments to certain priorities and ethical concerns, and Ruddick's picture of mothering offers perceptive insights into these dimensions of maternal caring. However, her stress on demands and responses tends to reduce the relationship to an isolated and naturalized cause-and-effect unit. And this reduction forecloses on conceptions of mothering as a potentially more reciprocal attachment between socially embedded persons with interdependent and shared interests. It also restricts analyses that point to the power of social structures in shaping the possibilities of mothering practices.

In part, Ruddick's tendency to isolate and reduce maternal care may originate from a conventional concern with those stages of mothering relations in which children's personhood appears to be constituted predominantly in and through their vulnerability, and their dependency on adults for their safety and well-being: the stages when mothering persons are fully occupied with their commitment to meeting these needs. The profound dependency of infancy and early childhood readily gives rise to conceptions of mothering as an activity whose demands emerge simply within the mother–child dyad, at least within the Western traditions with which Ruddick is familiar. But the temporary nature of this phase is surely a ground for questioning its dominance. As Chodorow and Contratto have suggested, a more inclusive investigation of maternal caring calls for examination of the ways in which mothering relationships develop and change for both mothers and children, and for an account of the ethical import of non-infantile modes of relating and cognizing.[43]

The work of Gudorf and Lorde, already noted with respect to the interactive possibilities of mothering relations, points to the significance of these kinds of concern and the enriched ethical potential of maternal care within the framework of reciprocity. Ruddick hints at this potential but her treatment of mothers as essentially responders to demands, and thereby necessarily more complete and integrated than their children, diminishes the possibility for developing an adequately nuanced account of their intrinsic interconnectedness. An unexamined, self-standing asymmetry becomes the hallmark of mothering.

Ruddick's conceptual isolation of mothering relations (like that of the current investigation) is, in part, the result of the logic of theoretical discussion itself and of the attempt to describe and reflect upon significant ethical distinctions. Any description must be selective, singling out some aspects of the subject and diminishing or omitting others. I have discussed her work at length here, firstly because it provides such an insightful description of the ethical values of mothering, and, secondly, to show how it is necessarily limited by its own process. The particularistic values she foregrounds suggest substantive content for our understanding of maternal care, and, in conjunction with other descriptions of mothering and those of other caring relations, ultimately caring, *per se*.

The specific oversights on which I have focused have been set out to direct attention to the limited perspective which my own work explicitly takes up: that is, gender-sensitive understanding of the ethics of multiply expressed practices of caring. From this perspective, the congruence of Ruddick's universalist philosophical perspective with the peculiar social organization that tends itself to isolate mothering relations by assigning sole responsibility for child care to mothers, frequently in an insulated household that makes such care their exclusive activity, is particularly worrisome. For the failure to take account of that context masks its contribution to her concepts and effectively normalizes the constraints it imposes on mothering relations and the predominantly female persons who are answerable to those constraints. As a consequence, that isolation and responsibility, and the economic, social and psychological difficulties they raise for its participants, remain unexamined. Ruddick's 'singling out' of a particular set of ethical concerns and commitments as characteristic of mothering practices, without adequate attention to their social constitution, seriously distorts their ethical possibilities for both mothers and children.

IV

A central theme of this book is that the kind of enabling and constraining condition of theoretical processes demonstrated in Ruddick's account of mothering can be readdressed by working through an array of examples of different theoretical approaches. To bring into focus and to correct some of the limitations of Ruddick's vision of maternal care, I want to contrast it with an alternative account of mothering that is more self-consciously engaged with its particular socio-cultural context. In this respect, Amy Rossiter's work, *From Private to Public: A Feminist Exploration of Early Mothering*, commends itself to attention for its determination to avoid abstractions that overlook the constitutive historical, linguistic and material contexts in which mothering relations are organized. The juxtaposition of Rossiter's study as an 'object of comparison' with Ruddick's perspective will illustrate some of the ways in which the 'constitutive social context', so frequently invoked in the last few pages, shapes the ethical possibilities of mothering and underlines the diversity of patterns of maternal caring. In addition it will enable us to understand more fully Ruddick's framework, and the particular values and constraints she describes. It is important to reiterate, however, that the point of this comparison of views is not to use one to trump the other. Each account has a different objective and is constrained by differing disciplinary parameters: each foregrounds and backgrounds different aspects of maternal care. My aim is only to show that understanding of maternal care cannot be achieved in a unitary way, but may proceed fruitfully by working through an array of examples. My account of the examples given by Ruddick and Rossiter is intended to make a start on this task.

Rossiter's study is motivated by the felt contradiction of her own experience of early mothering – the clash between her sense of the significance and value of her own caring attachment to her children, and the perception that her mothering is a response not simply to the demands of her children but to a social system that devalues her understandings and needs. For Ruddick this sort of contradiction is normalized either as part of the difficult territory of mothering or as a struggle identified by a maternal ideal like 'authenticity' or 'proper trust'; for Rossiter the contradiction signals the power of patriarchal social constructions in constituting her mothering practices and constraining their possibilities. As a result she champions the need for a structural reorganization of mothering that encourages both mothers' respect for their own need and ability to take care of themselves as well as social responsibility for child rearing.[44]

Analyses of individual maternal virtues and vices along the lines of Ruddick's work are overturned by Rossiter's assertion that her 'own experiences taught me that it wasn't me, with my knowledge of myself and my babies, that organized my life'. Rather than depending primarily on personal qualities, 'what I did as a mother', she claims, 'came from outside, came from a place that was different from the inner reason of my experience'

(FPP 19–20). These statements set out Rossiter's sense of the profound significance of social structures for mothering practices. More specifically, she argues that the conditions of isolation, financial dependency, work deprivation and exhaustion, characteristic of early mothering practices in her own white, Western culture, are produced by the structures of 'capitalist patriarchy' (FPP 241).

Given this framework, understanding requires an examination of the complex intersections of the personal histories of particular mothers and their children – of the actual, practical situations in which they participate and the socially available conceptions of their experiences. The possibilities of maternal care are formed in the interaction of these social forces. Rossiter's enquiry therefore traces the specific, concrete detail of the experiences of three young mothers from the final stage of their pregnancies through birthing until their children were six months old. Using data from extensive interviews with each of the women she interweaves details of their descriptions of mothering experiences, their personal biographies, and practical, material situations with her own reflections on their experiences to illustrate the ways in which their practices and perceptions of mothering – their pleasure, frustration, shame, anger – are engendered by the social contexts they inhabit. By comparing and contrasting the similarities and differences in their experiences, she highlights the connections between the particular possibilities of their separate practices, and the isolation and devaluation of maternal caring common to the patriarchal culture they share.

In contrast to Ruddick's normative generalizations, not only does Rossiter ascribe paramount importance to the social context in which maternal caring takes place, she also bases understanding of its possibilities in the overlapping dimensions of individual, concrete and specific relations. Instead of attributing a universal status to her claims, she demonstrates their validity in the continuity of particular relationships, pointing out their connection with the unique set of social structures that shape those relationships. Rossiter's detailed and contextualized accounts of particular mothers' experiences take us into the complexity, indeterminacy and difficulty of actual human lives. Unlike the pre-articulated examples which Ruddick sketches to demonstrate her generalized themes, Rossiter's concern with the integrity of each mother's experience in continuity with her whole life story underlines the significant, historical specificity of practices of maternal care.[45]

Rossiter's analyses are always conscious of the interpositions and impositions of her own socially formed consciousness and its interest in the general understanding of specific mothering relations with respect to their organization by particular material, historical and discursive processes. Comments on methodology provide explicit evidence of the self-conscious interweaving of meanings that takes her through the disparate and incongruous details of individual mothers' lives to the construction of patterns of possibilities and constraints. She talks about the co-production of understandings between each mother and herself, and the two-way illumination between concrete detail and general interpretative frameworks:

> Data were grounded on the subjects' actual experience; yet that actual experience was organized through my meanings, the subject's meaning, our shared meanings ... with an understanding that the goal of the account is to provide a text that is useful both to the inquirer and the subject in the process of naming their different realities... While it was critical for us to have a common base in the concrete events of the text, we had to be able to differ openly in our understanding of those events. (FPP 21–2)

Thus Rossiter's project moves towards a generalized, interpretative understanding of the power of structural forces in shaping mothering practices while affirming the intrinsic significance of the specificity of individual mothering relations and the integrity of each mother's perceptions of her own experience.

Her analysis is also distinctive for its basis in the sex specificity of early mothering. Ruddick's universalist account of mothering, in its bid for gender neutrality, attempts to minimize 'the biological fact that a small but significant fraction of maternal work is ineluctably female' (MT 48). She applies a conceptual distinction between birthing and mothering in order to 'celebrate the creative act of birth' without falling into romanticizations that ignore the potential ambivalence of birthgiving or the rich possibilities of non-biological relations (MT 48–9). Rossiter, on the other hand, is determined to explore the ways in which biologically based attachments may be connected with the constraints of social constructions of motherhood. It is her sense of the significance of this powerful, sex-specific attachment that prompts her to examine its social organization in specific mothering relations.

Starting from this baseline, it would seem that Rossiter's account of mothering is limited to these biological relations, and is bounded by the brief period of 'early mothering' when the imprint of this physiological connection is most significant. This constraint appears to endorse a form of biological determinism and thus to fly in the face of the not inconsiderable evidence of the indifference of some women to their biological offspring, and, more importantly perhaps, the profound attachment of all those primary caretakers who are not the 'birth mothers' of their children.[46] Such a reading of Rossiter is possible and may vindicate Ruddick's more inclusive approach. However, this reading misses Rossiter's central insight.

Her point is that the reality of the unique physical tie, through complex social manipulations, has produced – at least in the West – a normative conception of specifically female mothering, circumscribed by the function of sole-caretaking. Her focus on relations that are constructed in and through actual physiological ties serves to illustrate how the characteristic power of those bonds rationalizes a set of social arrangements that condition the possibilities of women's maternal (or primary) caring – and thereby, women's possibilities in general. We can now see how Ruddick's laudably inclusive objective, with its necessary diminishment of biologically based ties, overlooks Rossiter's perspective on the critical significance of the impact of the biological dimension for 'early' mothering practices.[47]

Further, Ruddick's account, as noted, seems to rely heavily on perceptions of the early stages of mothering relations for its general themes. It thereby reinforces identifications of mothering, *tout court*, with visions of caring for infant fragility. In contrast (if only by default) Rossiter's restriction of her discussion to relations with vulnerable and dependent infants, for all its own limitations, leaves open the possibility that maternal relationships may be significantly different at later stages of their development.

By use of Rossiter's work now however, I want to show that, even in the phase of maternal care that is characteristically dominated by infant dependency, analyses that remain abstract from the contextual detail and continuity of actual mothering relations are seriously limited. In this respect Rossiter's consideration of early mothering relations may serve as something of a limit case, pointing towards further possibilities for maternal care by way of analogous enquiries into other phases of its development.

Rossiter suggests the term 'containment' to describe the rich and complex practices of caring that occur in the first few weeks of mothering a newborn infant (FPP 65). In contrast with pregnancy when physical connection unites a mother's and her baby's needs, 'containment' is used to capture the sense of the inherently contradictory experience in which a physically separate person is incorporated into a mother's boundaries. This theme recalls the sense of intense relatedness and the expanded 'binary–unity' of selfhood mentioned earlier in this chapter. Where Ruddick, understandably wary of the dangers of self-loss, plays down mothers' experiences of 'binary–unity' by stressing the individuation of mother and child from the moment of birth, Rossiter's specific focus on the everyday activities of early mothering shows up what may be missed by this emphasis. For the details of mothers' daily activities reveal an 'in-between' process of attachment that defies conventional categories of identity and separation.

Rossiter describes this practice of 'containment' in terms of the requirement for babies' extensive needs to be included in the lives of their mothers. Drawing on accounts of the daily activities of one mother, she explains: 'The baby's needs became Maria's needs – she experienced the baby's needs as her own, and meeting those needs took precedence over meeting her own needs as a separate individual' (FPP 65). In this process the boundaries of the mother's identity change to include the baby, but at the same time the baby also remains distinct and separate for it is clear that one cannot fully contain a separate person within one's boundaries: 'the baby was included within Maria's boundaries, thus transforming the baby's needs into Maria's needs, yet in order for Maria to recognize the baby's needs, she had to see her as a separate person' (FPP 65).

Examining the details of Maria's early mothering practices, Rossiter indicates the different categories of activities involved in this process: the intense listening, the changes in sleeping, eating and activity rhythms, the engagement of different levels of attention at the same time enabling simultaneous incorporation of – and separation from – the baby. In the details of soothing, feeding, stimulating, changing, amusing, lulling, we see the intensity of the infant's vulnerability to her mother and the remarkable extension of the mother's awareness to the continuous inclusion of the baby's needs. Rossiter comments:

> Such work requires a tremendous fluidity of identity: suspending one's own identity to momentarily 'be' the baby in order to understand her needs, dissolving one's boundaries to admit a different rhythm, thinking with a constant sub-thought of 'baby' – all this means that mothering involves rather extraordinary transformations in identity. (FPP 244)

In addition, these transformations in identity are shaped by uncertainty about the explicit requirements of the relationship, and thus rely on trial-and-error learning with its anxieties and indeterminacies. All the while response to the constancy of the child's demands is played out in a state of exhaustion.

As Rossiter tracks the relationship over time, other dimensions of early maternal care become manifest. The accumulated 'containment' is deepened in a two-way dependency: the extension of the mother's boundaries to accommodate the baby's dependency overlaps and conjoins with the mother's engrossment in the baby and her pain at their separation. On the one side, the tasks of 'containment' are sustained and transformed in attachment, trust, communication and affection between persons, rather than between functionaries. Somewhere in the experiences of pregnancy, birth, lactation and the continuous, intimate responsibility of listening, adjusting and attending, the possibility for the fusion of attachment and responsibility is produced. With the realization of this possibility, the intrinsic value of the relationship itself becomes at once its own motivation and outcome. Yet, on the other side, the bonding is coincident with the ambivalence of separation from the baby. After investing an enormous amount of energy in the process of incorporating the baby into her world, learning to leave the baby creates renewed difficulties, tensions and anxieties for the maternal carer.

There are strong resonances between this account of 'containment' and Ruddick's conceptions of 'preservative love' and 'holding'. Ruddick's understanding of the tension between protection and risk, security and possibility, and the doubt, anxiety and fatigue of the struggle to balance these poles, catches the general dimensions of these mothering activities and their inherent instability. By taking us into the detail of particular relations during the first weeks of their development, Rossiter is able to show us the tensions as they are actually lived. We come to understand 'protection' and 'security', for example, in Maria's activities of incorporating the baby's constant needs for comforting, bathing, entertaining, nursing, and so on into her life, and 'risk' and 'possibility' in relation to the baby's activities independent of her mother.

By linking these processes of containment, attachment and responsibility with the social contexts of their enactment, Rossiter allows us to see the ways in which social arrangements tend to be produced by – and to reproduce and exacerbate – the instabilities of the relationship. Her discussion of the situations of each mother's experience of childbirth can be read as a prelude to this construction of their mothering relations. In each of the three cases, she describes how the relative difficulties or facility of the physiological events of giving birth were mediated by the expectations and socially constructed preconceptions with which the women approached the experience. In differing ways in each case, the enormous power of the medical apparatus to restrict the women's bodily potential and ignore their subjective needs, in conjunction with other culturally reinforced conceptualizations of women as passive and helpless, worked against the three women's active participation in the process.[48]

According to Rossiter, the restrictive medical practices are so powerful that they produce the understandings through which women order their experiences of their bodies and themselves. For example, following the birth of their babies each mother expressed subjective understandings of her birthing experience in varying degrees of disappointment, indifference and alienation from her active possibilities and needs.[49] Rossiter argues that the social arrangements that induce these self-interpretations are continuous with those that structure their child-rearing practices. Childbirth practices that devalue mothers' participation, and undermine their capacity to assert their needs, are continuous with the social relations in which their child care is practised.

The central element of this constitutive Western social context is isolation. The dramatic personal changes experienced during pregnancy, birth and postpartum recovery are accompanied, for most mothers, by radical changes in their relationship to the external world as well. Conventionally, during the first months of their mothering, they stop going out to the workplace, they cut back on their social activities outside their immediate family, and they are mainly confined to their separate households. As a result of these alterations in their possibilities for creative interactions in the social milieu, mothers experience physical and emotional isolation.

These experiences are often seen to be simply the result of the time-consuming and demanding work of caring for an infant. And, as Rossiter notes, much has been written about its oppressive effects.[50] However, as she follows the daily activities of each mother, we see how the minute and intertwined details of their physical, conceptual and social locations intersect with their preferential attachment and containment practices to produce that isolation. Maria's case is particularly instructive. Observation of her everyday life with her baby enables Rossiter to detect a wide range of factors that contribute to Maria's isolation: from her husband's long working hours, through the physical design of her apartment building, transportation possibilities, lack of facilities for babies in the public sphere and peer pressure, to her baby's attachment to her, and her own exhaustion and guilt about feeling isolated (FPP 241–51).

In this list of isolating factors it can be seen how actual material arrangements interact with cultural perceptions of mothering to reinforce each other. We can notice, for example, the reciprocal influence between the difficulties for Maria and her baby in using public transport and Maria's guilt about not feeling completely fulfilled in her relationship with her baby. When the connections between the ideology of fulfilment and the material conditions of its possibility are severed, mothers tend systematically to discount the significance of the actual organization of mothering for their experience. This neglect of material conditions in turn reaffirms the perception that fulfilment is intrinsic to the relationship, irrespective of the conditions in which it occurs. The isolation of mothering becomes an inevitable dimension of its practice, rather than an avoidable consequence of its social organization.

According to Rossiter, several entrenched features of Maria's society conspire to produce this isolation. At one level, the isolation of mothering from other social relations is a function of the separation of public and private realms of human activity. In contemporary liberal societies, this separation sets apart the functions and values of the political world from that of the family. Within this division, it seems that the confinement of mothering to the family sphere constructs the primary framework for its isolation. But this powerful organizational form is almost inseparably connected with the historically peculiar labour arrangements of Western capitalist economies.[51] Rossiter explains that two key commitments of the capitalist workplace intersect to sustain the exclusion of mothering relations from the public world: the priority of paid work over caring for the young and the requirement to protect the workplace from the threat of disruptive children. The assumption that it is not possible to work with children at hand neatly reinforces, and is reinforced by, the priority of paid work organized through the separation of childrearing practices from the workplace (FPP 280).[52]

The isolation of maternal care is further refined through the internal organization of contemporary families. The advent of the nuclear family – and its latter-day variants of single family households – in Western societies serves effectively to isolate maternal carers from each other and from other potential, familial caregivers. In this structure, so revealingly illustrated in the courses of the mothering relations that Rossiter studies, several conceptions of social organization coalesce: understandings of privacy, independence, security, economic viability, and so on. The outcome for mothering relations is their assignment to isolated households, away from and outside other culturally creative practices.

The functional dimension of mothering relations corresponding to this social isolation is the vesting of sole responsibility for the care of babies in their mothers. In a context in which mothers and their babies are cut off from other social relations, mothering comes to mean taking complete responsibility for the needs of babies, both in the eyes of the dominant culture as well as in mothers' own perceptions of their caring. With this understanding in place other interconnected ideologies become immediately plausible. For example: mothers are naturally capable of providing perfect care for their babies; mothers know what is best for their babies; caring for their babies is completely fulfilling for mothers. It is clear from Rossiter's analysis that these ideologies actively reproduce the legitimacy of sole responsibility and social isolation.

By following the course of the interactions of these socially constructed conditions with the daily activities of early mothering, Rossiter is able to locate the sites of deformation of the ethical possibilities of maternal care. Her analysis shows us how in conditions of isolation, the fluidity of identity – characteristic of 'containment' – is experienced as a loss of self, not because babies overwhelm their mothers but because mothers are cut off from the normal range of social exchanges in which identity is formed:

> Mothers are left without the social interactions which construct and produce identity; at the same time they are expected to perform work which demands a kind of diffusion of identity. In a very real sense, mothers feel they have 'lost' their selves. They have lost the world in which selves are co-constituted with and by other people. (FPP 244)

In this situation, strongly reinforced by the socially orchestrated self-alienation experienced in childbirth, mothers lose their general perspective on the possibilities of their caring. When the baby's needs become their only world, it is difficult to differentiate the varying imports of those needs. Uncertainty about the demands of the maternal relationship becomes uncertainty about the world in general, and the baby tends to be experienced as consuming her or his mother's self. As a consequence maternal caring becomes a course in self-sacrifice.

V

By setting this analysis beside that of Ruddick it is possible to explain Ruddick's framework. We can see, first, how her warnings to mothers against feelings of powerlessness and overprotectiveness, and her determination to distinguish the virtues of 'humility', 'cheerfulness' and a 'welcoming response to change' from the oppressive institutions of motherhood, are themselves shaped by alienating conditions. Instead of suggesting alternative ethical possibilities, these are precisely the virtues mothers need in order to cope with the isolating and self-diminishing social structure of their maternal caring.

Comparison with Rossiter's study also explains a second aspect of Ruddick's account. Because of their isolation and immersion in the work of caring for infants, mothers experience their own persons as insignificant. Accordingly, they become increasingly incapable of identifying, valuing and acting from their own independent needs.[53] In addition, the distorted maternal meanings produced through restrictive social organization feed back into practices of maternal care through dynamics such as self-castigation, shame and guilt, to reinforce this self-doubt and inability to trust one's own understandings and meanings. For this reason Ruddick places great emphasis on the requirement for mothers to trust their own judgements and to act out of their own self-appropriated understandings of dominant values in the face of these coercive external pressures. She realizes that mothers' own integrity and moral agency is crucial to the success of their maternal care. Yet once again we can see that these exhortations directly complement the structure that undermines mothers' sense of their own personhood and identity.

Third, we can appreciate how Ruddick's manoeuvres – to avoid understandings of mother–child relations in ways that might suggest an ethically unique harmony of identities – arise to counteract mothering practices that are socially shaped to encourage destructive forms of interdependence. Rossiter's study demonstrates how the material and ideological organization of mothering turns mother and child in on each other, making them totally dependent on each other for their life meanings. The damaging effects of this form of identification are all too obvious to Ruddick, and thus she steers her account of maternal care away from any recognition of the special union between (birth) mothers and their children. But in doing so she overlooks the potentially rich ethical possibilities of this bond in non-oppressive conditions.

Further, Rossiter's account also highlights the self-reinforcing dynamic of the invisibility of maternal care. The separation and concealment of mothering relations within individual households cut off from conventional social sources of affirmation and recognition – their difficulties ascribed to individual struggles with temptations and virtues instead of public priorities – erodes mothers' self-confidence and capacities to use their lived realities to generate their care. Concurrently, this lack of esteem and ability to attain public acknowledgement of the responsibilities, values and significance of mothering relations actively downgrades their worth, and their possibilities for shaping our understanding and conception of human interactions. As a consequence, (typically male) textbooks and courses in ethics completely neglect mothering relations as a source of ethical understanding. Thus a fourth aspect of Ruddick's framework can be explained. We can understand why she is determined to demonstrate the significance of mothering relations by placing their values in the relatively abstract and instrumental terms that are intelligible in the publicly established forums of ethics. And we can see the inherent flaws in this intent.

Rossiter's concern with the everyday accounts of individual mothers' experiences takes us to the ordinary daily places where, in different ways, the experiences of isolation and self-loss unfold in each mother's activities. For Maria, the slippage of her identity into her baby's, without other affirmations of her ego, brings on damaging feelings of guilt and depression at her sense of the need for help. Her only escape route is to return to the workplace. Tina negotiates her isolation with the voracious demands of her baby largely by imposing self-protective routines on the infant, 'protecting' time for herself but reducing her freedom to be with other people and the possibilities for them to establish independent relationships with the baby. For Natalie, whose actions express subjective experiences of extreme fragility with respect to the external world, isolation becomes an opportunity to conceal her lack of confidence and thus to further entrench her disempowerment.

In these stories, a tiny sample of the multitude of different possibilities that every mothering relationship produces, it is possible to see some of the outlines of damaging patterns of interaction constructed through the commonalities of their social contexts. For example, under the terms of isolation and sole responsibility, the contradictions of containment are produced as a clash of needs. Babies' needs constantly compete with their mothers', for each becomes the whole world for the other. Each mother arbitrates this clash in a different way, depending on her personal history and the actual situation of her mothering: 'escaping' back to the workplace and a possible superwoman role, imposing her requirements on the baby and teaching her or him not to need, or subsiding into the chaos of total alienation from self and 'treatment' with drugs and alcohol. From the infants' side, 'arbitration' of their needs ranges from undifferentiated satisfaction through curtailment of their participation in relational possibilities with other persons – perhaps most importantly with their fathers – to neglect and abandonment.

Rossiter suggests that this socially constructed pattern of conflict in maternal caring sustains the dominant conception of mothering relations. This conception then produces cultural paradigms for caring and for women in general. The relational conflict creates opposition between the needs of mothers and the needs of their children, and is resolved in maternal self-sacrifice. At the same time, the preferential attachment of birth mothers to their infants, and the vulnerability of infants to their mothers, create powerful identifications between the maternal, the womanly and the carer. As a result of these intertwined conceptual orders, selfless responsiveness to the needs of others and passivity with respect to their own needs become the marks not only of maternal caring, but of caring and women *per se*. Far from setting out possibilities for rich ethical enhancement and transformation, mothering relations become unacceptably constrained by their contribution to the disempowerment and devaluation of women. For Rossiter, the liberation of maternal care from these constraints can be achieved only through appropriate social change.

In contrast with Ruddick's discussion of the power of individual virtue and commitment in the creation of the ethical potential of mothering relationships, Rossiter's study exposes the refractory force of social structures in the overwhelming of individual possibilities. Doubtless this perspective permits irresponsible eva-sion and victimism. Perhaps few mothers would corroborate the uncompromising disavowal of responsibility: 'it wasn't me ... what I did as a mother came from outside' (FPP 19). To be sure, Ruddick's experience of her own participation in maternal care seems to contradict the location of primary responsibility in its social organization. Many other mothers – my own included – steadfastly vouch for and rejoice in the personal possibilities and responsibilities their mothering practices have given them. Thus it is clear that while subjective agency does not determine mater-nal possibilities alone, at the same time, individual commitments, attitudes and values are not simply the products of social forms. Ruddick's account of maternal thinking articulates, for many mothers, a rich understanding of the values and significance of their caring, and explains why they are so inspired by their maternal relations.

The strength of Rossiter's analysis, on the other hand, lies in the way it shows the constitutive importance of structural orders in shaping ethical possibilities. Accordingly, any account of ethical imports demands that attention be paid to the interdependence of social and subjective forces. In particular, the re-evaluation of subjective ethical commitments and aspirations is intimately bound up with re-assessment of the social conditions in which they arise. Thus the special potential of maternal caring for enhancement of the lives of both mothers and their children is dependent on a set of social arrangements that recognize and encourage that potential. These will be arrangements that reduce the possibilities of destructive conflict by avoiding closing mothers and their children in on each other and reducing their identities to a single function.

Chapter 2

Friendship

I

With the examination of the kinds of caring practices exhibited by relations of friendship, this investigation moves into a realm of social intercourse that is characterized by its informality and relative absence of controlling institutions, fixed rituals and conventions. Unlike mothering practices, with their organization deeply embedded in the social institutions of the family, and the more formally structured practices of nursing and citizenship, friendships call up a sphere of social activity that is both exhilaratingly free from regulation and profoundly fragile. The lack of publicly administered roles, activities, responsibilities and boundaries imbues friendships with liberating possibilities for interpersonal caring, unmatched by the more clearly defined structures of other social relations. But at the same time the potential for relatively unrestricted expression is hedged in by the constraints of its own uncertainty. The expansive promise of friendship, the possibility of freely choosing and being freely chosen, is conditioned by vulnerability to the vicissitudes of its participants and the exigencies of the more structured relations in which they are involved. The friendship that is given in freedom can also be withdrawn with impunity.

While it is clear that the absence of formal structures in the constitution of friendships permits endless variety in the range of attachments – endless diversity in the balancing of freedom and vulnerability – it is also apparent that intersections in that range map out distinguishable contours of caring possibilities. Through a discussion of the different possibilities of friendship, therefore, I hope to bring some of those contours into relief, and thus further my project of investigating the ethical import of the concept of care.

On the contemporary philosophical landscape the tendency to equate the moral with the impartial has diverted attention from personal relations towards more formal and contractual inter-actions. Duties to, and the rights of, indistinguishable others take centre field in deliberations on the moral life. Relations of friend-ship formed in that indeterminate and risky realm of personal preference and affectional influences have been largely removed to the sidelines of ethical concern.[1] But it was not always so. For the ancients, friendship was of central concern. In the work of Plato and Aristotle, selective affiliations – and self-chosen rela-tionships – combine qualities of wisdom, affection and goodness, without which no one can flourish.[2] The ideal of perfect friendship embedded in the Aristotelian claim that living and mutual sharing with friends is a constitutive feature of any worthwhile life echoes through the ages. Cicero, Montaigne, Bacon, and more recently, Thoreau and Emerson are notable examples.[3] But in the poetics of ideal veneration and heartfelt consolations, much of the essential connection with ethical life is diminished. Friendship becomes an expression of natural desire or inclination, no more a noble ethical achievement than an attachment of the slavish and weak.[4]

This kind of analysis might well be expected to be of interest to theorists concerned with gender sensitivity. Growing con-sciousness of the possibilities and actualities of enslavement and disempowerment, at the hands of putatively good friends, might suggest the relevance of exploring the ethical possibilities and limits of friendship to feminist ethicists. But the development of these connections has not been a central concern in the literature. Instead reflection on friendship has emerged from recognition of the focal importance of the maintenance of caring relationships in women's characteristic experience of moral life. The latter commonly derives from women's involvement in caring for dependent infants and children or the sick, aged and infirm, but it suggests a revaluation of interpersonal connectedness in general[5] and the examination of the ethical significance of more reciprocally based relationships.[6] In this context, friendships pres-ent the possibility of caring relationships that are connected with actively chosen sharing and reciprocity.

In addition, recent work in the genealogy of women's friend-ships presents evidence for the centrality of friendships to the realization of personal potential, identity and the maintenance of community values.[7] These studies form part of a programme that is more political than ethical in its inspiration. The examination of women's same-sex relationships from feminist perspectives is designed largely as a corrective to the persistent viewing of these attachments from within a masculinist framework that both demeans and undermines them: for example, as apprenticeships for relations with men, or as compensatory for the lack of men.[8] But the political and the ethical come together as these re-descriptions intersect with investigation of imposed asymmetries in relationships between females and males. Explicit exposure of the ethical distortions of relations of domination and dependency illuminates feminist explorations of friendship relations, from the other side as it were.[9] The revaluation of women's friendships and women's lives becomes, then, the site of enquiry into the alternative ethical significance of chosen, reciprocal relations.

In taking up the investigation of friendship as part of a survey of the ethical import of caring relations, this chapter is largely inspired by the suggestions of these projects. Friendships invite attention both in their potential for enriching understanding of the complexity and variety of caring practices, and in their signific-ance for the gender sensitivity of ethical enquiry. Once again, in keeping with my general claim that understanding develops through consideration of the differences and similarities of dis-tinctive examples, the discussion proceeds by juxtaposing differ-ing accounts of friendship.

II

I shall begin with a discussion of that most famous of accounts: Aristotle's treatment of *philia*. For despite its cultural discongruity and its central preoccupation with activities constitutive to the flourishing of a select band of men, Aristotle's description offers a picture of practices of friendship that sets out concerns and questions of enduring importance. Two important issues arise at the outset, however. First, Aristotle's term *philia*, is notable for the inclusion in its compass of a range of relations that are not customarily classified as friendships today: associations between family members, business partners and lovers. Our word 'friend-ship', of course, does not apply to a unified class of relationships, and we may well use the term in describing affiliations that are formed in more structured contexts like those of the family or the state, but it seems that *philia* links relations that are far less personal and weaker in affect, as well as those that are far stronger and more intimate, than our contemporary ascriptions of friendship imply.

Of particular relevance to the current enquiry, Aristotle discusses both maternal and citizenship relations as model cases of *philia*. This usage might appear to subvert my claims for the complexity and for the distinctions these different relationships raise for understanding the concept of caring. Why use Aristotle's *philia* to illuminate the specificity of friendship if *philia* itself is of such generalized import? The objection can be dissolved on historical grounds by indicating the impact of changes in social organization on conceptual categories. But in so doing, it is worth noting how the very possibility of this socio-historical move colludes with my project. For it is in the specific resonance of Aristotle's characterization of *philia* with contemporary usage of 'friendship' – its differentiation from contemporary usages of 'mothering' and 'citizenship', for example – that understanding of the complexities of friendship emerges.

Second, there is the troubled question of gender. Some explanation for the use of the writings of a philosopher who so clearly discriminated against women in his analysis of ethical possibilities is required. Blanket assertions indicating awareness of 'historical prejudice' and the necessity for opening up the highest realm of the ethical to women are deeply dissatisfying.[10] On the other hand, it is of some concern whether in fact the exclusion of women from the highest sorts of excellence is structurally intrinsic to Aristotle's conceptualization of ethical possibilities.[11] At least a gender-sensitive analysis of *philia* does not reduce straightforwardly to the exposure of explicit gender biases. Accordingly I shall retain Aristotle's gender ascriptions, refusing to overlook his bias while at the same time enabling it to raise questions concerning the possibilities for gender sensitivity.[12]

Explicit discussion of *philia* is given in Books VIII and IX of the *Nicomachean Ethics*, Aristotle's central ethical text. Both this locale and the substance of the analysis signal the integral interconnection Aristotle is concerned to assert between the morally good life and the practice of *philia*. It seems that *philia* and ethics are not only instrumentally connected but also, in some way, mutually constitutive: *philia* provides both the means to moral excellence as well as the conditions for its occurrence. *Philoi* assist each other in times of poverty and misfortune, weakness and ignorance – even in the 'prime of life' – providing aid, encouragement and pleasure that cannot be produced alone (NE 1155a9–16). But apart from the instrumental good of contributing to participants' independently defined goals, *philia* is a 'virtue, or implies virtue' (NE 1155a4) in itself. As Nancy Sherman explains, this intrinsic value attributed to *philia* is a 'pervasive sort, providing the very form and mode of life within which an agent can best realize her [*sic*] virtue and achieve happiness'. To have intimate attachments is to have 'persons toward whom and with whom one can most fully and continuously express one's character' interwoven through one's life.[13] In the course of Aristotle's discussion these two dimensions of the connection between *philia* and the active expression of moral excellence – the instrumental and the intrinsic – are worked through in more detail.

The primary criterion for *philia*, according to Aristotle, is mutuality in wishing the other well. The point is made by contrasting the love characteristic of *philia* and the love of wine. In the latter case there is:

> no mutual love, nor is there a wishing of good to the other (for it would surely be ridiculous to wish wine well; if one wishes anything for it, it is that it may keep, so that one may have it oneself); but to a friend [*philos*] we say we ought to wish what is good for his sake. (NE 1155b29–32)

Philia requires a mutuality – a shared giving and receiving of affection – that recognizes the other, the object of the love, as someone who has distinctive possibilities and needs in his own right. This 'mutual love' does not enable participants to possess each other, nor does it perform some kind of fusion process that incorporates the separate 'good' of each into the 'good' of the other. Rather, a true *philos* wishes the other well out of concern for his own, independent good; *philia* requires mutual recognition of each person's separate character and well-being. Other sources add that this wanting for another what is in his own best interests, has a necessary active, practical dimension.[14] Mutual well-wishing involves mutual well-doing.

With this essential condition in place, Aristotle goes on to describe the different kinds of *philia* that meet its requirements. Having observed that *philia* may occur in diverse social relations, he distinguishes different types of *philia* according to the different inclinations they serve. Persons may form bonds of well-wishing because they take pleasure in each other and find it enjoyable to be with one another. Alternatively, their association may be formed on the basis of the advantages that they derive from each other for the pursuit of their independent projects. In each of these cases the attachment seems to be motivated primarily by self-interest, rather than love of the other for what he is in his deepest sense of himself and his values. At the same time, however, these relationships are not purely selfish, for in order to be versions of *philia* it seems that the parties carry some disinterested concern for each other's well-being.[15]

Although it is not easy to interpret Aristotle's exact meaning here, his concern with the different grounds of friendship raises the question – if only by default – of the possibilities of multi-valent, self- and other-directed categories of *philia* (for example, NE 1156b35–1157a3). His classification points towards the very common experience of the complexity and varying strengths of the diversely based, selfish and other-interested activities and feelings that constitute our bonds of friendship. Sometimes mutual admiration of each other's taste in dress, or enjoyment in playing tennis, holds us together for the main part. Sometimes it is an exchange of books or child-care, or emotional support, that forms the basis of a relationship; perhaps more frequently a combination of pleasures and profits sustains the connection. But if the relationship is deemed to be one of friendship then at some level it seems that the participants also care about each other's well-being without selfish motivation.[16]

Aristotle's appreciation of some of the complexity and contingency of the various types of *philia* is evident as he explores the nature of the 'pleasure' and 'advantage' kinds of *philia* by comparing them with the third and best kind. Relationships of utility and pleasure, he says, are somewhat transient and unstable since they are based on interests that are only incidentally connected with the well-being of each *philos* on his own account (NE 1156a20–2). The third type of *philia* – that is, attachment based on mutual concern of each person for the other for his own sake – is however far more durable and profound. For in these relationships it is the qualities of each person that are most fundamental to each, as the particular person he is, that is the primary basis for the affiliation (NE 1156b9–12). As Martha

Nussbaum explains, the qualities at stake are those 'that are so intrinsic to [each partner's] being himself that a change in them would raise questions of identity and persistence'.[17] This sort of *philia* is therefore a far more lasting form of mutual caring in which the independent and enduring good of each of the participants is fostered by the other.

According to Aristotle, it is also the most worthy form of *philia*: such mutual loving, when it enables active expression of the qualities of human flourishing in each partner's innermost self, is ethically excellent because goodness is living the life that is true to the fullest expression of oneself. 'Perfect friendship [*philia*] is the friendship [*philia*] of men who are good, and alike in virtue; for these wish well alike to each other *qua* good, and they are good in themselves' (NE 1156b7–9). In the perfect form of *philia* it seems that loving the other for his own sake is, for Aristotle, coincident with loving the qualities of 'objective' ethical excellence that the other displays – as well as actively expressing 'objective' virtue oneself.

The effective collapse of the distinction between the intrinsic particularity of the *philoi* and the 'alike' virtue which they express, a collapse implicit in this description, is both complex and confusing.[18] Is the moral worth of *philia* grounded simply in love of the virtues of the other, rather than concern for the other person for his own sake?[19] Has the 'alikeness' in virtue of each (good) *philos* rendered the significance of care for their individual particularity and independent goods null? Is the realm of morally excellent attachments limited to persons who are wholly and completely virtuous, ruling out the deep and abiding relations between ordinary people who are characteristically a mix of virtues and imperfections?

There are no easy answers to these questions, for they call on elucidation of the intimate interrelationship between objective values and their concrete moorings in individual's lives. Emphasis on objective values may overlook the particularistic value of friendship in its nurture of each participant's essential uniqueness; emphasis on those values' moorings may dissolve the moral worth of friendship into support for any beliefs, aspirations and choices that may be deeply held. A judicious balance draws attention to the way in which we are concerned for both the character and values of our friends.[20]

While different interpretations are debatable, it is clear that

Aristotle's conception of the most significant kind of *philia* takes us to the heart of the issue of what it means to be concerned for a person, for that person's own sake.[21] The discussion of his account, thus far, indicates that this kind of caring is constituted in the complex set of relations between persons' love for each other's particularity, the affinity of their values, and the connection between individual particularity and values. These are complicated and messy concepts, perhaps intractable for determinate analysis. For Aristotle, their elaboration occurs through discussion of the active practices that are crucial to this kind of mutual affection, and an account of its differences and similarities with respect to relationships based on pleasure and advantage.

Essential to 'virtue *philia*' is the requirement that *philoi* must 'live together', enjoying each other's company, conferring benefits on each other, and sharing the social, intellectual and political activities that produce the intimacy relevant to their human flourishing (NE 1157b7–8; NE 1172a2–9). Living together is significant in enabling physical proximity and the possibility of spending time together. Both of these factors are conducive to creating effective opportunities for sharing diverse and numerous activities and becoming intimate with each other (for example NE 1157b22; NE 1158a9; NE 1171a4). Correspondingly, distance and lack of time together limit these opportunities for active sharing, and may cause the relationship to lapse (NE 1157b10–12). It seems obvious that because *philoi* are attracted to each other and enjoy sharing activities, they will naturally want and choose to spend time together. But, more subtly, going through time together itself strengthens the bond and its value (NE 1156b25–7). Here the point is that the intimacy connected with caring for a person for his own sake requires a history of sharing not only especially chosen and valued activities but the mundane and everyday practices that are also part and parcel of a flourishing life. Typically, Aristotle talks about the activities in which men are involved outside the domestic sphere: eating, drinking, conversing, financial dealing, politicking. Sharing in as many of the activities of the other as possible – and thereby gaining a thoroughgoing experience of his character, values and habits – is constitutive of loving him for his own sake. With this insight Aristotle confirms his understanding of the way that ethics, the practice of what is most valued in life, is firmly rooted in the concrete details of the everyday –

though the everyday lives of the male elite to which Aristotle refers may seem rather rarefied. Ethics is a matter of daily living, not just heroic or monstrous moments, and *philia* is a central constituent of an ethical life.

His emphasis on the extent of sharing resonates with the familiar experience of the way bonds of friendship and love are enriched and deepened through the accumulation of activities and events that have been 'lived together' with a friend or lover. In part this strengthening of bonds is related directly to the sheer quantity of shared activities, their number, diversity and repetition bringing a wide-ranging experience of what the other's own sake might be and enlarging the possibilities for the relationship. Perhaps more importantly, the quantity of repeated activities facilitates that kind of habituation with respect to mundane routines that frees up the relationship for the development of more profound dimensions of mutuality and intimacy. The accumulation of shared activities may function as a process of 'enculturation' into the communal practices of the relationship: the kind of practical immersion in which 'know-how' is acquired in the actual performance of sharing (NE 1095a30–1095b13; NE 1103a-1103b6).

Something more than the weight of numbers is involved here. The quantity of accumulated sharing seems also to be qualitatively constitutive in the ethical bonding of persons who genuinely care for each other for each's own sake. Changes in consciousness, knowledge and values, and in the possibilities of intimacy, become interwoven in the extensive practice of sharing activities. It is this qualitative potential of 'living together' – especially apparent in the sharing of discussion and thought – that Aristotle claims distinguishes *philia* from non-moral, unreflective sharing (NE 1170b10–13).

The trust that is crucial to the best sort of *philia* also depends on 'time and familiarity'. Aristotle quotes the proverb 'men cannot know each other till they have "eaten salt together"'; and goes on to claim 'nor can they admit each other to friendship [*philia*] or be friends [*philoi*] till each has been found lovable and been trusted by each' (NE 1156b28–9). Here the two very palpable elements of 'living together', the sharing of space and of time, conjoin with the possibility of reciprocal knowledge of each other and receptivity to each other in a bond of shared meaning and value. At its best, *philia* requires the ability to receive one another's love with trust and openness, without fear of betrayal or misuse by the other and without the intrusions of one's own self-centred defensiveness and jealousies.

We have seen from Ruddick's description of mothering that this kind of trust, though it originates there in necessity, is vital to ethical relations of maternal care as well. In both cases, the willingness to accept each other acquires its value in its mutual recognition, for without reciprocal acknowledgement of each other's openness and responsivity to the other, trust is insecure, and the relationship can only be an expression of good will. For friendships, as well as mother–child relations, this recognition and trust is clearly a process of development, inextricably bound up in acting and living together through a shared history. Indeed Aristotle even hints that the duration of time spent in shared activities may be a 'test' for the value and genuineness of the relationship when he says that 'people cannot live together if they are not pleasant and do not enjoy the same things, as friends [*philoi*] who are companions seem to do' (NE 1157b23–4).

For maternal relations, however, this 'test' is less valid since, by comparison with friendships, mothering practices are supported by the more strongly structured kinship arrangements that encourage 'living together' even when trust is minimal. Without this institutional framework to ensure a measure of care, friendships are much more centrally dependent on trust and vulnerable to its misuses. For Aristotle, therefore, the thoroughgoing trust that is so crucial to caring for the other for his own sake emerges only when *philoi* can live together happily and share in all the activities that are relevant to the good of their independent lives (for example, NE 1157a16–24).

This is no small demand, and although *philia* is enhanced by extensive sharing, its full ethical potential can only be actualized when a well-developed sense of virtue is shared and exercised by both persons (NE 1157b25–8). And for Aristotle, of course, virtue is virtuous because it is an actively developed quality that harmonizes practical wisdom and choice with the claims of the emotions, physical capabilities and the contingencies of personal history. The ethical value of *philia* lies not in the happy coincidence of sharing a sense of what is 'good and pleasant' with someone else, but in expressing and responding to expressions of this faculty of cultivated feeling and choice (1157b28–33). Here Sherman suggests how the moral worth of *philia* is continuously sustained since the practice of spending time together – which is the hallmark of

genuine *philia* – involves choice, not so much in terms of initiating
the relationship, but rather in 'a capacity to share and co-ordinate
activities over an extended period of time'.[22] Thus the bond
of mutual trust and receptivity is composed of complexly intertwined strands of shared commitments, mutual affection, reciprocal choices, familiarity and habituation.

Once again the overlapping and divergence of themes familiar
from the discussions of maternal care are apparent. Trust in
oneself and in others, openness to change and difference, are
intimately interlinked with the capacity for choice: to be able to
choose with integrity to one's own values is ethically central to
maternal care, though there may be constraints on the subject of
one's choice. In friendships of the 'best' kind, choosing whom one
cares for, and choosing for oneself, are continuous and mutually
reaffirming.

Given the significance of sharing, trust and intimacy for the active
and continuous expression of one's character and identity in the
fullest and most genuine sense, Aristotle claims that nobody
would choose to live without *philoi* even if he had everything
else that he could want. This kind of personal connectedness is
part of what it is to be fully engaged with oneself and the world.
For this reason we praise those who love their *philoi*, and we
think that *philia* is one of the greatest goods (NE 1155a5–6;
NE 1155a29–31). So too, Aristotle likens the disposition one has to
one's friends to the feelings one has for oneself, explaining that
the latter feelings, which are psychologically prior, present the
clearest case of the kind of relations that are characteristic of the
former.[23] 'A friend is another self'; or a good man 'is related to his
friend [*philoi*] as to himself' (NE 1166a29–31). Here the equation
between *philia* and 'self-love' affirms once more that *philoi* are
integral parts in the fullness of each other's lives.

But the worth of this bond inheres not only in the intrinsic value
of sharing, trust and intimacy to the fullness of life. This ethical
import is interconnected with more individual and directly instrumental gains for each partner. *Philia* is also self-love in the sense
of its returns to one's independent interests. Recognition of, and
effective concern for, the worth of another person has a direct
reflexive value to oneself that in turn redounds to the intrinsic
possibilities of the relationship. It is important to remember here,
however, Aristotle's distance from the modern moral tradition

that has been preoccupied with pitting self-interest against other-interest. He defends the moral worth of *philia* both on the basis of the intrinsic value of intimacy to the self and in terms of its more direct contribution to the self's individual values (NE 1168b9). But here the benefits to self are not merely the satisfaction of interests arising independently of the relationship, but rather that enhancement of a person and his virtue that is only available insofar as he is actively engaged in a relationship of love for another person for that person's own sake.

In the face of conventional self/other distinctions, this position has a paradoxical ring. But closer examination of Aristotle's understanding of this self-love and the ways in which it is fostered by genuine *philia* reveals a constitutive realm of compatibility and harmony between self and other that is frequently overlooked in theories that emphasize conflict between persons. In this respect his emphasis on the reflexivity of *philia* and its vital connection with the ethical value of the relationship resonates strongly with the ideas of reciprocity and reflexivity that have already arisen in the examination of maternal practices in Chapter 1. Aristotle's description of the ways in which *philia* is constitutively linked with self-love enriches our understanding of the significance of this reflexive dimension of caring, but we can also see how it takes a contrasting form in this different sort of caring relationship. In addition to providing direct instrumental benefits in the form of help, support and enjoyment, *philoi* who respect and care for each other's well-being are able to provide inspiration for the development of each other's virtue. As Aristotle puts it, *philoi* 'are thought to become better too, by their activities and by improving each other; for from each other they take the mould of the characteristics they approve' (NE 1172a12–14).

Intimate relations between genuine *philoi* also enable enhanced self-knowledge and understanding. The deep affinity between *philoi* allows each to function as a mirror for the other, their eyes providing the reflection. Since close *philoi* are very much like each other – 'another self', as it were – each can gain valuable insight into his own character by studying the other. For while it is very difficult to see directly what sort of person we are, without bias or emotion, 'we can contemplate our neighbours better than ourselves and their actions better than our own' (NE 1169b34–5). As Cooper explains, *philia* serves as a 'bridge by which to convert objectivity about others into objectivity about oneself'.[24] And the ethical value of this self-knowledge seems self-evident, for in Aristotelian terms the fullest expression of one's identity and life crucially involves knowledge about that sort of life and why one is leading it.[25]

Again, by joining in one's pursuits *philoi* can provide a source of continuing stimulation for one's central goals and interests when one's own self-motivation is flagging (NE 1170a4–9).[26] Accordingly, *philia* becomes a source of self-validation and confirmation. For the experience of sharing the activities that are most important to one's identity and values strengthens one's sense of their worth and increases their possibilities. Since this depth of sharing is only possible between those who are alike in their commitments, and in their receptiveness to each other for what each truly is, it is clear that Aristotle's conception of *philia* provides an account of caring between persons in which concern for the good of the other and the enhancement of self-understanding and self-esteem are intimately interconnected.

Implicit in all of these possibilities of love and care, based in the reciprocal concern of each *philos* for the independent and particular good of the other, lies an understanding of irreducible ethical uniqueness. The meaning and value of the relationship is dependent on the character of just these two unique individuals. Each person stands in relation to the other in a way that they stand in relation to no other person, for it is the specificity of the other for whom each is in himself that is the focus of their love. Importantly it is this constitutive uniqueness or particularity of concern that generates the ethical possibilities of the relationship.

But this exclusivity and uniqueness also signal its vulnerability and ethical limits. The picture of virtue and harmonious stability that the intense intimacy and durability of genuine *philia* evokes is circumscribed by the complex conjunction of variables it demands. From a contemporary perspective, the concurrence of the conditions that are conducive to such a long-term and demanding commitment, tailored so specifically to the characters of two unique persons, seems close to miraculous. Although he does not say much about the contingencies involved in the formation of such relations in the first place, Aristotle is aware of some of the difficulties of maintaining genuine concern for another in the face of the complexity and uncertainties of human lives. For example, he remarks early on in his discussion that age is a significant factor in the possibility of enjoying genuine *philia* (NE 1157b13–14; NE

1158a1–5). And as he works through his account he mentions some of the familiar stock of deformations, divisions and reproaches that may threaten and destroy the best of relations, for example: misinterpretation, changes in character, deception and conflicts (NE 1165a36–1165b36; NE 1171a5–8), in addition to the absences and lack of time already noted.

These remarks indicate some recognition of the fragility of relations formed on the basis of self-directed concern and love for another without a supporting institutional framework of rights and obligations. The centrality of trust, and the emphasis on extensive intimacy, familiarity and habituation in his description, also suggest dimensions of vulnerability in these kinds of caring relationships that are not as significant in mothering relations, for example, where social organization is geared towards protecting the connection. Further, Aristotle's claims about the essential engagement and interdependence of both emotions and 'choice' (or reason) in the maintenance of the reciprocal affection, imply that *philia* requires protection from the capriciousness of raw feeling as well as the indifference of abstract ratiocination. Again his mindfulness of the vital power of reciprocity and trust, of the ethical import of the reflexivity and particularity of the relationship, are marks of his understanding of the significance of its freedom from impersonal regulation. In the contours of these limits and possibilities we can grasp the outlines of a practice of caring between persons which maps much of the familiar and complex ethical terrain of what is currently understood as friendship.

In setting out this ground, however, Aristotle's discussion takes its bearings from a social order that is strongly structured in favour of an elite group of males, and his conception of ethical value displays a marked correspondence to the distribution of this social order. Not only does the potential for the highest possibilities of virtue and goodness reside within the structures of the aristocratic class, and the activities and relationships that are typical of its members, but those activities and relationships fashion the possibilities of ethics itself. In the case of *philia*, perfection and the practices in which it is expressed – close and extended sharing of activities, thoughts and ideas – are accessible only to free adult males. For although he frequently invokes family relations, especially relations between mothers and their children, as models of the special affection and uniqueness characteristic of caring for another for his own sake (NE 1059a26–33; NE 1161b11ff.), Aristotle's description of the sharing and reciprocity of 'living together' clearly precludes relations between persons who are 'unequal' in their social possibilities from reaching the highest sort of *philia*.[27]

This interdependence of ethical and social hierarchies is of particular interest to my enquiry at two different levels. First, and almost by default, Aristotle's survey of different kinds of loving and concernful relations between persons identifies for us a significant distinction between the possibilities of mothering relations and personal relations between mature and socially equivalent men. For in the discussion of mothering, we have already seen some of the ways in which this distinction influences practices of caring. In Ruddick's account, for example, the dependency of children – that is so characteristic of mothering relations – structures the ethical possibilities of practices of 'preservation', 'nurture' and 'training'. Thus, insofar as it endorses the distinction between 'unequal' and 'equal' relations, Aristotle's expansion of *philia* to include both these types of caring attachments provides positive evidence to the current investigation of the complexity of the differences and similarities of caring relationships.

Second, the correspondence between the highest form of *philia* and the highest social order produces specific emphases in his account of the nature of friendship itself. In particular, the link between ethical value and social status creates a vision of perfection and harmony that is relatively secure from the range of individual and systemic contingencies characteristic of the flow of personal relations within more loosely structured and more mobile social orders. Even though, on Aristotle's account, *philia* is notable for the engagement of personal preferences rather than institutional obligations, its formation and practice are bounded by the homogeneous structure and values of the social elite. The apparently diverse possibilities inherent in the ethical particularity of *philia* are therefore tightly constrained by their conjunction with the generalized values of the *polis*. As a result, the 'likeness' between persons that is characteristic of members of a close-knit elite with relatively uniform values and aspirations – more particularly, likeness in virtue, as the quality that is most lovable and typical of a person in himself – becomes the determining factor for the attachment.

This stress gives Aristotle's account of *philia* its characteristic political force: the understanding that the kind of affinity expressed in the intense intimacy of *philia* is also the 'glue' of political relations, holding states together by inducing harmony and like-mindedness between their citizens (NE 1155a23–5). Accordingly, for Aristotle, the bonds of intimacy resound beyond the personal sphere providing the basis of communal congeniality; in its turn, the end of politics is the production of *philia*.[28]

I have already noted, however, that Aristotle's emphasis on the role of 'objective' (or communal) virtue in the attraction of *philia* raises questions concerning the significance of individual differences to the relationship. And while it is clear that a deep basis of affinity facilitates friendly relations, at the same time recognition of independence, and acceptance of idiosyncrasies as well as emotional and ethical differences, are intrinsic to the creative complexity of caring for a friend for the friend's own sake. Backed by its confinement to a relatively commensurable and compact social class, Aristotle's conception of 'virtue *philia*' diminishes the role and tensions of these differences between friends, as well as much of the complexity of internal changes in character and values within each friend. Although he is not oblivious to some potential for conflict and change, the minimization of moral disparity inherent in his orientation towards likeness and 'objective' virtue misses the ethical riches of that deep-rooted connectedness which comes of trust developed in the face of imperfections and differences. It also defuses much of the creative vulnerability incurred in maintaining genuine concern for the different, complex and uncertain life of another person.[29]

Further, the connection between *philia* and the practices of the aristocracy shapes the kinds of activities that are deemed relevant and valuable to friendly sharing. Thus activities displaying physical, intellectual and political domination and pleasure preponderate in the domain of *philia* to the detriment of practices in emotional responsivity and expression, the communication and sharing of one's 'inner-life', self-revelation, and the conveying and support of personal biography and identity.[30] Indeed, in an especially telling passage that shows a singular lack of understanding of the dynamics of emotional support, Aristotle explicitly scorns the sharing of emotional distress as a 'womanly' pastime, justifying 'manly' emotional repression as liberation from the pain of causing another pain at seeing one's suffering (NE 1171b5–12).

Close involvement with one's *philos* requires caring for him and his aspirations as one would for one's own, but this intimacy is mostly a matter of 'doing' together the sorts of things that show strength and independence: activities that avoid showing one's limits and vulnerabilities. The kind of sharing that apparently incorporates another into one's most personal and vulnerable sphere neglects and even disparages activities of inner disclosure that support 'being' together for the sake of connectedness. It seems that the likeness of the parties and the equivalence of their status produce independent identities that can somehow be taken for granted in the relationship – or where inequalities in status are involved, a quantitative calculation of proportions that is free of problems of self-doubt, vulnerability or contention (NE 1158b12ff.).

In addition, of course, the sharing that is characteristic of *philia* is structurally insulated against the trials of servility, poverty and oppression latent in systemic social constructs of difference. Though they may be mortally vulnerable to betrayal and treachery, Aristotle's *philoi* are blessed with considerable freedom from the pressures of material survival, and structural dependence on the will of others. They are able to engage with each other with a degree of personal confidence and security that is largely inaccessible to those whose lives are systematically degraded, enslaved or spent in the struggle for material subsistence. To this extent, issues of identity, choice and reciprocity in relationships become relatively straightforward and unproblematic. Thus important questions concerning the particularity, vulnerability and differences between friends are muted in Aristotle's examination of *philia* in favour of a focus on affinity of virtue and character, durability and 'alikeness'. The complexities of identity are masked by the enframing interdependence of social order and ethical values. At the same time however, his account carries, at least implicitly, the psychological complexity which gives rise to these concerns, and in some respects – for example, on the question of the connections between self-knowledge, self-esteem and friendship – his insights provide an explicit opening.

In its insights and oversights, openings and closings, Aristotle's discussion supplies evidence for my general claim that every description is essentially perspectival. My presentation of it here,

however, is also more specifically motivated by the rich and
influential example of understanding it provides of the ethical
value of friendship. I want now to move the process of understanding further, by considering other views and their contrasts
and resemblances to this Aristotelian picture. The overall aim of
this movement is to enhance recognition of the constitutive role
of social structures in conceptions of identity and the possibilities
of friendship – even more specifically, the structures of gender. In
many ways, however, the themes that emerge directly in relation
to the impositions of gendered structures overlap and inter-
connect with issues of particularity, identity, self-disclosure and
vulnerability latent in the Aristotelian picture of *philia*. Before
turning attention to explicit questions of gender, therefore, I
shall first examine some accounts of friendship in which these
important issues are developed more directly. As well as enriching understanding of the ethical possibilities of friendship, this
procedure aims to help in placing the perspective of Aristotle's
work.

III

Lawrence Blum's exploration of the possibilities of friendship as
a practice in the morality of partiality and 'particularism' (cited
here as FAM) draws out the implications of a feature that is
intrinsic to Aristotle's account but apparently of little special
significance in his classical context. In a context dominated by
conceptions of morality as generalizable constraints on self-
interest, Blum highlights the moral significance of personalized
affection, concern and compassion in fostering the good of other
persons for their own sake. From this perspective, friendship
becomes a practice of affective beneficence – that is, activities
directed towards ameliorating the 'weal and woe' of others. The
relational, or intrinsic, ethical importance of friendship which is
so crucial to Aristotle's discussion, is thus largely assimilated in
the moral value of personally oriented altruistic dispositions.

Blum's emphasis on the personal, affective nature of the attachment is oriented towards his case for the distinctive moral
importance of friendship. Compared with the gains of an operative
morality of impersonal relations, he claims an irreducible ethical
significance for friendship's non-self-interested, but personally
motivated, benefits to its partners. The caring that is characteristic
of friendship is constitutively emotional and direct, in contrast to

the (allegedly) rational decision-making processes on which impartiality is based. Expanding on Aristotle's insight, Blum insists that this deep-felt care and affection is an active learnt achievement in which cognitive and emotional dimensions of understanding inform each other (FAM 12–15ff.). It involves a responsive grasp of the other's condition or of what the good for the other might be, as well as being affected, touched and motivated to take action to address that condition.[31] The movement into action, although it is direct – in the sense of not requiring consultation with universal principles – is deepened with learning and experience, rather than being an instinctive reaction. A person brings to the relationship their compassion and habits of sensitivity and attention to others: 'what to notice, how to care, what to be sensitive to', developing and learning from their responsiveness in each new situation.[32] Judged by the most rigorous standards of rational theory, the responsiveness that is integral to friendship is a moral achievement – though one that does not rely on impartial and generalizable precepts.

The key moral feature of this practice of friendly responsiveness, for Blum, is its 'particularism'.[33] Most obviously friendships are particularistic insofar as they connect us to other persons in, and indeed because of, their uniqueness. While the extent of our affection varies in different relationships, primarily we care for our friends because of their particular individuality: for their specific needs, beliefs, aspirations, behaviour and whole way of being that makes them who they are. We respond to their highs and lows, their successes and failures, their values and interests, because we are committed to them as unique persons, not as instances of generalized rules, holders of universal rights or subjects of institutional obligations.[34] Blum argues that this personal quality is constitutive for the moral significance of friendship. The quality of our responsiveness, the responsibilities we take on, our loyalty and concern, are all grounded in this particularity. It accounts for the enormous difference in value we experience between acts of friendship, and support given in the name of beneficence or charity.

His insistence on the distinctive morality of particularism deepens our understanding of the ethical meaning and potential of friendship. Although this possibility may be embedded in Aristotle's description of well-doing for a person's own good, it is diffused by his central preoccupation with the affinity of the virtuous. In contrast, Blum's analysis points directly to the deep human value of being cherished for the sake of one's own particular identity and personhood, of being connected to others as an irreplaceable person, and the special kind of responsiveness that this connection requires. From this perspective we can also see how friendship plays a direct role in the affirmation of self. For it is clear that mattering to someone, on the basis of whom one is in oneself, contributes to the validation of one's own sense of self-worth (FAM 150).

Blum has explicitly linked this particularist position with Iris Murdoch's account of the ethics of 'loving attention'.[35] We have seen, in Chapter 1, how Ruddick also highlights the way in which this kind of particularistic and affective caring for a child's individuality, inflected by the less personal demands of training, is critical to the nurturing characteristic of mothering relations. Thus, Blum's work on friendship confirms the significance of an insight that is central to analyses of the practices of caring in personal relations. And in this respect it is continuous with analyses of the ethics of caring developed extensively in the writings of feminist ethicists.[36]

Importantly for Blum, the particularism of friendship is also a relational quality. The concern and care that we have for our friends take their meaning and significance from the particular friendships in which they are expressed. 'It is integral to the significance to the friend of what I do for him', explains Blum, 'that my act is an expression of our particular friendship, of the particular concern and care which I have for my friend; rather than say, an expression of a general responsiveness' (FAM 56). The kinds of feelings and behaviour that are appropriate to each relationship, the kinds of things that are relevant to comforting a friend, are dependent on and grow with the history of their particular attachment. Here Blum seems to tie the value of altruistic affection back to an Aristotelian sense of the intrinsic relational value of friendship. It is not simply responsiveness to the particularity of the individual parties that gives value and meaning to our practices of friendship but the particularity of the relationship itself, the shared attachment and intimacy for its own sake.

It is this characteristic value that motivates friends to remain understanding and supportive, to sustain the relationship, despite our mistakes and failures in meeting their expectations.[37] It is the value that enables us to distinguish friendly acts from those performed out of general duty. For Blum it is also the value that allows us to see how moral calculations based on separable individual interests may be flawed. The holistic value of friendship is irreducible to the interests served or waived by its individual participants. The balance of interests, 'the different sorts of emotions and feelings which the friends have towards one another get their meaning and significance from the entire relationship of which they are a part'. The nature of my caring about the weal and woe of my friend is integrally bound up with our mutual liking, trust and personal importance to each other (FAM 76–7).[38]

Where Blum foregrounds the relational particularity and beneficence of friendship, other theorists elaborate on its potential for self-validation. Once again Aristotle's account provides a prelude. I have shown how he presents the intense sharing and intimacy of friendship as a vital source of self-affirmation: how self-knowledge and understanding are developed through seeing one's mirror reflection in the other, how sharing one's most important projects and values supports and affirms identity. I have also suggested that in Aristotle this conception is limited by his emphasis on the strong affinity of the parties and the characteristically manly expressions of their mutuality and affection. When the highest ethical imports of friendship are unshackled from their connection with the lives of a confident and homogeneous male elite, other possibilities come into sight.

Lillian Rubin, for example, in her analysis of the views of American men and women on friendship, *Just Friends*, unpacks some of the ways in which friendships allow people 'to test out various parts of themselves'.[39] Like Aristotle, Rubin uses a mirror metaphor to convey the connection between friendship and self-understanding. But unlike the Aristotelian reciprocal reflection of likenesses, Rubin's mirror is a more creatively critical instrument of self-knowledge. Our friends' eyes reflect tensions and differences as well as affinity. But she explains, 'what we see there, whether it pleasures or pains us, helps to affirm those parts of self we like and respect and to change those whose reflection brings us discomfort'.[40] It is through the receptivity and sensitivity of those whom we cherish and trust in their meanings and values, that we are able to see where we have strengths and where we disappoint. By seeing what kind of person it is who loves and cares for us, what kinds of interests, needs and aspirations they have, we can gain some insight into our own qualities and limitations.

An important dimension of this 'reflected' self-knowledge is that it exposes us to the possibility of emotional insecurity and distress. Since we are complex and fallible beings, self-knowledge has its disturbing side. Self-knowledge goes hand in hand with self-disclosure which may not only threaten our own equanimity and sense of who we are, but allow another person the opportunity to take advantage of us. Rubin does not overlook this painful dimension of self-discovery, and our vulnerability in a process that reveals our weaknesses to the desires of another. She notes that without institutional forms and rules to define their roles, friends are likely to tolerate far less emotional distress and conflict than, for example, family members.[41]

However, along with the potential for suffering and abuse in the unmasking of 'our darker side' is the possibility for dimensions of self-affirmation, inspiration and development that are less accessible in role-defined relations. Rubin presents accounts of friends calling out the best in each other, affirming and acknowledging all aspects of the other, even those of which the other was unconscious, or that were not accepted by the wider world or seen as 'freakish' and marginalizing, as well as confirming turning points and major changes in their lives. She tells of friends whose excellences inspire self-development through emulation, whose love and attention elicit responses that overcome fears of self-centredness and defensiveness.[42] Underlying this validation and anchoring of self-image is the quality of affection and concern that conveys the feeling that we matter to our friends for who we are: that we are persons who are worth loving and befriending.

There is some overlap here with Aristotle's remarks concerning the ways in which *philoi* may advise, correct and inspire each other with respect to the qualities they value in each other, but Rubin's conception is based in a much more complex exposition of personal psychology. Individual persons, she claims, are a 'shifting amalgam of various and complex facets', with varying competences and blind-spots that have been developed or hidden in compliance with the demands of external social relations. Instead of the model of a relatively stable and unitary man of virtue reflecting off his alike *philos*, Rubin's image is of an intricately woven 'tapestry' in which different threads are picked out through the 'many ways we see ourselves mirrored in the eyes of others'.[43]

Different friends illuminate different threads in the cloth, often threads that we did not know existed, thus confirming who we are, in ourselves, while offering new possibilities.

Marilyn Friedman has talked about these sorts of possibilities for confirmation and growth that friendship offers in the more specific realm of moral development.[44] According to Friedman, the context of trust and shared perspectives that friendship provides allows us to participate vicariously in the very experience of moral alternatives. Our friends' different lives and values, their 'needs, wants, fears, projects and dreams ... can frame for us new standpoints from which we can explore the significance of moral values and standards'.[45] The trust of friendship allows us to rely on our friends to confide their experiences 'authentically, sensitively and insightfully'; the intimate sharing of perspectives facilitates the reproduction of experience with a detailed and rich 'narrative specificity'. 'Living through' a friend's moral life in this way enriches the range, and enables transformation, of our moral resources. Here the intricacy and tension of criss-crossing differences and similarities between friends is key to enhanced self-understanding.

Underlying these intertwined processes of self-validation, understanding and development are the activities of reciprocal self-expression and knowing of each other; the conveying of each person to the other on his or her own terms – that is, in a way that breaks down the barriers of ordinary social distance. This mutual communicating of each friend's self to the other[46] is a complex, subtle and difficult process that engages every significant aspect of each person. Where friendships between free men of the ancient *polis* are the source of ethical insight, the close and continuous sharing of everyday physical, intellectual, administrative and political activities become the favoured means of reciprocal communication. But consideration of a wider range of exchanges suggests that other practices of shared self-expression may offer different possibilities for intimacy, self-validation and moral understanding.

One of the strongest contenders in the field is verbal communication. We have already seen, in Chapter 1, that Ruddick claims conversation and storytelling as central moral resources for mothering relations. Stories told with vitality and compassion by mothers provide children with continuities, connections and expanding horizons where possibilities for response are otherwise limited. In friendship, too, conversation that draws on the fullness of each partner's experience and commitments provides subtle possibilities for establishing mutual understanding and self-development. Friedman, for example, claims that growth in personal understanding relies upon the communication of experience through stories and verbal disclosure of intimate information. After considering accounts of friendships based on a variety of different practices of sharing, Rubin also favours the superior possibilities that words offer for communication and understanding our lives. Except in rare instances, she claims, even 'the warmth and intimacy of a companionable silence' – events of unspoken communication – depend for their meaning ultimately on past words, the verbal exchanges of earlier events.[47]

Perhaps there is an element of verbal elitism here. No doubt a strong case can be made for the power of non-verbal expressions of self, for physical closeness, crying and laughing together, playing sports or providing mutual protection, for example. But Rubin's important point is that the possibilities of intimacy for self-understanding, esteem and development are dependent on 'some willingness to allow another into our inner life, into the thoughts and feelings that live there'.[48] While close and continuous sharing of each other's interests and projects, daily routines and habits, can secure mutual companionship, loyalty and trust, it is the sharing of the thoughts and feelings about ourselves that offers the most profound possibilities for self-affirmation and enhancement. It is this voluntary self-disclosure of intimate information that is not generally available to those who watch, listen and participate with us as we go about the activities of our social roles – this relaxation of wariness about who we are most importantly in and for ourselves – that marks the particular lack of constraint characteristic of friendship.

From the other side, reciprocity requires a characteristic attentiveness and responsivity that establishes the possibility for the other's self-disclosure. In order to know and support our friends, to be able to enter their inner selves and to participate in mutual self-affirmation and enhancement, an environment is required that is hospitable to their integrity – an environment which they can inhabit as persons on their own unique terms. Where disclosure is bound up with validation and self-esteem, responsiveness demands specific attention to hurts, sensitivity to emotional damage and lack of confidence, and the maintenance of commitment to the value and significance of our friends' needs, interests and aspirations. It involves sustaining the freedom to reveal imperfections and weaknesses without threat of betrayal, abuse or condescension; maintaining a friend's spirits and sense of her or his own worth through losses and doubts; providing the affection and support that nourishes strengths and fosters abilities to cope with vulnerabilities.

It is clear that the dimensions both of self-disclosure and responsiveness which are engaged in these practices of mutual communication and understanding make them full of risk and difficulty. Friends risk violation to boundaries they did not intend to relax, without the refuge of social forms, they risk the uncertainties of giving friends the freedom to follow their own heads without the parameters and norms that produce predictable outcomes, and they are vulnerable to loss of their self-chosen attachments without the insurance of structural guarantees.[49] The difficulties of maintaining this complex relation of self-expression and attentiveness, unprotected and uncoerced by institutional constraints, may be transcended in the protections volunteered through the bonding of choice, mutual affection, trust, loyalty and supportiveness. In their different ways, the power of these relational values secures our willingness to share our innermost selves with our friends. In its turn, reciprocal self-disclosure builds the attachment, trust, loyalty and support that ensure the mutual understandings and enhancements of friendship.

Central to the risky venture of friendly care is recognition and commitment to the intertwined values of attachment and autonomy. A focus which highlights one of these values to the detriment of the other incurs the dangers of self-loss on the one side, isolation and alienation of self on the other. For Aristotle, who explicitly denigrates the value of some important relational practices of inner life sharing, supporting social structures can substitute possibilities for habituation in the value of attachment among those men raised to celebrate the exercise of their manly autonomy. The tension between attachment and autonomy can be maintained. For the women of the *polis*, of course, recognition of womanly affectional exchanges and shared intimacies – in the absence of corresponding support for female self-affirmation and autonomy – leads to only partial and imperfect opportunities to partake in the highest ethical possibilities of *philia*.

IV

It is precisely this kind of neglect of the implications of systemic deformations of social possibilities that is the source of feminist interest in practices of friendship. For despite its relative freedom from the constraints and protections of social institutions, compared with other caring practices like mothering, for example, it is evident that friendship is not immune from the impacts of more generalized structural orderings, like that of gender.[50] At its most general level, this concern emanates from reflection on the connection between the characteristic confinement of women's social opportunities to the realm of personal relations and the conventional omission of personal relations from the scope of ethical theory. The exploration of the ethical import of personal relations is thus a central focus of attention. Hence, insofar as accounts of friendship aim at elaborating the value of personal connectedness as intrinsic to the flourishing of human life, and thereby claim friendship as a practice in ethics, they overlap and support this concern.

More specifically however, feminist interest in friendship relations is impelled by the correspondence between the effective exclusion of women from the practice of ethically significant friendship in the tradition, and the relegation of women to social relations of secondary importance and to dependency on men. Aristotle's account of *philia* stands out as exemplary here, its direct correlation between ethical possibility and social independence explicitly excluding women from the highest forms of both realms. Before considering directly the concerns raised by theorists who are alert to these questions of gender bias for caring practices of friendship, however, I want to underline their significance by examining a contemporary discussion of male friendship. My aim is to show that understanding the ethical possibilities of friendship from the perspective of gender sensitivity cannot be achieved simply by including women in the realm of perfection. The fine balance between attachment and autonomy on which ethical friendships for all persons depend requires reconception of the values of differing practices of intimacy as well as restructuring social institutions that encourage their support.

Stuart Miller's disturbing narrative of his personal search for friendship, *Men and Friendship*, provides a remarkable example of the intractability of gender biases in accounts that fail to recognize their complex structural dynamics.[51] As we follow Miller through his tentative excursions into the realm of friendship with other men – certain only of the emptiness of a life without the support, shared tenderness and personal exchanges of close, male attachments – we catch a sense of the fragility of interpersonal intimacy in a world without established forms for its expression. Without the hospitable social milieu that allows Aristotle's perfect friends to build trust and affection in shared activities, Miller's self-conscious intent to establish a context in which he can enjoy sustained sharing of his inner thoughts and feelings is constantly unsettled by the 'deep habitual tension' and 'generic wariness' of living 'in a world of alien, seemingly tame but ... potentially dangerous males' (MF 11).

Expressions of tenderness, and willingness to drop the armour of defensiveness and competitiveness, are hedged in by suspicion, fear and incomprehension from potential friends as well as his own doubts about taking the risk of exposing himself to this particular person. He must rely almost completely on attempts to establish attachment through self-disclosure in a society that does not recognize the ethical possibilities of such intimacy, is suspicious of – and demeans – its practices. As a consequence, his halting attempts to break through these barriers are a clumsy mix of general apprehension, formal gestures, personal awkwardness and uncertainty, occasionally marked by fleeting moments of recognition (MF 36–8). Miller's frail attachments display palpable evidence of the lack of social models, of formal understandings that establish 'getting down', confronting feelings, showing uncertainty, talking about oneself and the meaning of the relationship, that permit the very quality of particularity and personal affirmation on which friendship thrives (MF 67ff.).

Interestingly, his account indicates some of the powerful social forces that militate against the formation of friendships. Ideological structures of individualism and self-sufficiency, the material conditions of work organization and family life, the demands of physical mobility, competitiveness and technological innovation, combine to squeeze out time and opportunity, and so impede the course of friendship in his middle-class, white, male American life. Miller thus gestures to the complex intrication of social structures in the possibilities of friendship but, as we shall see in respect of gender orderings, his analysis falls short of exploring the differential influences of these structures for the different social groups they maintain.

Miller also describes the complications of 'unreason' that check his intent. By this he means the subtle blend of personal and social factors that constructs his psychic possibilities. More explicitly he names 'the unreason of our own states of being': the primary states of anxiety, worry, anger and annoyance when we lose balance in our lives. And then there are our second-order evaluations of these difficult states: feelings of shame, shyness, neediness and touchiness (MF 99). The search for friendship shows up the disabling effects of this complexity, the uncertainty and unreliability of one's feelings: 'this back and forth, this approach and avoidance, this careful dancing' (MF 99), that experience and commitment to the mutual trust of 'real' friendship characteristically handle with confidence.

From the other side his quest points to some of the difficulties inherent in the responsivity of friendship. The notion that friendship may provide safety from a threatening and competitive world is repeatedly opposed by references to the dangers of covering for a friend, taking a stand for him should other men strike (MF 11ff.). And beyond the hazards of protection in a milieu seen as a universe of adversaries, Miller also mentions the difficulties of maintaining intimate responsiveness itself. He talks of the energy and patience required in receptively attending to a friend, the cognitive and emotional tasks of following another's behaviour and moods, the risks of rejection, hurt or the imposition of their truths, that come of allowing them to go through the experiences vital to their integrity (MF 105–6). Finally, he notes the central problem of understanding: recognition of the other's intent, aspirations and values (MF 186–7).[52]

Miller's story thus uncovers tangible layers of risk that are embedded for him in the characteristic caring of friendship. The poverty of his personal strategies for inducing mutual affection and sharing is overwhelming. We are reminded of Aristotle's perception of the significance of habituation and interactive learning, that friendship is a way of being, rather than a possession or a technique.[53] Along with this important insight we are also reminded of social impacts on friendship with respect to gendered constructions of the ethical possibilities of friendly caring and intimacy. It is a commonplace of contemporary Western discussions of interpersonal relational practices that characteristic differences in social roles, and socialization for those roles, for men and women produce characteristically different capabilities and valuings of intimacy.[54] Typically men's relational practices lack the intensity of intimate personal exhanges of self-knowledge and understanding that are common to female attachments; it is the freedom for affirmation and development of individual skills, personality and imagination – rather than the attachment itself – that is of primary importance.[55] Miller's importunate quest is a poignant illustration of these differences. For many of the difficulties he experiences originate in the confusing relationship he bears to his special world of contemporary manliness, with its biases and defensiveness with respect to women's relational possibilities.

Much of the risk of close affectional attachments for Miller derives from his perception of manliness, of what it is to be a man amongst men. This perception embraces qualitative principles that are directly antithetical to the personal relatedness he craves. For example: public expressions of emotions are a sign of weakness, relations between persons are competitive and adversarial, individual self-sufficiency is a strength. Miller's struggle to achieve affectionate intimacy with other men can be seen as an attempt towards a radical change in this ideology, part of the culture of a more sensitive, more 'humane', masculinity. At the same time, however, its professed celebration of manliness also engages conceptions of friendship relations that draw on a context of institutionalized male social supremacy and female oppression.

This troublesome dimension of Miller's project is evident in his unproblematic affirmation of 'the great tradition of male friendship, celebrated in the West' as his reference point for affection and intimacy. More specifically he names Homer, Aristotle, Cicero, Montaigne, Shakespeare and Pope as purveyors of this tradition, along with 'the terrible wrath of Achilles at the slaughter of his friend Patrocles, the love of David for Jonathan, the heroic self-sacrifice of Oliver for his friend Roland' and more recently the images of *The Deerhunter*, *Butch Cassidy and the Sundance Kid*, and *Breaker Morant* (MF 2). Apart from the limitations in the conception of intimacy already noted, at least in the work of Aristotle, it is clear that these celebrations of masculinity thrive on the exclusion and explicit denigration of women's ethical capabilities. As Jeffrey Richards points out in his discussion of the overlap of the 'tradition' with conceptions of 'manly love' in Victorian society, many men became enthusiastic proponents of male comradeship in a world in which life revolved around all-male institutions and women were sidelined, exploited as sex-objects or worshipped as goddesses.[56] And even where oppression of women is not intentional, it seems that the failure by men to express their inner thoughts and feelings may result in this social bias.[57]

Miller's search for the intimacy that expresses that ultimate 'mystery', the male element, is articulated in terms of difference with respect to friendships with or between women. But references to the draining away of 'vital masculine energy that might be used to bond with another man', and 'a sense of being suffocated in the arms of the Great Mother' in relationships with women (MF 27), indicate that that 'difference' is not neutral, that it depends on breaking away from female corruptions. Accusations levelled at the 'progressive liberation of women' for placing 'manliness' in jeopardy and pre-empting possibilities for close, non-homosexual relationships between men (MF 135), as well as defensiveness concerning 'feminine' capacities for intimacy (MF 143–52), provide further evidence for this misogyny. Given the social context of gender inequity in which Miller writes, therefore, his enthusiasm for maleness appears to uphold values that are complicit with the derogation of women's ethical possibilities. As a consequence, the quest for rejuvenated male friendship and increased possibilities for male intimacy sounds more like an extension of contemporary male solidarity based on superior economic, political and physical power, than a commitment to the relational values of friendship's caring and intimacy.

The ethical implications of sidelining women and women's friendship relations, in favour of men and men's relations are perhaps most directly visible in friendships between women and men. For here the 'reciprocity' of the relationship is at odds with the dominant patriarchal social structure, and runs the risk of at least surreptitiously reproducing its asymmetries. In a context in which women are largely dependent on male-dominated institutions and individual men for our psychic and material survival, when our social status is judged and legitimized in terms of our relations with men, our personal relationships are readily compromised in accord with the deformations of that context. The ethical value of reciprocal caring determined by the particular interests and aspirations of a friend whose concern and affection is determined by our own unique identity and values, is vulnerable to invalidation when our identity is the source of oppression and dependency. Under conditions of systemic inequality in social power, women's practices of friendship with men are in danger of becoming instrumental practices in securing personal safety and protection on men's terms.

Claudia Card's work on friendship offers acute insights into these constraints.[58] Critically cautious with respect to Gilligan's claims for women's characteristic ethical competence in intimate relations, Card suggests that the much heralded 'ethic of care' may frequently be a survival strategy for women whose institutionalized dependence on men gives us reasons to be responsive to men's interests and values. Women's sense of the intrinsic value of close, personal attachments and our affectionate concern for our (male) friends' different and distinctive needs, beliefs and aspirations, may be the result of our own poor self-definition and the desire for approval.[59] In other words, the basis of the caring expressed in women's friendships with men, and thus its ethical import, is seriously constrained by the social context in which it occurs.

As Card explains it: 'when people are affiliated with "protectors", their affirmations of those affiliations may have little to do with love, though the language of love be the language of their discourse'. Accordingly, what is frequently taken as an ethical attachment in women's participation in friendship relations with men, is more likely to be 'the misplaced gratitude women have felt toward men for taking less than full advantage of their power to abuse or for singling them out for the privilege of service in return for "protection"'.[60] Card's point is that when gendered inequalities in power are factored into personal relations between women and men those relations may well be understood as inherently flawed and conducive to vice rather than ethical enrichment.

Sandra Bartky has unpacked some of the elements of these socially constructed constraints on women's ethical possibilities in friendship with respect to the specific activity of providing emotional support for our social superiors.[61] She points out that the continual provision of the kind of caring attentiveness that validates one's friends on their own terms and enhances their self-esteem runs the risk of producing epistemic and ethical 'leans' in the carer. Perpetual immersion in the world of one's friend in order to affirm one's concern for her or his beliefs and values tends to dissolve one's sense of one's own reality. As we have already seen, it is clearly in the nature of friendly responsiveness that we suspend our own projections in order to understand and share in our friends' meanings and values for their own sake. But Bartky's claim is that in relations where there is no corresponding affirmation of our own world, as is frequently the case between women and men, we actively assimilate the other's perspective through our concernful and affectionate attention. And perhaps more perniciously, we may silence or compromise our own values in favour of supplying the requisite emotional support, approval and validation.

For these feminist discussions, the critical question for the ethical value of friendship is the reciprocity of the relationship. The very lack of formality that produces the ethical possibility for valuing persons as unique particulars rather than as bearers of impersonal rights also presupposes a finely tuned sense of fairness and reciprocity. Card suggests that since enforcement of behaviour is not sanctioned, 'if anything, to be a good friend, one needs a *better* sense of fairness than for other relationships'.[62] However, this ability – as is evident from Blum's analysis – is not simply the rational application of impersonal principles to cases of competing claims, but a practice of particularistic responsiveness that, with respect to reciprocity, is sensitive to 'what others deserve from oneself and . . . to what one deserves from them given the history of one's interaction with them'.[63]

The issue of reciprocity is of course at least as old as Aristotle's lectures and remains integral to all subsequent analyses. Where, for Aristotle, cases of unequal *philia* are presumed to be part of the natural hierarchy of ethical possibilities and readily amenable to a calculus of proportions, contemporary theorists righteously reject his ethical hierarchy and presume equality of reciprocity. In so doing, however, they tend to overlook the profoundly significant role of socially structured inequalities. Card's analysis reminds us that the transparency of this structure to friendship relations between women and men may result in ethically flawed practices in which misplaced gratitude – or manipulation, cunning and deceit – masquerade as virtuous affection and concern. Bartky's discussion brings some of the complexities of this process of deformation to attention. She details some of the ways in which persistent provision of unreciprocated emotional support results in a self-denying displacement of one's meanings and values towards those of one's friend.

Thus the vital connection between reciprocity and identity comes to the fore again. For it is clear that the identity-enriching potential of friendship is seriously impaired under conditions of non-reciprocity. While we would expect lack of reciprocity in self-affirmation to result in the dissolution of friendship relations, analyses like those of Card and Bartky show us that systemically structured inequality may be either invisible or inescapable. Under these conditions an 'ontological lean'[64] occurs: one may either deny one's own meanings and values in favour of those of one's friend, or else identify and merge them undifferentially with those of the friend. More specifically, in the context of a gendered hierarchy of status and power, women's sense of their own identity, interests and values tends to be both directly disregarded by the structure as well as prone to active self-devaluation.

In view of this generalized self-loss, the fundamental relation of ethical 'self-love', on which Aristotle can so straightforwardly base his claims for the significance of personal relations of mutual sharing, completely collapses. Constant engagement in practices of unreciprocated support and concern for others may result in lack of self-definition and the psychological priority of 'other-love'.[65] It is with this deformation in mind that Janice Raymond, in her important work on women's friendships, reminds us of Aristotle's vital presupposition by converting his adage – 'a friend is another self' – to 'the Self is another friend'.[66] As a final turn in this investigation of practices of friendship, therefore, I want to consider Raymond's account. For, in enriching the discussion through its feminist concerns, curiously it takes us back to themes of central significance to Aristotle's vision.

V

Raymond begins from the position that the gendered structure of society has robbed women's social relations of much of their ethical import. In particular, the historical denigration of women's independent capacities with respect to ethical values deemed important to men has resulted in the devaluing of women's same-sex friendships. Montaigne's description of women's 'ordinary [in]capacity ... for that communion and fellowship which is the nurse of this sacred bond'[67] provides the benchmark here, but evidence from contemporary accounts of women's lives seems to confirm the view that women's female friendships are unimportant to their identities. Raymond notes the influence of Freudian theory that interprets and constructs female friendships as aberrant, the use of descriptors such as 'exceptional' when the power of women's same-sex relations is acknowledged, the conversion of female relations into categories that are congruent with male domination, as well as direct silence about women's affection for each other (PF 173–81).[68]

Her project, then, is to describe a conception of female friendship that is of central significance to the full empowerment of women's identities and lives, that is, a relationship chosen according to women's own needs, desires, interests and values. Thus where the feminist analyses discussed earlier sound warnings concerning the implications of women's characteristic lack of power and loss of identity with respect to men, Raymond's aim is to move away from this latent victimism by reclaiming the ethical possibilities of women's own individual agency in their friendship relations.

Her description of the kinds of practices in which this vision is realized unfolds in the interconnected insights of three different approaches to the project of reclamation. First, she uses a genealogical method to search out examples of communities in which women's attachments to women are of primary importance and a source of identity – validation that resonates beyond a socially designated status as passive, derivative or superfluous. Second, she examines contemporary, socially constructed obstacles to these kinds of passionate female attachments. Finally, she articulates the nature and possibilities of the practice of friendships in terms of her vision of the ideal conditions in which women are for each other for their own sakes.

The genealogical section of the work comprises accounts of medieval convent life in Europe, and the houses instituted by Chinese 'marriage resistors' in the nineteenth and early twentieth centuries. Raymond's description of these communities immediately takes us to the heart of her understanding of the vital connection between passionate relations among women and societies in which the full possibilities of women's lives are allowed to grow and flourish (PF Chs 2 and 3). Friendship is not simply a supplement to the fundamental needs of life, nor does it merely amount to the personal activities involved in the movement of one person towards another. For Raymond, female friendship – or as she terms it, 'Gyn/affection' (to avoid confusion with weaker conceptions of purely personal admiration and generosity) – is itself fundamental to the expression of women's lives in all their worldly, social, economic and political dimensions. Accordingly, she describes the emergence of women's particular attachments in these two sets of communities where living together and sharing property, the everyday domestic tasks of survival, economic viability, administration and public commitments, foster women's general development. As a result of this institutional support, Gyn/affection establishes, both materially and psychically, a sense of space and place of their own for the participants, a sense of self-created independence and worth.

It is clear that this conception of friendship relations embeds a strong sense of their political potential for nurturing and expressing the values shared by their participants. The ethical import of the development of a shared commitment to the significance of the emotional, material, social, intellectual and cultural good of each woman for her own sake is continuous with the grounding of a political context in which that value is fostered. Friendship provides women 'with a common world that becomes a reference point for location in a larger world', Raymond claims.

> The sharing of common views, attractions and energies gives women a connection to the world so that they do not lose their bearing. Thus a sharing of personal life is at the same time a grounding for social and political existence. (PF 152)

More powerfully Gyn/affection – as a relation entered into not only by individual women but by political beings who claim social and political status for themselves – has the expansive political possibility of creating a world in which women's values and meanings can flourish.[69] And, with this political prospect, we circle back to Aristotle's description of *philia* again.

By exploring the obstacles confronted by Gyn/affection in the gendered structures of contemporary North American society, Raymond elaborates on the implications of the public dimensions of the relationship (PF Ch. 4). Her point is that the contexts in which many women currently live militate against their living and expressing themselves fully in the public realm, and thus from forming the passionate and politically consequential friendships that would in turn affirm and facilitate the enrichment of their identities. She supports this claim by cataloguing the different orders of alienation that create this situation and drawing attention to the way they undermine important aspects of women's identity and expression that are the vital source and potential of their Gyn/affection.

The discussion begins with the effects of women's direct 'dissociation' from public life due to relative lack of involvement in political, intellectual and financial realms of existence; their lack of self-conscious traditions of reflection and politics, of a history of their participation in the material world. In the face of these dissociations, women's lives tend to take their meaning in the sentient sphere rather than the material, in the inner world of emotions and feelings, rather than the sphere of action and thought in which they move and live. Consequently, the communication of emotions frequently becomes definitive of their realities, and friendship relations often become activities of sifting and sorting through feelings and psyches, rituals of emotional expression for the sake of expression itself, imperatives to 'let it all hang out' in endless confessions.

While the mutual conveying of oneself to another seems to be integral to the nature of friendship, Raymond warns that when the emotional dimension of life is severed from its vital connections with inner reflection and external activity, relationships run the risk of becoming practices in the management of confessional sessions. The potential for self-empowerment is lost in the preoccupation with attachment itself, shifting the focus of energy from a wider world of meaning and significance to the activity of relating for its own sake. We catch the sense of her conception of the strength of a worldly integrated identity when she contrasts these relational exercises in shared emotional expression with the self-demanding and self-affirming practices of passionate and reflective sharing of 'the fruits of a thoughtful and creative existence' (PF 164).

Raymond shores up this notion of identity in the discussion of two further contexts of 'worldlessness' that obstruct Gyn/ affection and the validation of women's sense of their own individuality. She talks about social mechanisms by which women's identities are 'assimilated' to men's definitions of their possibilities and worth (PF 164–81). For example, the 'new women' who work the double shifts of 'masculine' careers and 'feminine' marriages often repress their real selves in conformity with male definitions. Sexual liberationists, both heterosexual and lesbian, tend to equate individuality with sexual expression and thereby put themselves back in place as sexual objects. These are the kind of moves by which women silence and tame themselves in deference to male-dominated definitions of who they are. In contrast, full self-expression and the Gyn/affection that produces it involve initiating activities that are significant to women on their own terms.

Other women, aware of the gendered structures of social power, are impeded in their friendships by assuming a stance of 'victimism'. The historical and cross-cultural reality of their abuse is transformed 'into a psychosocial identity whereby women take on the status of victim as a primary self-definition and role' (PF 181). Signs of this tendency are the reduction of attachments between women to activities of consolation and sharing of pain, the reduction of collectives to communities of resistance, and the reduction of individual lives to expressions of shame and guilt. Once again Raymond emphasizes the multitude of ways in which women's identities become passive to their derivative status and dependence on male determinations.

There is much that is troubling in these analyses, however. Raymond's clear-cut understandings of the contrasts between deformations of identity and women's own needs, interests and values frequently belie the complexity of the interconnected personal and social forces in which our sense of self is constructed. Her facile identification of all heterosexual meanings with women's passivity and subordination denies the validity of many women's experience of themselves and their choices in their social relations. However, her discussion forcefully reminds us that the key to empowering friendships, the ability to value and realize oneself in personally, passionately and reflectively meaningful ways, is integrally linked with one's social and political possibilities. More specifically for women this means that friendship depends on intimacy that is continuous with forms of social, political and economic life that are significant to our own sense of our needs, interests, desires and values rather than those prescribed for us by men.

Raymond borrows Alice Walker's term, 'rigors of discernment', to describe the cognitive dimension of this strong sense of self-connection and identity. Discernment is a reflective quality that conveys the active role of mind and heart in the formation of friendships. It grounds the crucial element of choice in our friendships, overcoming the 'passivity and uncritical mindset' that prompts women to form 'nondiscriminating friendships', or that fosters the attitude that all feminists can be friends (PF 171–3). Importantly, for Raymond, this reflective quality with respect to our friends is at the same time an instrument of self-empowerment. It gives us a vital, self-activated appreciation of who we are, our values and aspirations. 'Discernment', as she explains it, 'helps us to regain perspective about our Selves and others. Without this habit of reflection, we lose the feel of our own Be-ing, the sense of integrity that makes us who we are.' The practice of discernment also encourages confidence in ourselves and sustains that confidence in interactions with others (PF 164–73).

These comments recall the component of choice we have noted in Aristotle's conception of the affection between *philoi*. The notion is used to distinguish the integrity of the attachment to the overall characters and values of its participants from the attachments of raw feeling. The idea of choice, if not explicit, is at least implicit in the other accounts of friendship investigated. For choice is the very condition of the possibilities for mutual self-enhancement that the relationship offers. With her feminist perspective, however, Raymond shows us that the capacity for choice or discernment, an integral connection with our own character and values, may be a hard-won achievement. In contexts that are structurally antagonistic to active expression of ourselves, our relationship to our sense of who we are may be ill-formed and deceptive. The acquirement of discernment is crucial to the strong sense of self-definition that is the keystone to Gyn/affection. And she reminds us that it is a habit, a way of being, that is produced and continually renewed and revitalized in an active learning process.

Raymond's final move to reclaim the ethico-political possibilities of female friendships is an account of the 'conditions' required for Gyn/affection. Her elaboration of this vision, in terms of 'thoughtfulness', 'passion', 'worldliness' and 'happiness', once again stresses the notion of individual responsibility and capacity to be with another in a mutually empowering and politically significant connection. Her account of thoughtfulness, for example, explicitly claims the basic relation between self-regard and friendship. As thinking enriched with attentiveness, considerateness and respect for the other and her needs (PF 220–1), thoughtfulness seems to have much in common with the idea of responsivity that we have already met in Blum's discussion. However Raymond's additional stress on the self-discursive nature of thinking brings out the importance of one's friendly 'intercourse with oneself' (PF 222). On this view, she claims, the capacity for affectionate discourse with another depends on one's ability to be at the same time a companion to oneself. Thus 'friendship begins with the affinity a woman has with her vital Self' (PF 5).

Here we see Raymond directly setting out her feminist turn on the Aristotelian heritage: the inversion that emphatically insists 'the Self is another friend' rather than 'a friend is another self'. But for Aristotle, too, self-love of this kind, the valuing of one's integrity to one's own active and full expression of oneself, is central to the ethics of friendly relationships. For, as we have seen, it is the model as well as the end of *philia*. But where Aristotle is concerned to dispel its confusion with self-interested ambitions, Raymond's primary focus is on its deformations and occlusions. Thus Aristotle, presuming a well-defined sense of one's own needs, interests, values and beliefs, stresses that this form of self-regard relates to the kind of enrichment of a person that is only accessible insofar as it is actively engaged in an affectionate attachment to another for his own sake. From Raymond's perspective, Aristotle's presumption is properly a social product that in the contemporary, gendered social hierarchy is rendered largely invalid for women. Hence she emphasizes the other side of the intrinsic link between self-regard and friendship: empowering friendships are only possible to the extent that we have a sense of the integral value of our own meanings and values.

Her discussion of happiness reinforces this position, making the link between happiness and the fullest experience of life as a self-directed activity of the whole self. And, again, Raymond stresses the political dimension of this ethical possibility. The 'thoughtful passion' of Gyn/affection to arouse, inspire, influence – and to be aroused, inspired and influenced by – another woman, is not merely a matter of personal affection; it is the passion of 'worldly' women who claim social and political status for themselves. 'In addition to being a personal space, Gyn/affection is a political space, a female enclave created by conscious female effort in the world that men have fabricated' (PF 232). By constructing a world

in which women can live in integrity with their own selves, it is a
profoundly political act.

Once again, the force of her account – and she acknowledges
this herself – circles back to the familiar terrain of Aristotle's
discussion. For it is clear that for Aristotle, too, friendship is
co-extensive with citizenship. The best sort of *philoi* are politically
active participants in the *polis*: the affinity of virtue that is the
basis of the ethical particularity of their affectionate relationships
with each other is likewise the grounding of the generalized
values of their state. In this respect, their intimacy, like that
envisaged in Gyn/affection, resounds beyond their personal lives
in their social and political existence.

Thus Raymond's analysis converges with that of Aristotle, claiming that friendship supports the vital bonds of communality. And
like the account of her Greek predecessor, it suffers from important oversights and omissions. For, while from one perspective
friendships have the potential to sustain and reinforce the kind
of commonalities to which political connections aspire, the
assumption of similarities between participants – on which this
perspective relies – fails to take notice of the inherent differences
and potential for conflict among persons, which it excludes. By
placing these discussions beside those of Miller, Card and Bartky,
it is possible to see that the connections between friendship and
politics are far more complicated than the overlap between
Aristotle and Raymond may suggest. For these differently framed
investigations of friendship make the point that the ethical possibilities of these relations are shot through with political effects
of contradictory kinds – structural constraints on reciprocity, and
self-definitions of identity and choice, for example – that frequently rupture and produce oppositions between intimacy and
political life.

The further juxtaposition of the perspectives of Blum and Rubin,
however, places these concerns with the ethico-political imports
of friendship in an even more complex array. By foregrounding
the special particularistic quality of friendship relations, these
theorists draw attention to vital dimensions of the ethical caring
practised in friendship that take their value from the degree of
independence from political constraints that they express. From
this perspective, friendships provide the freedom to recognize

and care for inherently idiosyncratic, non-generalizable or non-generically constructed dimensions of our lives and our identities. The survey of views that juxtaposes these different insights thus enables us to understand the range of the complex ethical possibilities for the practice of caring in friendship relations.

Chapter 3

Nursing

I

The structured context of professional nursing relations stands in sharp contrast with the characteristic freedom that marks the possibilities of caring in friendship relations. Nursing care is constituted in the relations of response to determinate pleas for help. Its practices are enacted within an organized framework of self-conscious needs and purposes that lie beyond the intrinsic values of relations between people freely chosen for their own sake.

In this sense there are significant areas of overlap between the values of nursing relations and those aspects of maternal caring that are primarily structured by the explicit dependency of infants and children on their mothers. For mothering practices, insofar as they involve responsiveness to children in virtue of their needs for help, also have constitutive instrumental claims. But here too, apart from substantive differences in the kinds of dependency, the context of nursing care is typically more formally organized, its practices more directly regulated by external forces than the realm of personal volition in which maternal practices are embedded.

Relations of nursing care are formed between people whose connection with each other is primarily governed by the responsibility of one person to respond to and to service the needs of the other. Most frequently the parties are strangers to each other, not personally involved in each other's lives through ties of blood or friendship. As a consequence, the caring practices of nursing are subject directly to the determinations of publicly administered norms and structured by the demands of publicly sanctioned conduct.

This is not to deny the ground where practices of nursing care,

those of lay carers for example, may be infused with the freedoms
of the private domain[1] and thereby eschew many of the constraints
of institutional care – or correspondingly those mothering practices like 'daycare' that take their bearings from externally administered commands. The point of introducing nursing relations by
way of this distinction, that seems so brazenly to contrast the
domain of personal freedom and engagement with that of public
regulation and responsibility, and to deny to the latter possibilities
of intrinsic value accorded to the former, is not to assert absolute
conditions. More importantly, it is not to neglect the profoundly
significant interconnections traced in the critical work of earlier
chapters between personal relations and socio-political orders.
Rather, my aim is to direct attention to a recognizable terrain, a
ground that at least in common parlance is characteristic of the
caring practices under investigation in this section.

Thus, following in this line of 'recognizable' distinctions, the
discussion of nursing relations moves the current investigation
into the ethical import of caring practices across that immensely
important ethico-social construct: the public/private division.
Whereas the practices of caring discussed in the sections on
mothering and friendship occupied a common region on one side
of this partition, professional nursing care inhabits the other side
of the divide. The examination of nursing practices, then, in as
much as they are conventionally designated public practices of
care, provides the opportunity for exploring some of the ways in
which terms of public organization and accountability directly
influence the nature of caring and for understanding the ethical
possibilities of impersonally administered relations of person-to-
person care.

At the same time, however, my adoption of convention to set
the context and orientation of this discussion of nursing care is not
uncritical. The relevance and meaning of the distinction between
personal and public domains is frequently a matter of dispute. The
overlap already remarked in cases of lay nursing, for example,
cannot be so cavalierly dismissed when conventional 'wisdom'
interprets the (public) value of lay practices entirely in terms of
satisfaction of personal desires. Or again, as we have seen in the
chapter on mothering, the divide becomes problematic and potentially dangerous when the loss of self, which many mothers
experience in the course of their early mothering practice, is
unquestioningly attributed to their personal characters. It is clear

that the relationship between personal and public domains of activity is complexly interlayered and holds multiple possibilities of meaning. With these complexities in mind, my identification of nursing practices by their location in the public domain carries within it the potential for self-reflexive questioning and the possibility for challenging the familiar terms of this location. In this way the investigation of nursing offers the opportunity for clarification of different understandings of caring – with exploration of the possibilities of practices of care in a different context – while concurrently interrogating the conditions of that context.

There are other dimensions of nursing relations that make them a particularly rich example[2] for the purposes of the present investigation of the import of caring. The special circumstances of their formation – as a response to a recognized breakdown in the functioning of personal, embodied well-being – create characteristic dilemmas and tensions for their practices, and corresponding unique implications for their ethical possibilities. In the first instance, the breakdown signals, in the most powerful of ways, the contingency and vulnerability of human life: the ever-present susceptibility of every person – infant, child and adult – to accident and affliction. In particular, the loss and incapacity of illness expose our intrinsic limits and dependency with respect to relations with others. As a result, nursing relations express the actuality of this sensitive and difficult dimension of existence. They are inherently unequal insofar as patients' abilities to participate are limited by their disabilities and the primary lines of concern are focused in one direction: from nurse – or self-reflexively from patient – to patient.

Second, the forms of concern elicited by the breakdown involve massive objectifications of patients' being and functioning. Taken-for-granted subjective experience is transformed by illness into experience of the concrete objectness of oneself for oneself. The incapacity brings the impaired part of oneself into consciousness as an obstacle or something alien to one's normally smooth-functioning existence.[3] This self-objectification invites and is reinforced by the objectifications of medical science methodology. Consequently, concern is directed to the breakdown and its possible repair as to a malfunctioning object that is comprehensible in terms of spatio-temporal quantities and functions rather than to a subjectively experiencing person. Caring in these conditions involves negotiating the tensions between integrity and dependency, responsibility and control, as well as mediating the interconnected aspects of patients' subjectivity and objectivity, interposing the often conflicting claims of physiology and the spirit, science and humanism.

The specific organizational structure of the public institutions within which nursing care occurs brings other significant factors to bear on the possibilities of its practice. Most notably, nursing relations are usually characterized by exceptional functional interdependence and overlap with other relations in the health care organization, together with a clearly delineated ranking with regard to social value and status. Relations with patients are closely tied into relations with other members of the institution, and importantly influenced by the terms of their place in the hierarchy. Nursing care thus occupies an 'in between' position in the organization of the public response to the patient's need,[4] and is infused with the tensions of sustaining interdependent but differently focused relations with different levels of authority.

The most outstanding feature of this functional organization and its hierarchical ranking is its sex-defined roles.[5] Nursing practices are overwhelmingly carried out by women, and the activities, responsibilities and status associated with them call upon the kind of social capacities and standing that women have typically exercised in their traditional domestic roles. Accordingly the gendered social order is a crucial constitutive factor in the practice of nursing.[6] In keeping with the dominant norms of this order, nursing care is encumbered with much of the social apparatus that operates to undermine both the value of women's practices in general and the social possibilities of their practitioners.

The example of nursing relations, therefore, offers yet another opportunity to re-examine the connections between ethics and gender. At one level re-examination involves uncovering the largely invisible, ethical significance of nursing as a caring practice. At another level recognition of the 'external' context of values, within which nursing relations are enmeshed, directs attention to the ways in which that context affects nurses' social and personal possibilities. As a consequence, consideration of the needs and well-being of nursing practitioners becomes an important dimension of the ethical import of their relations with patients. To this end, the current investigation tracks the complex interconnections between the distinctive values that emerge within the person-to-person practices themselves, and the socio-political ordering of the values of their participants' personal lives. By examining nursing practices in this way, marking along the route the areas of overlap and disjunction with the examples of caring practices already discussed, this chapter aims to further the gender-sensitive project of enhancing understanding of the ethical limits and possibilities of caring.

II

By taking up seriously the question of what nurses actually do in the particular situations in which they care for their patients, nursing theorist Patricia Benner provides one of the richest descriptions available of the nature of clinical nursing practices and their distinctive ethical possibilities.[7] From the outset of her early work, *From Novice to Expert*, Benner is concerned to show how it is situated caring interactions, the personal, embodied and idiosyncratic dimensions of nurse/patient relations, rather than abstract models of their context-free variables, that provide the key to understanding the nature and significance of nursing care.

Through discussions that are brimming with examples of specific incidents of practice, she emphasizes the specificity and relational aspect of each situation, the way behaviours, symptoms or interventions take on their meanings and relevance with respect to the particular context in which they occur. And while Benner aims to use these incidents as exemplars to identify different levels and domains of practical competence, she firmly warns against reification of her interpretations. Like the situations they describe, her characterizations and orderings are constrained by their context (FNE xxii). Instead, she encourages the collection of more examples, arguing that although the fuzziness and variety of actual clinical practice resists systematization, it gradually yields to the understanding of an expanding fund of similar and dissimilar situations.

This perception, that the specificity and contextuality of actual situations limits the possibilities of textbook descriptions, is central to understanding Benner's notion of excellence in nursing. Her main point is that the decision-making and action required in the practice of nursing rely on kinds of 'perceptual awareness' and 'discretionary judgement' that cannot be pre-articulated or formulated according to abstract rules. While skilled nursing clearly depends on formal education with respect to knowing what to consider and how to organize information about patients, how to operate equipment and how to monitor vital signs, excellence in caring emerges through more intuitive understanding that 'responds to the demands of a given situation rather than rigid principles and rules' (FNE xx).

In examples of nursing excellence, the vague hunches, gut feelings and sense of uneasiness through which nurses express their understanding of situations, are shown to illustrate capacities to cope with the ambiguities and complexities of real-life circumstances that defy the possibilities of analytical models or lists of context-free criteria. Drawing heavily on the description of practical skills produced by Hubert and Stuart Dreyfus,[8] Benner's work with Christine Tanner identifies crucial cognitive dimensions of these intuitive judgements: for example, the ability to grasp the importance of relevant details, to 'recognize "fuzzy" resemblances despite marked differences in the objective features of past and present situations', to integrate body activities with equipment and to 'try on' alternatives.[9] When expertise is understood in this way, it is clear that the possibilities of nursing are intimately bound up with its inherently practical activities, and the special capacities these generate and engage.

Benner insists that such excellence is grounded in experience. Expertise develops, she claims, from the experience that accrues in the process of interpreting, confirming and disconfirming preconceived ideas and principles in actual practical situations (FNE 3). Clinical know-how, the ability to make finely graded distinctions in patients' conditions, to interpret the importance of subtle changes before measureable alterations occur, to recognize problems that ought to be solved and to implement strategies for their resolution, comes from many hours of directly observing and caring for patients. Time spent with a specific patient together with cumulated experience of caring for many different patients gives nurses a wide base from which to assess and grasp the needs of a new patient. Nursing is a practice that is learnt through its practice and in this respect, despite differences in intent and location, these professional caring relations display their similarity to the mothering and friendship relations already described, underlining the inherently practical aspect of the ethical possibilities of caring.

But learning through practice – as Aristotle also notices – is not simply a matter of heaping up hours with patients, or repeating procedures so frequently that they become unconscious rules or reflex actions. Benner claims that practice provides the possibility for its own transformation. Experience is a dynamic process of progressively refining pre-articulated ideas and theories through many actual situations with patients, situations that add nuances or shades of difference to theory. Gradually concrete experience replaces abstract principles as the paradigm for practice, and nurses learn to see what is relevant in a complete situation rather than a composite of equally relevant factors (FNE 13). Analytic procedures of attention are transformed into synthetic perception that produces understanding of significant configurations and relationships in a situation that cannot be captured in pre-specified components. Nurses' descriptions of the enhancement of their abilities with experience provide persuasive evidence of this dimension of their caring.[10]

These transformations in nurses' abilities to recognize and look for salience are not merely mental phenomena. The practical expertise of nursing care also has a crucial bodily component: skilled know-how, Benner claims, is dependent on 'embodied intelligence'. Using phenomenological insights[11] as well as empirical evidence from medical research, Benner and Judith Wrubel argue that our bodies play an important role in action and knowing (PC 67–80). As a result, they claim, the complex skills of nurse experts rely on a 'bodily takeover of the skill to some degree' such that the body is oriented appropriately in relation to the kind of activities the skills encompass (PC 53). In the use of medical interventions, for example, perceptual 'takeover' transforms the instruments into extensions of the nurse's body: an intravenous catheter tip becomes an extension of the nurse's fingers; the regulation of an intravenous drip, the visualized responses in the patient's veins. This is not simply a matter of physical dexterity and co-ordination, but of bodily insight understanding how different resistances feel, and what the relationships between different responses are. Embodied intelligence sees the patterns and understands the complexities of the situation for the nurse in rapid, non-explicit and non-conscious ways.

Taking together the themes of experiential learning, and bodily integration, Benner's account of clinical practice entails a considerable degree of active, personal involvement from nurses in their caring relations. The progress from novice to expert is accompanied by 'a passage from detached observer to involved performer' (FNE 13). The nurse no longer stands outside the situation but is personally engaged in it. Since nursing 'situations' are specifically constituted by special person-to-person relations, this engagement also requires emotional involvement and a deep grasp of social meanings.

The examples Benner and Wrubel hold up, of judgements and activities through which nurses have made positive contributions to their patients' well-being, describe qualitative relationships that meld more rational, instrumental approaches with emotional guidance and expression. Standard distinctions between 'taking care of' and 'caring for and about'[12] – between instrumental and ethical activities – dissolve in these practical situations. In contrast with cognitive or behavioural viewpoints that understand emotions as unruly bodily responses that are obstacles to rationality and objectivity, Benner and Wrubel maintain that emotional connections are central to our involvement in situations in an integral way. Controlling or detaching oneself from one's emotions – or indeed denying their influence – results in partial understanding, or alienation from much that is significant. Emotions give access to the kind of global understanding and attunement to the complexity of the patient's world that is the hallmark of expert nursing care. As Benner and Wrubel put it: 'We do violence to caring when we separate in our practice the distinctions we are able to make conceptually between the "instrumental" role and the "expressive" role' (PC 170).

This kind of personal, emotional attunement is also dependent on the context of social meanings in which the 'situation' is embedded. Nurses' participation in the common culture – in the shared human language of emotions and lived experiences, in communal meanings – enables them to 'tune into' patients, to recognize in their bodily holding and their expressions how they are experiencing their illness and what it means to them, how the course of their disease is changing, and how they are coping with those changes.[13] A deep grasp of social meanings and language enables nurses to translate a patient's tone of voice, eye focus or eating style, into an assessment of their needs, of how their anxiety can be relieved or their pain diminished, how a sense of possibility and hope might be most appropriately nurtured. For even though the nurse may not personally hold the same beliefs as a patient, an attentiveness that draws on, and responds to, a shared culture enables access to the patient's world (PC 88).

Benner and Wrubel's exemplars provide countless illustrations of the ways nurses practice this sort of attentive caring, drawing on their clinical experience, the cultural meanings they share with their patients, their personal bodily, emotional and perceptive capacities to recognize and respond to the particular concerns of individual patients. They give us Clare Hastings, for example, assessing a woman with 'terrible rheumatoid arthritis', communicating by the way she looked at the woman's joints, the way she touched her hand and fingers, that she had seen these kinds of things before, that she knew 'what they are', and that she understood the meaning of the swellings and pains for this woman's personal life (PC 9–11). They present Mary Cucci reading the body language of a terrified heart attack victim, reflecting and clarifying his feelings, selecting an approach that matches his goal-oriented way of working, challenging him with humour and commitment to meet each day's objectives, teaching him to monitor his own progress, gradually rebuilding his belief in himself (PC 16–17, 247–51).

These descriptions have a strong ring of familiarity. Although Benner's account, as I have presented it so far, has been produced mainly from the perspective of nurses' capabilities, rather than a consideration of the ethical import of the kind of relations in which they are involved, her descriptions of their practical skills and involvement recall several important themes articulated in earlier chapters. In particular, aspects of 'attentive love' mentioned by Ruddick and Blum with respect to mothering in Chapter 1 and friendship in Chapter 2 come to mind. As already noted, both these theorists draw on views articulated by Iris Murdoch to explain the work of emotionally engaged attention as an ethical activity that depends on responsiveness to the unique particularity of another person. According to Murdoch, the cumulative work of attention that refines our grasp of the dynamic and endlessly complex situations in which we find ourselves provides ethical possibilities for action that outstrip the simplifications of rule-bound moral frameworks. Just and loving attention orients this grasp of situations in ways that enable its practitioners to respond to other persons for whom they particularly are in themselves.[14] The sorts of perceptual awareness and engagement that Benner detects in clinical practice show a striking resemblance to this account.[15]

It is worthwhile pausing to reflect on these overlapping conceptions. For, despite its historic origins in the mobilization of capacities allegedly developed by women in their close, personal and family relationships, nursing, as Benner notes, has largely defined itself through the establishment of 'distance' as part of professional relationships (FNE 163–4). Nurses are warned about becoming too involved with, and attentive to, patients as individuals; professional behaviour entails the avoidance of any personal interactions and the limitation of one's role to the exercise of scientific, technical and managerial capabilities. These injunctions are designed to answer the problems of face-to-face caring relations in the public sphere.

Nurses learn early that 'distance' – using themselves as lifeless instruments – protects them from embarrassment while performing awkward and intimately associated procedures, and from emotional depletion and personal suffering when dealing with, and inflicting, pain. Ideally patients are also saved from embarrassment, from intrusions into their privacy, exploitation of their personal resources and possibilities, and the risks of biased judgements.[16] Thus, while we might willingly embrace the kind of ethical possibilities provided by caring attentiveness in the realm of personal relationships, as for example, Ruddick and Blum do, with respect to maternal and friendship relations, it seems that nursing relations fall into a conflicting domain.

Yet Benner's exemplars of nursing excellence seem to defy this conclusion. Clinical nurses are actively involved with their patients as whole persons and express their perceptive, experiential, deliberative, emotional and cultural selves as well as their scientific and organizational abilities. At the same time there are also crucial differences in commitment, compared with the personal caring of a mother or a friend. The well-structured context of clinical nursing care with its established domain of tasks and expectations does not evoke detached as opposed to engaged, or impersonal as opposed to personal care, but rather a distinctive kind of ethical concern that rides the tension between these conflicting dispositions. Blum has suggested that this personally engaged, professionally structured connection can be understood by considering the vocational dimension of professional practices of care. Accordingly, nurses learn to respond to their patients in a mode that personally invokes and interprets the values and ideals that are socially and objectively associated with their profession. Though their role and the distance it entails are objectively prescribed, their orientation to these prescriptions is suffused with their personal endorsement of the ethical traditions of nursing.[17]

The engaged caring of nursing practices is also distinguished from that of personal relations, like friendship, by its uni-directional focus. While being personally engaged with their patients, professionals' attention lacks the mutuality and 'world-defining'[18] concern implicit in personal relations. Nursing does not depend on receiving reciprocal attention from the patient to make the relationship valuable; experience is not shared for the intrinsic value of sharing in the life of the other in itself. And although personal relations like friendship and mothering may also exhibit a dominant one-way concern, their characteristic goals of life sharing and mutuality place a limit on this dynamic.

Philosopher nurse, Sally Gadow has discussed the distinctive uni-directional focus of nursing involvement in terms of its special 'intensity' and 'perspective'.[19] In contrast to the shared immediacy of feeling that tends to be primary in friendships, the nurse's 'external' perspective facilitates the integration of feelings and knowledge, this integration being aimed at liberating patients from the limits of their immediate feelings. This perspective gives rise to a more reflective, directed intensity of involvement. According to Gadow, it is this possibility for conscious, directed intensity of involvement that overcomes the risks of emotional burn-out and prejudice often associated with personally engaged concern. These ills typically result from the sort of involvement in which the nurse identifies with the patient's emotion, and consequently succumbs to the same sort of involuntary and unconscious immediacy that the patient experiences. The nurse's intentional emotional participation is quite different from this kind of emotional infection. The professional's directed focus, conscious emotional intensity and 'external' perspective assists patients to develop a unified sense of themselves; it understands and supports their emotional complexity, without falling prey to the isolation and partiality generated in the immediacy of their distress.[20]

The suggestion here is not that intimate relations suffer from excessive emotional infection, but that nursing care offers the possibility for a distinctive kind of involvement. At the same time, because it requires participation of the whole person, nursing is not immune from feelings of pain and loss, joy and relief. Benner and Wrubel quote nurse Sallie Tisdale's poignant account of 'treading lightly' between the poles of burdensome emotional identification and that severance from the person in pain that creates a schism in the nurse's own experience. Anything more than this 'light tread' is self-indulgence, anything less, self-estrangement (PC 375).[21]

From these discussions it is evident that the engaged and perceptive attentiveness of expert nursing practices is not simply a matter of active knowing as such. In the first place, although the nurse's experiential and embodied knowledge is ultimately translated into objective meanings in order for decisions to be made, there is no precise, one-to-one correspondence between the multiple relations of an actual situation and knowledge. Nursing judgements are always hedged with ambiguity and are vulnerable to unexpected configurations and outcomes beyond the ken of their emotionally guided, culturally dependent intelligence. Nor is clinical caring merely a subtle way of discovering salient facts, prying out hidden, privileged information that increases control – and domination – of another. Benner and Wrubel indicate that 'overinvolvement' may signal an attempt to gain control in order to overcome the inherent vulnerability of caring (PC 373–4). Nursing care is a particular way of entering the world of another person, and thus a unique practice in ethics.

And it is primarily the situation of the 'other person' that constructs the distinctive possibilities of this practice: it is the illness of the other that calls out the particular ethical import of nursing practices. The patient's perspective adds crucial insight to understanding here. 'It is the *accident* and the *vulnerability* of affliction which manifest the moral order', explains Richard Zaner referring to his experience of renal dialysis.[22] Illness presents us with explicit and indisputable evidence of the pervasiveness of chance and vulnerability as inherent structures of our lives. As the sufferers of assaults of happenstance, we experience the inescapable 'objectness' of our bodies – or in more complicated ways, our minds: the defenceless, thing-like fragility of body or mind is experienced in opposition to our purposes and values. Nursing care is a response to the specific experiences of affliction, that carries the meaning of this essential dimension of our humanity.

There is a continuity here, of course, with the vulnerability of childhood and the mothering it elicits. In his stress on the centrality of illness to 'the moral order', Zaner displays a characteristic forgetfulness of the fragility of infancy and the vital ethical significance of the nurturing that facilitates the transformation of children's capacities into maturity. Discontinuities are evident as well. The inherent dangers of childhood are less self-consciously experienced, more expected, perhaps more readily defused and more distant, except for mothers and their children. The vulnerability of illness is experienced as a loss, a deformation of what could or should be, and therefore its lessons are somehow more acute.

Zaner goes on to detail the nature of the vulnerability from the perspective of the losses and strictures of dysfunction experienced by dialysis patients. He talks about the way one's body takes centre stage, constricting movement, sight and reach, consuming one's attention and energy; the way one's ability to make a variety of choices and decisions is impaired, one's capacity to expect is confounded, one's ability to plan and direct one's own history is constrained. He describes the way ordinary relations with others are distorted, the isolation and humiliation of having to place oneself in the hands of others, and how one is deprived of a crucial sense of self, integrity, and much of what one values about oneself.[23] Renal failure is, using Benner and Wrubel's terms, not only 'a manifestation of aberration at the cellular, tissue or organ level' but a complex interaction of physiological malfunctioning with the 'lived experience of the body' (PC 8ff.). Zaner's affliction is not simply a mechanical breakdown, but an attack on his personhood, a rupture of the unity between himself and his grasp of his reality.

Ironically, this sense of fragmentation is deepened in the world of institutional health care. The patient's shattered but private, lived experience becomes a public object transformed by the conceptual categories of clinical science into precise, pathological phenomena.[24] The impersonal organizational routines of the institution, designed to make the patient's alien and problematic otherness accessible for treatment, intensify the disempowerment. Almost every aspect of the professional clinic, from the allocation of caregivers to the colour of the floor, functions for ends beyond the personal, subjective needs of the patient. The administration of personal care, itself an intrusion of others, is frequently mediated through the use of unfeeling instruments and machines. The expert nurse is able to manipulate instruments as if they were an extension of her own body, but for the patient the 'otherness' of instruments that symbolize transcendence of bodily limits remains. And since, as Gadow points out, the difficulty lies in integrating what is beyond or alien into the personal sphere, the more complicated the technology the more disruptive is its presence.[25] Finally, professional care frequently involves the in-fliction of pain: perhaps the ultimate symbol of human unfreedom and objectification. The therapeutic response, in this form, acts on the pure materiality of the patient, and, in so doing, reduces the patient's whole world to an entirely negative, bodily sphere of existence.

By contrast, the clinical nurse moves with ease, undisturbed by the possible disruptions of embodiment. Fully clothed, sometimes gloved and masked, the professional's body is wholly intact and hidden from intrusive eyes and instruments. Sight, reach and spoken language function normally to enable participation in the projects and relations that produce a unified sense of self and meaning: the clinical environment is familiar, both physically and culturally; the abstractions of science, the categories of conditions are also part of the professional's own forms of access to the patient. Most importantly, professionals have expertise in inter-preting the patient's illness, both formal scientific knowledge and experience that give them markers and signs that are unavailable to patients in making assessments. It is this expertise on which patients are dependent for the alleviation of the fracture in their lived experience.

It is interesting here to consider the way in which this institu-tional vulnerability compares with the vulnerability that was so central to the discussion of friendship in Chapter 2. As we have seen, Rubin, and most notably Miller, emphasize the vulnerability of the freedoms of friendship relations: the anxiety and un-certainty inherent in a kind of caring that lacks established forms for its expression. In the case of nursing relations, however, the vulnerability of illness is largely a matter of happenstance amelior-ated and exacerbated by institutional provisions. The formally structured relations established to overcome vulnerability also contribute to its intensity. But in both examples of care, vulnerability is central to their ethical force. Mothering relations are also constituted in vulnerability and in this case yet another constellation of factors is in play. Children are vulnerable to accident and abuse in a way that makes them dependent for protection as well as for healing; mothers are vulnerable in virtue of their emotional investment. But the social organization of family life and the responsibilities it obliges, while less formal than institutional nursing, provide something of a buffer against these fragilities, too. In each case, the different dimensions of these vulnerabilities give rise to the specific shape and ethical significance of the relational responses they elicit.

It is clear that nursing relations are constitutively structured by the vulnerabilities of inequality and dependency at many different levels; it is also evident that it is attending to the 'objectness' of the patient that constructs this gulf, yet is central to their practice. The complexity of nursing care is such that it both contributes to and aims to overcome patients' objectification and dependency. For as much as it aims at alleviating the patient's subjective experience of distress, nursing is also strongly rooted in the reality of attending bodily functions: dirt, hunger, excreta, breakages and decay, the 'stuff' of the experiential rupture.

Gadow quotes Tisdale describing the 'oddly unbalanced intimacy' nurses share with their patients:

> Always in the mind of the nurse is the desire for the wound to heal, for the infection to cease, and for the skin to be whole again. But that desire isn't separate from skin on skin, from the exclamation of burning when the medication is applied, from the tears, the pleas, and the gratitude for tenderness, which is no more and no less than itself – direct, exact, real.[26]

With this eloquent account of nursing practice Tisdale conveys the inexorable force of objective concerns enmeshed in the subjective desire for healing: the unmediated bodily directness and pain of 'skin on skin'. But in so doing she also captures, with matter-of-fact simplicity, the way in which her direct involvement in the patients' world of 'wounds and decay' is interwoven with the tenderness of caring that participates in bridging the gulf of inequality and dependency that separates her from them. It is crucial for her patients' well-being that Tisdale ministers to their objective concerns, but her feeling engagement with their bodies prevents their reduction to the moral status of objects. The tenderness that elicits their gratitude is witness to a relationship in which the objectivity gulf is overcome by mutual subjective involvement.

Here we see the two interconnected ethical dimensions of nursing relationships: on the one hand, the helping and healing activities of coping with the experience of rupture; on the other, the interwoven practice of breaching the relational chasm that those activities, in part, create. Alleviating the patient's condition is a practice of focused engagement that involves ensuring that that chasm is never uncrossable: 'where no assault is permitted unless it can be redeemed, not by its future effect, but by the immediate, present caring of the nurse'.[27] Perhaps there is an analogy here with the complex of protection, training and nurturing Ruddick discusses in mothering practices. The protective and training aspects of maternal care can be seen to interweave objective concerns with the subjective and redemptive practice of supporting children's own development and integrity. Through caring that attends to the caring relationship for its own sake, in this way, both nursing and mothering manifest their most significant ethical possibilities: the reconciliation of the child's and the patient's dependency and dignity, their vulnerability and self-esteem.

There are many related ethical dispositions involved in this complex and conflicted process of bridge building. Gadow discusses the activation of nurses' 'clinical subjectivity':[28] the disclosure of nurses' embodied, emotional involvement that enables connection with the patient's experience and well-being, and which produces the refinements of physical ministration that alleviate suffering and create the trust that subjectivity will not be betrayed. Benner talks about creating the possibility of giving and receiving help by providing a climate of trust which enables patients to appropriate the help offered and to feel that their identities and their experiences are being supported (FNE 44ff.). She elaborates her account with stunning examples of this caring practice.

Each of her examples bears witness to the unique situated forms of this creativity but she also detects common themes. She identifies caring practices that mobilize hope for the nurse and the patient, that provide comfort, manage or reduce pain, encourage patients' participation and control in their own recovery, and their ability to use their own social, emotional and spiritual resources.

Through touch, nurses affirm the subjective significance of the patient's body; through coaching and teaching, nurses make what is foreign and fearful to patients familiar; through their presence as whole persons, nurses express their involved participation in their patients' experience. There is no determinate set of activities that catches the essence of these 'healing relationships', but Benner's examples point to the fund of imaginative possibilities through which committed caring practices traverse the gulf between nurse and patient, engaging the personhood of the nurse in the protection and enhancement of the patient's own unique personhood.

In *The Primacy of Caring*, Benner and Wrubel unpack the nature of those possibilities by considering the facets of personhood that influence – and are influenced by – the stress of disruption to the ordinary smooth functioning of a person's embodied existence. Central to this analysis is the idea that the experience of illness depends on its personal meanings to the patient or, phenomenologically speaking, 'the existing conditions of possibilities that the person experiences in a situation' (PC 58). Beyond biomedical factors, these conditions include the interrelated roles of the lived meanings evident in a person's bodily and emotional holding, their sense of the connections between the present situation and their past and future purposes, the cultural meanings of the illness, and the personal commitments of the patient (PC 57–103).

The significance of these dimensions of experience is explained through the presentation of copious illustrations of their expression in particular nursing relations. Habitual bodily capacities that have been disrupted are encouraged and restored by practices that understand the alterations in the patient's experienced embodiment and the need for a sense of bodily integrity in rehabilitation. A new synthesis of past, present and future can be developed by practices that enable exploitation of present possibilities in face of the apparently interminable distress of the moment. Recognition of the meanings for the patient that arise out of cultural understandings of different illnesses – the psychological stigma of cancer, the lifestyle assault of a heart attack, the scepticism concerning unidentifiable and chronic degeneration – allows caring to cope with this dimension of stress. Perhaps most importantly, understanding of each patient's own personal involvements and commitments allows nurses a healing entrance into their disrupted world. Thus, revisiting examples cited earlier to illustrate nurses' clinical attentiveness, we can see that the 'other side' of Clare Hastings' and Mary Cucci's personal involvement is their outstanding comprehension and affirmation of what is personally important to their patients. Their directed concern enables the interpretation of body language, emotions and words that 'builds a bridge to the patient's lived experience of the illness' (PC 12), thereby supporting and affirming its unique significance.

By accepting the patient's whole phenomenal world in these ways, nursing care transforms the meaning of dependency and vulnerability from alienation and demoralization into a sense of personal integrity and dignity. And although physiological factors are often crucial to this change, it is clear that the transformation is not necessarily dependent on positive alterations in the disease process. Coping with chronic and terminal illnesses clearly illustrates the transformative power of nursing care in which finding an acceptable sense of personal identity, and the conditions of possibility, is bounded by the way the person is in the situation, rather than objective criteria of medical progress and health.

It is noteworthy, however, that although the relation is unidirectional in the sense that it is focused on the patient's well-being this transformation of meanings is a process of collaboration. The mutuality of personal involvement is evident as nurses redeem their assaults on patients' vulnerability through disclosure of their own subjectivity. From the other side, the discussion of the kind of trust caring requires indicates the importance of patients' capacities to appropriate the care offered, to feel that they in all their unique particularity matter, and are thus directly involved in their own care. Benner's example of an expert nurse's caring for an alert young man with a broken spine, whose anxiety was producing a dangerously high respiratory rate, captures this sense of 'collaboration'. The nurse explains how the patient could not relax until he recognized that he could trust the medical team's appreciation of his personal involvement in the recovery process. He needed to know, she says, 'that we cared about *him*, as an individual, not just another helpless patient. . . He needed to be involved, not just prescribed to.' Only then could he trust his carers (FNE 52–3).

This trust is not simply an act of blind faith that relinquishes responsibility; nor is the nurse's care a philanthropic gift or a paternalistic judgement that marks dependency. Still less does this care defer to the 'patients' rights' lobby that ensures merely that patients' authority to make their own decisions is protected.[29] Power is not wielded in this either/or style. Despite the gulf between his extreme incapacity and her practically informed assurance, they are able to pool their resources – his personal, immediate involvement, her professional perspective – to participate together in the clarification of his possibilities. While caring cannot be reciprocal, it succeeds through joint practices that engage the persons of both patient and nurse. This mode of 'collaboration' resonates with the example of trust that we have already seen in practices of mothering: the caring trust of a mother in the potential for reciprocity that transforms passivity in the face of vulnerability into active collaborative trust of the child. Indeed the climate of trust created in practices like mothering serves as an exemplar of and support for the trust required in the case of the vulnerability that occasions the need for nursing care.

Benner claims that both patients and nurses gain personally from this practice of caring. The former seems obvious: the relationship is structured by this end. For nurses the direct personal rewards are less clear. Benner refers to the self-reflexive values of caring that have been discussed in earlier chapters of this investigation: the self-enhancing and affirming outcomes of engaged participation in the lived experience of another, as well as the increased perceptive possibilities, understanding and emotional capacities of witnessing and co-operating in the support of another person's meanings and values (FNE 213–14). This opportunity for learning is intensified by its context. Compared with friendship relations, for example, where the stakes tend to be lower, nurses participate in the parts of peoples' lives when they are most vulnerable, when there are fewer possibilities to hide behind appearances, and when everything that makes life most meaningful is at risk. Nurses are a party to human possibilities that many other persons never experience or observe.[30]

In addition, the formal organization of nursing under the rubric of paid work carries reflexive possibilities for nurses. Here, apart from providing the means to economic security – itself a crucial requirement for self-esteem and independence – the paid work in which a person is employed tends to be significantly implicated in her or his sense of self and values. At least work that is satisfying and challenging, in which one can become involved, committed and interested, in which one participates in determining how it is done, and one's competence is recognized appropriately by others, is potentially rewarding in this way (FNE 195–7). Personal identification with the ethical ideals and values of the profession that mediates ethically engaged nursing care is simultaneously a source of self-validation and empowerment.

Coming towards the end of her paean to clinical nursing, Benner's self-reflexive claims have considerable plausibility, for she has shown us caring in its richest and most outstandingly responsible practice. However, even given this context of actual examples of excellence, Benner is not unaware of some of the barriers to the realization of this potential. Indeed her whole project of uncovering the nature and significance of nursing care is largely propelled by the state of disillusionment, demoralization and devaluation in which clinical nursing is practised in North America. Her important response to this crisis is the provision of detailed and persuasive evidence of the crucial significance and the scope of the possibilities embedded in the actuality of nurses' relations with their patients. Revaluation of caring along these lines opens the way to the recognition and rewards that will allow nurses to enjoy the sense of self-worth, identity and commitment that is their due.

But here her project seems to lose some of its strength, for in her focus on individual instances of practice she seems to have underestimated the structural components of the crisis. Benner's stated aim is to 'offer a resounding rebuttal to the skeptic [of excellence in actual nursing practice] and a ray of hope to the disillusioned' (FNE xviii). Her determined emphasis on situated excellence of caring in the face of 'troubled nurse–physician exchanges', and a lack of 'formally acknowledged nursing functions' (FNE xxi), is designed to avoid the traps of victimism and the paralysis of impotence that often follow from confrontation with entrenched institutional obstacles. But in its accolades to the creative possibilities of nursing, her discussion often slides over the complexity and immensity of the disempowering structural relations in which clinical nursing is enmeshed. Her acknowledgement of the profession's lack of recognition, and of nurses' lack of participation in the decision-making that is vital to their practice, for example, is followed by challenges to nurses to provide 'descriptions of nursing practice [that] match the significance and scope of nursing as it is practiced' (FNE 204). By buttressing personal morale in the face of powerful and oppressive institutional structures, this focus runs the risk of encouraging damaging self-effacement.

The problem here is the familiar difficulty of perspective and emphasis. While it makes possible understanding of certain aspects, Benner's perspective inevitably overlooks others. In her later work with Wrubel, more space is allotted to consideration of the disablements of clinical caring, though the discussion of the oppressive social context of nursing relations comes in the final pages of a study that has immersed the reader in moving illustrations of nursing's profound possibilities for individual empowerment. Connections between the invisibility and de-valuation of nursing care on the one hand and the gendered division of labour on the other are announced, and the difficulties of working in conditions of financial duress and rapid scientific development are noted (PC 365–9). Yet, in my view, the discussion is shaped in ways that tend to diminish the power and dislocating impact of socially constructed impediments.

'Coping with caregiving' – that is, dealing with institutional impediments to caring – seems to be framed in the same way as the preceding discussions of 'coping' with illness. As a result, meanings related to the assault of chance and a situation of vulnerability inherent in the human condition are evoked for this situation of socially constructed disablement. The scene appears to be set for the 'healing' transformation of meanings that will ameliorate the stress of happenstance, though in this case there are no 'external' caregivers to assist those who are suffering. Despite suggestions that the difficulties require the dual responses of uncovering the significance of nursing care and restructuring its institutional support and status (PC 368–9), concern for struc-tural impacts on caring is deflected with morale-raising talk of the special values of nursing care. Attention is drawn to inherent difficulties: how nurses find the right level of involvement, acknowledge the pain and losses, deal with anger and fear, recognizing personal strengths and weaknesses, and shaping practice towards strengths. And while 'it is insulting to talk about individual strategies to cope with ... an untenable situation' (PC 384), the challenge of caring seems to remain with individual nurses and their nursing administrators, rather than the 'external' social relations through which health care is organized.

In the discussion of mothering relations in Chapter 1, I have pointed to the complex of interconnected ways in which Ruddick's

account of mothering tends to underestimate the profound constitutive power of the socio-cultural field in which those relational
practices are embedded. We have seen how the dynamics of
'idealization', 'individualism' and 'essentialism' operate in her
work to mask the contribution of social structures to her concepts,
and effectively to normalize and naturalize the constraints they
impose on mothering relations. Although Benner's approach is
substantially different, her efforts to render visible the hidden,
significant work of nursing as a caring practice share many of
these oversights. Where Ruddick's universal claims lead to the
identification of mothering as a struggle under guiding ideals,
Benner's determination to uncover excellence in existing situations tends to establish a corresponding set of ideals. In each case,
despite distinctions between actual practices and abstract goals,
the outcome is much the same: the production of a context in
which the excellences and the deficiencies of caring tend to be
related to the personal capacities of the care-givers.

Benner is anxious to avoid romanticization or censure of nurses'
practices but the stress of her focus on the possibilities for
excellence lends itself to these corruptions. Examination of the
significance of clinical practice, like Ruddick's analysis of mothering, is an important part of understanding the nature and ethical
value of caring, and of helping care-givers maintain self-respect.
Without a counterbalancing perspective that takes the realities of
its deformations seriously, however, her account runs the risk of
affirming structural relations which in contemporary North America, at least, often endorse and encourage the exploitation of
nurses' capacities and hold them personally responsible for the
failures of nursing care. When nursing is displayed in its full
virtue, offering nurses and patients alike the rewards of a committed, meaningful relationship, and the goods of personal help
given and received, the interwoven perceptions that all difficulties
can be surmounted individually, and that the practice provides its
own intrinsic compensations, gain considerable reinforcement.
The impact of structural contributions both to the forms of
excellence and to the massive problems of nursing relations, is
largely neutralized, and rendered irrelevant to the ethical possibilities of care.

The particular orientation of Benner's discussion of individual
practices further compounds this inattention to the disabling
effects of the socio-cultural context of nursing. With her specific

interest in the deep interrelations between the personal and the social in the construction of patients' possibilities and the responses of expert caring to these dimensions, she seems to overlook the ways nurses' possibilities are structured by their interconnection in a network of different social relations. Consideration of the effect of the clinical environment on patients' experience, for example, is not matched by similar regard for its effects on nurses. Nurses' discomfort in talking about the co-ordination of patients' interactions with doctors is elided by accounts of 'excellence' in this area due to 'commitment to the patient as an individual and engagement in the situation' (FNE 135–44). We learn nothing about the misplaced authority of physicians[31] that produces this discomfort or how it might be challenged. Neither the structural features that cement physicians' power in unassailable forms, nor those that are conducive to the requisite courage in advocacy, are considered in the discussion of nurses' successes in this domain.

Similar, more far-reaching oversights occur at the cultural level as well. Benner foregrounds the ways in which caring must traverse not only the inequalities and vulnerabilities of accident and health care institutions but also the cultural values that militate against acknowledgement of dependency. Making a point reminiscent of Miller's discussion of the difficulties of forming male friendships within the flourishing ideologies of independence and self-sufficiency in North America, Benner and Wrubel call attention to the way patients' feelings of dependency are culturally loaded. A 'culture where self-esteem is based on individualism, self-control, independence and self-reliance', they claim, creates both reluctance to ask for help and difficulty in receiving help when it is offered by appropriate others (PC 366). Nursing care therefore also involves nurture of values and ideals that encourage non-threatening expectations of the relationship.

In *From Novice to Expert*, when noting nurses' sensitivity to this matter, she explains how they 'covered' their help by joking about it or assuming an air of unconcern. 'In all cases', she remarks approvingly, 'they took special care to limit the patient's sense of obligation and tried to establish a context of attentiveness that was central to being a "nurse" and not dependent upon a social contract or exchange on the patient's part' (FNE 47). Such caring masks the culturally depreciated dependency it signals by injecting equalizing and distancing stances of 'humour' and 'nonchalance' into the inherent inequalities in order to minimize the patient's sense of incapacity or obligation. Further, by establishing a domain of responses characteristic of being a 'nurse', nurses call forth in that domain another tradition of values that allows caring to be accepted without damage to identity. Patients are able to interpret their dependency as harmonious with an established context, yet free of conflict with celebrations of autonomy and independence in the wider culture.

But Benner fails to point out that the social constructions of being a 'nurse' that support this possibility, like those of mothering relations, frequently also sustain gendered assumptions that are damaging to the relationship. In continuity with cultural devaluations of women's caring, nursing care may conventionally be perceived as a right of service from inferiors. Correspondingly, through deep enculturation processes, being a 'nurse' may be understood as a practice of self-effacement combined with the establishment of relationships that are worth little valuation from patients, or society. In these terms caring begins to smack strongly of self-sacrifice, or perhaps even self-established exploitation; dependency and vulnerability begin to look as if they become palatable if caring is invisible or given by a self-sacrificing, and thus insignificant, 'nurse'. In many ways nursing care works against cultural ideologies of self-reliance, but by invoking its difference without a view to its own social context it runs the risk of being constructed in an oppositional way that entails the sacrifice of nurses' own sense of self.

As was clear in the case of mothering relations – and as Benner and Wrubel have affirmed in their discussion of the phenomenology of illness – the domain of ethical possibilities is complexly constituted in the interrelations of generic human, personal and socio-historically determined factors. But nursing care is not simply a response to the complicated interconnection of these factors as they play out in the world of the patient. It is also the response of nurses to the particular social system within which their caring is organized. Benner's tendency to pay less attention to this dimension of clinical caring, despite being directly motivated by the context of societal devaluation of nursing, runs in danger of supporting its ideals. Nonetheless, her rich and insightful description of the possibilities embedded in actual practices of care comes from a deep understanding of, and an unwillingness to give up, the values and significance of nursing caring. I have

discussed her work at length precisely because of this understanding, the way it brings the values of nursing relations into
such vivid relief and shows us why nurses are so strongly
committed to their caring even under oppressive conditions. Its
perspectival character is, following the approach adopted in this
investigation, a condition of its very articulation. Accordingly,
understanding of nursing entails approaching it from a variety
of perspectives.

III

Given my interest in gender-sensitive understanding, in this
section I want to set out for view approaches that trace the ethical
impact of some of the multiply intertwined components of the
socio-political construction of professional practice. Here the
influence of cultural understandings of gender roles and values is
intertwined with the complexities of institutional organization
designed to provide for needs that outrun the resources of
individual care-givers. Tracking gendered effects on the possibilities of practice is caught up in investigation of the concurrent
force of institutionalizing care.

Anne Bishop and John Scudder's recent 'philosophy of nursing'
focuses specifically on this latter dimension. Their account aims
to highlight the inherent teamwork of institutional care and
nursing's distinctive 'in-between' possibilities within the network
of patients, doctors and administrators.[32] In a discussion comparing the different institutional locations of nurses and physicians in the United States, they note the many ways in which
nursing care is determined by its institutional relations rather than
by the personal needs of patients. Time is allocated in accordance
with physicians' orders and hospital schedules; resources are
determined by hospital budgets and patients' financial situations.
Hospital schedules, efficiency requirements and physicians' demands structure relationships with patients; hospital policy, routines, shifts and so on, dictate tasks and standards. Even financial
rewards are fixed by hospital administrations rather than being
indexed to effort, concern and patients' requirements of service.[33]
As a result caring is carried out within a set of regulatory relations
which in many ways fit uneasily with the shifting, uncertain
character of the personal relations that are central to nursing.
Further, the contractual relationship between nurses and their

institutional employers creates tensions in allegiance and commitment to patients.[34]

According to Bishop and Scudder, the structured context of
nursing care plays out in a set of moral 'dilemmas' that are
constitutive of nursing's unique possibilities. Some of the ways in
which caring that is attentive to patients' personal needs negotiates intrinsic institutional and medical objectifications of patients
have already been considered in this chapter. Seen as part of the
product of practice in the health care 'team', however, this tension
between personal caring and impersonal contexts appears to be
directly related to 'the conglomerate of intentionalities which
have developed over time in the health care professions'.[35] Most
notably in the United States context, individual patients' needs
come into conflict with economic interests in profit-making, as well
as the promotion of medical and nursing professionalism; efficient
work schedules, medical science developments, specialization and
high-tech interventions compete with the establishment of personal healing relationships between patients and nurses. Given
these institutional conflicts, nurses act from a 'privileged in-
between position to foster the good of the patient'.[36] Their caring
is characterized by the ethical potential to communicate between
different members of the 'team' and to encourage co-operation
and accommodation among those involved.[37]

Far from viewing this process of consensus-making as the
unavoidable compromise of moral principles, Bishop and Scudder
claim that this broader context – unlike Benner's nurse–patient
focus – constitutes the situated ethical significance inherent in
health care provision. Institutional health care is a communal
practice requiring the contributions of medical/nursing knowledge and skill, patients' aspirations and values, and hospital
policy and procedure. Within this community nurses occupy the
special inside position that provides the possibility for securing
the requisite situated, ethical practice.[38] From this perspective
health care institutions supply nurses with the security and
protection, financial support, facilities and resources that allow
them to fulfil the complex ethical possibilities of collaborative
caring.

This emphasis on communal practice is developed in part as a
counter to the pervasive stress on rights and autonomy in contemporary discussions of medical and nursing ethics.[39] Bishop
and Scudder rightly insist that ethical nursing care is constituted

by situated, organizational and interpersonal limits and possibilities. They remind us that clinical nursing is an intrinsically co-operative practice, providing resources, knowledge, skill and commitment that individual patients or lay carers are unable to supply. Additionally, they foreground the sorts of tensions and dilemmas that are inherent in the forms of this co-operative enterprise: the complex of diversely motivated relations that comprise the institutional response to patients' needs. In acknowledging the organizational conditionality of nursing relations, however, they assume a level of communal solidarity and 'in-between' privilege that seems to overlook the widespread conflict and dissatisfaction that is such an outstanding feature of nursing practice in contemporary Western institutions.

Nurses' discontent is marked simply as a misdirected demand for autonomy and the protagonists are roundly chastised for their failure to understand the inherent co-operative nature of their caring and its value. Protests objecting that systematically created obstacles prevent nurses in hospitals from exercising the freedom of action necessary for ethical patient care are dismissed as products of a flawed individualism that refuses to recognize the practical reality of the community discipline of health care provision.[40] As a result, an analysis designed to affirm the constitutively social character of nursing relations leads back to ascriptions of individual praise and blame. Once again the burden of responsibility for the realization of the ethical possibilities of nursing care seems to fall squarely on the now privileged shoulders of individual nurses themselves.

As Benner has shown, individual clinical nurses are able to perform outstanding feats of excellence in their caring, including gaining appropriate and timely responses from medical and administrative members of the health care team. But it is also clear that disillusionment with institutional nursing, and the belief that the organizational and social constraints in hospitals render nurses impotent, are widespread in the professional culture (FNE xvii–xviii).[41] That the source of this impotence is more profound than a misunderstanding of the intrinsic tension between institutional forms and personal involvement is also evident. In a study of Canadian nursing, for example, Sarah Growe explains the ways in which 'community discipline' involves the systematic devaluation of nursing care and mistrust of nursing judgements. Hierarchical hospital organization, budget containment techniques

and an increase in high-tech medical procedures, all combine to
create a situation in which nurses have no authority to control the
clinical patient environment, yet at the same time they are held
accountable for patient care.[42] Chronic short staffing, lack of
recognition, lack of possibilities for professional growth, strained
relationships among hospital personnel, and insufficient time to
establish the intimacy that is the hallmark of good nursing, are
the creation of powerful socio-historical interests that command
nurses to care while refusing to value caring.[43]

Like the diminishment of the significance of socio-cultural
factors in Benner and Wrubel's description, Bishop and Scudder's
failure to question the structural constitution of clinical nursing –
who controls the health care team? and to what ends? – overlooks
the power of organizational factors that constrain ethical co-
operation in institutional provision of health care. The disavowal
of serious discord among the members of the health care team
community in the assertion that, 'physicians and hospital bureau-
crats have the same moral commitment as nurses in that they are
to promote the physical and psychological well-being of the
patient',[44] disregards the force of vested interests in the organization of institutional care. The focus on nurses' day-to-day
ethical practice of compassion and commitment, 'in spite of the
circumstances',[45] underestimates the implications of the systemic
devaluation and subordination of nursing care. In the light of
disabling ideological and material forces, the claim that the ethical
possibilities of nursing are centred in the obligation 'to sustain
excellent practice in the face of unreasonable demands which deny
the legitimate authority of nurses',[46] is highly problematic. In the
absence of countervailing perspectives, it may even open the way
to encouraging nurses' collusion in the exploitation of their care.

IV

In order to loosen the perception of inevitability latent in this
understanding of caring, Susan Reverby suggests that examination of the history of nursing offers a way to rethink its possibilities. According to Reverby, the obligation to accept the duty
to care without the authority to control the activities performed in
its name has been a central organizing factor in the development
of the nursing profession in the United States.[47] From the earliest
beginnings of the institutionalization of their activities, she claims,

nurses were expected to take on their obligation to care as part of the expression of their natural identities rather than as work chosen and performed by autonomous and self-directed agents. Following this line, Reverby's fascinating history of the profession charts the ambivalent dynamic of this obligation that, on the one hand, provided nursing with an ethical and practical legitimacy while, on the other, constrained attempts by nurses to take control of their practice and profession.[48]

The key feature of this history is its profound entanglement with conventional social constructions of women's character and roles. Modern hospital nursing drew on the social virtues of caring as an act of love and obligation to the needs of family and friends, held to be embedded in the natural character of women, rather than a vital function of nurses' work, valuated by time, expertise and money. The vocation and duty to care which were so deeply rooted in the culture of nineteenth-century British and American womanhood, not the need for or right to work that suited their skills, was the theoretical justification for the mobilization of women's labour in the public sphere. Consequently, the training that became the mark of professionalism was a disciplined process of honing womanly virtue. For those women who needed work, however, the conception of nursing that legitimated their identities in this way offered them a new realm of respectability – 'a livelihood and a virtuous state'[49] – outside the family. For these women, the duty to care with its accent on their feminine capabilities seemed to coincide with their governance of their caring practices.

By calling on sex-typed roles in hospitals, the system also endorsed a strict separation of nursing functions from the all-male medical sphere. Nursing was a distinct field of concern that in no way encroached upon the physicians' preserve. According to Nightingale, nurses neither needed nor desired any of the doctor's skills or prerogatives. His concern with medical therapeutics and surgical care, based in the masculine realm of scientific thought and practice, was but a small part in the function of hospitals compared with nurses' disciplined feminine abilities and responsibilities for the broader hospital morale. In line with Victorian family models, the complementarity and putative political equality between these two spheres was to be secured through nurses' relative independence and their treatment of doctors' authority with deference and loyalty – though not with blind servility.[50]

The locus of the discipline and obedience associated with the professionalization of nursing was the strict female hierarchy through which orders were passed down from superintendents to probationers, and through which the control and standards necessary to keep the hospital environment clean and conducive to healing were maintained. Reverby points out that this plan for order and health embedded in an appeal to women's special moral character was thereby characterized by stratification from the beginning. Two categories of nurses were to be trained: the 'gentlewomen' who would have the 'qualifications which will fit them to become superintendents', and those women 'used to household work' who would be regular nurses.[51]

The subsequent history of the profession saw the reproduction of these founding themes of sexual division of labour, training, hierarchical organization – duty, obligation and obedience – as they interacted with the developing interests of the male medical academy and the hospital administration, suppliers and financiers. The call to womanly duty provided hospitals with a willing corps of cheap labourers whose commitment to the virtues of pleasing, sacrificial service, acquiescence and subordination was ingrained in their sense of female identity and conduct. For these women, confrontation or movements for change in the face of difficult working conditions created a conflict with the innermost core of their being, an assault on the natural obligations of femininity.[52] Lacking any cultural or financial clout, the skills of female character seen marshalled at the patient's bedside in selfless devotion were readily translated into absolute duty and obedience to physicians and hospital authorities. Thus integrity to self – to one's 'feminine' identity and capacities – was constructed in continuity with the inherently contradictory requirement for absolute submission to male authorities.

The 'training programmes' at the heart of nursing's professional status offered the perfect forum for this co-opting of the womanly duty to care, turning it into obedience to external authority. Reverby explains that hospital administrators were quick to recognize that opening a 'nursing school' ensured a ready supply of low-cost and disciplined young labourers who were eager to offer their services in exchange for the professional training offered. Frequently, however, the hospital's nursing school and its nursing service were identical. The needs of caring for increasing numbers of acutely ill patients and financial pressures on the institutions rapidly compromised education in favour of long and heavy hours of mindless, repetitive work on the wards. Emphasis on womanliness as the most important factor in successful nursing, stressing its meanings in terms of submission and self-sacrifice, obedience to orders and unswerving loyalty to doctors rather than initiative, innovation and advocacy, gave ideological justification for this abuse.[53] The alleged exchange of service for training amounted to unwitting compliance in their own exploitation on the part of the trainees.

As Jo-Anne Ashley recounts in her work, *Hospitals, Paternalism and the Role of the Nurse*, the apprenticeship system of training in hospital nursing schools became good business practice. Independent of public regulation, there was little concern about quality of education or exploitation of nurses. Schools were geared to production of minimally trained 'nurses' with narrowly circumscribed spheres of activity, disciplined to self-denial and lack of growth, and dependent on physicians' guidance. Attempts by nursing reformers to use training to broaden the knowledge base and social skills of nursing in the interests of clinical improvements and professionalization continually ran against the deep-seated cultural assumptions concerning gendered capabilities and functions embodied in the roles of the doctor and the nurse. Hospital authorities and the medical establishment were able, therefore, to play on these sentiments in order to maintain their supply of cheap, servile labour whenever there was a nursing shortage, or whenever nurses tried to define their caring as more than assisting doctors. In its turn, the constant flood of poorly trained nurses from the hospitals ensured the low image and status of the occupation, devaluing the contributions of nurses to health care, demoralizing those in the field, discouraging more independent and qualified young women from entering, and justifying low wages and oppressive working conditions. With few alternative choices of work open for women, the training programmes were able to perpetuate the subordination and dependency that secured their commercial success.[54] In this context it was extremely difficult for nurses to organize around shared goals that could transform their obligation to care into active participation in its terms. As Reverby puts it, 'nursing remained bounded by its ideology and its material terms'.[55]

The force of gendered subordination and servility could not be redressed within the profession itself. Indeed the hierarchy of

power and class stratifications built in from its earliest organization has brought further disempowerment as nurses with
conflicting class positions and sensibilities clash over the appropriate definition of nursing, a coherent strategy for change, and
the meaning of womanhood.[56] Underpinned by society-wide
perceptions of women's possibilities and roles, this hierarchy has
fallen easy prey to the forces of industrialization which have
reproduced and further entrenched its disabling impact on the
caring possibilities of nursing.[57]

In the first place, efforts by the nursing leadership to throw off
the shackles of gender subservience through control and up-
grading of training schools has exacerbated the problem of hierarchy and fragmentation of vision. Emphasis on increasingly high
educational standards in order to earn credibility and control – the
measurement and formalization of character and duty – has
caught nurses in the bind of striving for established symbols of
status and value. The weight of gender ideology against the
revaluation of the unique ethical potential of practices that confirm and engage with the inherent particularity and vulnerability
of persons has led to the neglect of these values by the educated
stratum.

The push for high educational qualifications has therefore
produced elitist tendencies that threaten the values and ideals of
the majority of nursing practitioners outside its terrain. The move
towards four-year degrees seems for many nurses to be antithetical to the caring born of shared 'time, embarrassment, pain,
intuition and loss ... [a] quiet word, a stroked cheek, a sharp
retort held back in spite of demands and deadlines', that lies at the
heart of their practice.[58] In defence of their stance, the loyalties of
the highly trained professionals are diverted inwards to the
profession and away from the care of their patients. The unifying
ideology of womanly labour conceals this division in the assignment of nursing tasks and values, while the caring ethic is
transformed into a professional ethic that allows registered nurses
to identify with the doctor-managers whose interests dominate
the structure of institutional health care.[59]

The graded nursing workforce encouraged by this narrow
professionalism has left hospital administrators free to mobilize
the feminine services of those outside the elite by creating
new subdivisions of 'practical' or 'vocational' nurses to fit their
budgetary interests. In this way the hierarchy, with its gendered

confusions and conflicts, is further elaborated and consolidated. These 'auxiliary' nursing categories, with their differential training requirements, work to blur the distinctions between professionals and non-professionals, threatening credibility and maintaining the generalized cultural associations of caring with minimally important domestic work. Growe's account of Canadian nursing suggests that professionals who are reluctant to perform the trying tasks of mother-based caring pass them on to aides and orderlies. At the same time, however, they recognize that their nursing identity is built on care, and so argue that auxiliaries do not have the training to do that professionally.[60] In this context the whole question of what counts as a nursing skill and its ethical import, how it is to be valued and taught, becomes caught up in conflicting political agendas that distort and fracture the possibilities of practice.

Following Reverby, other efforts to overcome the links between the service ethic of nursing and minimally valued expression of womanly virtue and obedience have fared little better. The hope that adoption of techniques of scientific management and efficiency would provide the key to the status of 'objective' practice and the associated rights to assert the priority of self-determined caring values have also been deflected by the powerful and recalcitrant conjunction of hospital interests and gender subordination. Speed, not quality, in performing tasks has been the concern of nursing and hospital administrators in most institutions. As a consequence the introduction of the methods and tools of efficiency experts has been used to subdivide and increase the work output rather than upgrade nursing. As Sandra Harding has pointed out, hierarchical control of this 'industrialization' of nursing has meant that workers at the lower levels of nursing are increasingly alienated from the content of their work. Suggestions and innovations from the ranks are perceived as disruptions to the smooth functioning of the hospital machinery; the service ethic that motivates much of the health care work force is thus forcibly subverted into industrial conformity.[61]

Increasing unionization of hospital workers has not helped to counteract the divisions among nurses and the alienation of their caring ethics. The professional associations have always had difficulty with moves to align the exalted moral calling of womanly nursing with more pragmatic labour issues, for the former feeds off understandings of the virtues of female character and integrity that are considered to lie outside the material calculations of marketplace exchanges. Early challenges to hospitals' demands for self-sacrifice issued by 'worker-nurses' with claims for better conditions and wages sparked accusations of commercialism and derogation of duty from nursing administrators.[62]

The historical split continues today. From the perspective of the ward floor, nursing management is seen to be supporting the short-term efficiency goals of the institution; from the other side, implementation of standardized concepts of care is seen as imperative to unitary professional accountability.[63] Further, established bargaining practices of unions usually succeed by getting more pay for jobs rather than challenging the organization or the quality of the service delivered. The result is the ultimate subversion of caring as increases in wages are passed on by hospitals to the medical consumers, implicitly pitting the needs of nursing staff against the needs of patients.[64] Recent union activity in Canada, concerned as much with working conditions and patient safety as wages, has seen authorities exploiting the power of this almost sacrilegious notion of conflict of interests to hold nurses hostage to the duty to care. The image of Nightingale 'turning in her grave' while greedy nurses 'use patients' lives or health as bargaining tools' is vigorously promoted to shame striking nurses into submission.[65]

Underwritten by ideologies of womanly obligation and self-sacrifice, its practitioners kept relatively ill-paid and weakened from within by conflicting class interests and ideologies, nursing has had little chance to give substantive form to its own vision of caring under the impact of the enormous expansion of health care institutions in North America following the Second World War. The particular priorities of the major players in the system – in the United States the academic medical empires, the financiers, and the hospital suppliers and drug companies[66] – have continually constrained nursing's claims for recognition of its ethical and practical possibilities and the right to determine those possibilities. The powerful interests of medical research and education, financial efficiency, and profitable high-tech supplies and treatments, have divided and alienated nurses further from their own caring potential.[67]

One of the most direct examples of the constraints imposed by gender-based cultural and institutional biases is nurses' troubled relationships with physicians. Despite beginning with a model of largely separate but equal spheres of responsibility, as we have seen, economic interests led to the rapid corruption of nursing's culture of female obligation into wifely obedience to male doctors. With the explosion in the development of scientific medicine, and the interrelated consolidation of medical power and authority in recent decades, nursing has not been able to shake off this aspect of its gendered stereotyping. Studies indicate that 'most doctors see the nurse "as a provider of a conglomerate of insignificant services" such as "mother, child, secretary, wife, waitress, maid, machine and psychiatrist"', while the public image of nursing also reflects all the ambivalent meanings of womanhood.[68] In comparison with medical authority, nurses' knowledge is downgraded, even in areas where medicine has no demonstrable expertise. Doctors are regarded as the only legitimate 'knowers' in the health care system, and nurses are therefore expected to remain within the boundaries set by doctors' orders.

This deep-rooted asymmetry in power generates a context of conflict between the different orientations of nursing and medical relations towards the patient, conflict that impinges directly on nursing judgements. The point is not that one or another perspective is 'correct', rather that each has a different function in the patient's well-being and merits consideration by the team. The terms of legitimate knowing, however, dictate that when the practical experiential knowledge of nurses, born of the relative continuity and intimacy of their relationships with patients, is at odds with doctors' medical claims, their experience may be directly discounted by the superior validity culturally accorded to and presumed by doctors' claims.[69] Not surprisingly then, discussions of clinical practice are rife with references to the ways in which oppressive nurse–physician relations obstruct caring.[70] Nurses' caring for patients is disrupted by the rules of the 'doctor–nurse game' in which their special expertise must be compromised and shrouded in deference to medical authority so as not to damage the physician's status. Manipulation and deceit become the imperatives of practice. Assertion of their own knowledge by nurses, on the other hand, is encumbered by the risks of destroying their working relationships with doctors and their professional credibility.[71] It is clear that under these conditions nurses lack the necessary authority to allow them to fulfil the possibilities of their caring relations.

A more subtly mediated but perhaps more far-reaching dis-
tortion of clinical care is found in contemporary applications of
budgetary management. Here the gendered origins of nursing's
subordination are reinscribed in formulaic practices that completely undermine the distinctive ethical import of clinical care.
As new technology, new equipment and expanding medical
services keep up the pressures on hospital budgets, the weakest
interests in the health care team are affected most severely.
Spiralling costs and decreased government subsidies are not
reflected in physicians' incomes or pharmaceutical and hospital
supply company profits. Although historically the major part of
hospital incomes has derived from selling nursing services –
especially in the early part of the century when medicine had few
services to offer – invisibility in billing and on the governing
boards of hospitals has made nursing care the obvious source of
cost control.

The political weakness of nursing inherent in its dominant
ideology of duty, obedience and submission, and the captive
labour market produced from cultural subordination that has
limited women's opportunities for work, have meant that nursing
care has always been severely and disproportionately constrained
by health care budgets. Foremost among current strategies is
the rationing of care through the assignment of pre-determined
'target hours' and 'patient classification systems'. Formulas set by
hospital management experts and medical diagnoses are used to
provide an empirical rationale to cut nurse–patient ratios down to
the minimum. Nurses are left to organize tasks so that 'un-
necessary' or 'wasted' activities are eliminated in the drive to
provide 'fewer and fewer services to more and more patients
faster and faster'.[72]

Marie Campbell's work, on documentary methods of decision-
making in the contemporary organization of Canadian nursing,
points out some of the ways by which these formulaic practices
distort and reduce caring. Acknowledging the structural role of
documents in the ordering of nursing practice, Campbell argues
that increasing reliance on the use of documents in recent decades
signals nurses' 'implicat[ion], against their commitments to patients, in implementing budget cuts in their own practice'.[73]
She explains how documentary procedures transpose personal
experiential knowledge into an objective organizational mode.
The rich dimensions of intuitive, emotional, embodied knowing

that are central to nursing care are reduced to abbreviated forms and standardized categories of tasks that are amenable to quantitative manipulation. These formal measures then become the interchangeable and transpersonal data of care.

The documentation of examples of nursing expertise, when – as in the case of Benner's descriptions of excellence – it is heuristically directed towards the elaboration and valuation of practical knowledge, has the potential to enrich and extend understanding of the possibilities of nursing care. In a context of industrial management, however, documentary systems are designed not for advancement of understanding of the specificity, complexity and practical possibilities of nurses' caring but for systematization and standardization. They provide the 'ruling apparatus'[74] with the capacity to control, regulate and order practice, far from the particular bodily reality of each bedside caring relation.

Using the example of Patient Classification systems, Campbell explains that the documentation process '"works" as a control mechanism through making objective a heretofore individual professional judgement about patients' needs for nursing care'. The 'objective needs' generated in this way can then be managed according to costing formulas. Documentation transforms the material reality of particular patients' needs into ciphers that are 'adjustable to management's cost-constrained "realities"'. As a result, says Campbell, 'what constitutes good enough care, previously a professional judgement, becomes established by how much staff [time] is made available'.[75] Disjunctures between documentary accounts, and the caring relationship experienced by nurses and patients, are 'solved' not through caring 'bridge-building' but by the authority of the 'official version'. Thus the silencing of nurses' voices is reproduced anew, for in situations of conflict their experiential judgements are overruled by the documentary reality.

Quality assurance formulas, powered by analogous erasures of personally experienced responses, have even more invidious potential for the corruption of caring. For while nurses themselves produce the records of activities in which 'quality' is 'objectified', emphasis on documentation rather than practice – keeping the record categories 'straight' rather than interpreting the patient's actual condition – in conditions of severe time constraints, provides little assurance that records will reflect caring accurately. Instituted to offer objective guarantees for the quality of professional practice and to protect institutions from blame when untoward incidents occur, these records provide almost no protection for the documenting nurses. Nurses remain personally responsible for the actual outcomes of their care, whatever conditions they are given to work in, as long as the documented version shows that staffing is 'adequate' and 'quality' care is being given.[76] In this kind of environment, nurses are caught in a double bind. From the one side, their personal, experientially grounded responses are overridden and discredited; from the other, their personal actions are the bearers of full accountability and responsibility. Far from the engaged and personally sensitive caring Benner describes, or the special collaborative opportunities Bishop and Scudder suggest, the possibilities of nursing are reduced to rule-bound, documentary-controlled adherence to the least dangerous routines.

By placing this understanding of documentary care beside the caring excellences described by Benner, we can see that it constitutes something of a reversal of the latter. Following Benner, experiential learning enables nurses to transform the abstract conceptual models and standardized versions of nursing theorized in textbooks into the perceptual awareness and discretionary judgements that lie at the heart of excellence in nursing care. The documentation procedures described by Campbell, on the other hand, have the capacity to translate hunches, 'gut feelings' and embodied knowledge into organizational judgement, feedback and information which, she argues, is used to support management ends against patients' and nurses' subjective needs. This contrast of approaches to the same practice brings the different aspects of nursing with which they are concerned into sharp relief.

Campbell, like Benner, is aware of the limits of knowledge that is abstract rather than grounded in the practical specificity of nurse–patient relationships, and she is critical of corporate uses of documentation that put cost calculations ahead of nursing judgements. I have introduced her study here because it provides further evidence of the ways in which descriptions of nursing that fail to take account of the institutional and gendered constraints on care are seriously flawed. The suppression of the experiential reality of particular nursing relations effected by the crushing power of hospital management priorities over the gendered and devalued claims of nursing care both explains the context and accounts for the limits of perspectives like those of Benner, and Bishop and Scudder. We can see how the approaches of the latter theorists are motivated by the oppressive contexts from which they arise, and how at the same time their celebration of professional nursing values depends on minimizing the constitutive force of institutional and ideological structures on their practice. Like the analogous juxtaposition of Rossiter's and Ruddick's accounts of mothering relations, the contrast with Campbell's discussion shows us how the caring practice of nursing is a more complex field of possibilities, and that understanding its ethical significance requires viewing it from many different perspectives.

Taken together with Reverby's account of nursing practice, we can also see that Campbell's study of the ways that document-based management systems control and corrupt care identifies a contemporary form of the disjunction between the 'phenomenological' possibilities of professional nursing and its practice in institutional work settings. Reverby's socio-historical perspective draws attention to the deep grounding of this disjunction in gendered understandings of the nature and value of nursing. Nursing care can never be understood simply as a set of phenomenological possibilities, nor yet as a product of structural forms. In particular, gender-sensitive understanding requires recognition that different aspects of its practice are intricately interwoven and differently expressed in changing socio-historical contexts.

Both Benner and Campbell acknowledge that dimensions of formal knowledge and institutional organization are integral to nursing practice. Abstract theories and rules provide systematic frameworks that help nurses order their thinking, organize their tasks, and appreciate considerations that lie beyond the immediate activities in which they are involved. Institutional standards and systems offer the possibility for monitoring and accountability, especially in large and increasingly unmanageable institutions with proliferations of specialisms. They enable nurses to make connections between their different tasks and to transfer information to other persons in the health care team. However, Reverby's detailed study of the first hundred years of institutionally organized nursing in the United States, indicates that the historical consolidation of nurses' obedience to authoritarian demands, has largely thwarted their claims and capacities to define their own practice. The nexus of formal knowledge, authority and institutional control has characteristically overwhelmed the claims of personal, experiential and responsive caring that are so central to ethical excellence in nursing.

Chapter 4

Citizenship

I

My aim in this final chapter is to extend the investigation of the ethical possibilities of caring into less familiar terrain. Thus far, the interpersonal practices I have discussed constitute relatively well-established contexts of care. Though they range across varying patterns of social organization and personal freedom, dependency and choice – and are oriented towards diverse dimensions of needs and desires – mothering, friendship and nursing fall within a recognized terrain. All strive for that intimate engagement with another, for her or his own sake, that is the hallmark of caring relations between persons.

In this chapter I want to take up the case of citizenship relations – the bonds between citizens and the state, as well as those among individual citizens – where reference to the possibilities of caring may seem at best supererogatory, and at worst unjust. Indeed, the formal associations of 'citizenship' are frequently used to distinguish precisely those aspects of relations between persons in which intimacy is constitutively limited or in which the partiality of personally engaged attentiveness signals undue bias and favouritism. Unlike the case of formally organized nursing relations, for example, there are no injunctions to practitioners to balance the tension between organizational demands and intrinsic caring values. Citizen relations are more likely to denote interpersonal connections that eschew the values of intimacy and personally engaged care.

'Citizenship' is used here rather loosely to designate a range of relational practices characterized largely by their association with the public sphere.[1] Citizen relations are public in terms of access, participation and impact, and in terms of their connection with practices of collective government, administration and institutional organization.[2] Accordingly, although not unambiguously, 'citizenship' points to practices that express the most generalized forms of interpersonal interaction, where the personal attributes of the participants appear to be relatively insignificant, and where predictability, stability and control of the outcomes of activities are predominant goals.

In contrast with the kinds of intimacy and particularity that are characteristic of maternal, friendly or nursing care, citizen relations conventionally call up norms of conduct that emphasize the impersonal, the interchangeable and the impartial.[3] The contexts of attachment, responsivity and flexibility, variously evident in the caring relations described in earlier chapters, are frequently suppressed by requirements for order, decisiveness and consistency.[4] Or in more specifically moral terms, citizenship allegedly signals the replacement of care with justice, commitment with duty, and the priority of rights over goods. From this perspective the connection between citizenship and interpersonal caring relations which is the focus of this chapter suggests movement into an alien domain, from the established ground of the investigation.

But by using the term 'citizenship' to designate the variety of connections that exhibit these public, impersonal, institutional dimensions, I also want to signal continuities with the sets of relations between persons considered in earlier chapters. Despite apparently radical disjunctions in norms and purposes conveyed by associations with 'the public' and 'the formal', seeing citizenship as part of a survey of relatively specific sets of interpersonal relational practices is intended to highlight a shared terrain. For my aim here is precisely to dispel some of the power of those conceptions that understand citizenship solely through this oppositional construction. The common ground of interpersonal relations upon which mothering, nursing, friendship and citizenship are practised permits the suggestion that there is no impenetrable boundary surrounding some relational practices that excludes them from the ethical relevance of caring; nor are there any determinately specifiable conditions that fix the nature and possibilities of caring itself. In this context citizenship relations provide yet another set of interpersonal practices in which the diverse possibilities of caring may be considered. In the light of this suggestion, this chapter attempts to progress through the persistent distinction erected between the ethical dimensions of intimacy and communality, private and public, personal and political. I want to show that far from being antithetical to ethical practices of care, citizenship relations offer their own particular caring possibilities.

A suggestive contextual manoeuvre, however, cannot overcome the difficulties of challenging the limits of conventional boundaries. From the outset the project may seem to beg the question. The association of citizenship with caring appears to deny the very terms and practices within which citizenship has been constituted, and thus appears to invalidate its distinctive relational meanings. The differentiating characteristics that determine the import of citizen relations are themselves under review, rendering the whole process of categorization problematic.

But such a view, I want to claim, is underpinned by a faulty logic. It rests on a perception that aligns the conceptual opposition between citizenship and intimacy with allegedly corresponding oppositions between universality and particularity, order and responsivity, duty and commitment, rights and goods. In calling up the distinction between citizenship and intimacy, whole clusters of traits are presumed to be simultaneously operative as included or excluded features. Accordingly, traits associated with intimacy – particularity, responsivity, commitment and so on – are automatically removed from the possibilities of citizenship. In this way, the original distinction, no matter in what terms or context it has been constituted, cements in place associations that may have limited contextual validity. The functions of public welfare services, for example, may be seen as precluding concern for recipients, for their own sake, because the norms for citizen relations are associated with values such as accountability and predictability, that are apparently antithetical to such concern. Emotionally engaged concern with one's professional colleagues may be defined as out of bounds because the value of emotional attachment is associated with the oppositional context of intimacy.[5] In order to challenge these stereotyping dynamics, investigation of relations among citizens in terms of practices of care involves uncoupling these clustered oppositions. The ethical possibilities of both caring and citizenship require developing a transformed understanding of the nature of social relations, their organization, practice and values.

This is no easy task, for the conceptual habits of clustered associations and oppositions are reinforced by social practices and the habituated understandings they encourage. Since the intelligibility and viability of such a transformation depends on connections with previously established constructions, its articulation entails holding some aspects of meaning in place, while simultaneously indicating inadequacies in others. Given the strength of conventional understandings, however, such a process runs the risk of producing confusion, the kind of confusion that results from misunderstanding the transformation as an illicit identification of incompatible meanings or a false generalization of one set of meanings to an alien context.

It should be evident at this stage, however, that the reconception proposed is not a matter of simple identification or generalization. My aim is not to show that citizenship relations amount to citizens being 'nice caring persons' towards each other, or indeed, that political values and responses are or should be structured solely by caring relations and responsibilities.[6] For, just as the preceding chapters have shown that the values and perspectives that structure the interactions and decision-making involved in mothering, for example, are not exactly the same as those involved in friendships or nursing, so too my (relatively uncontroversial) claim here is that citizenship relations present their own important and distinctive ethical characteristics. Varying shifts from relatively non-voluntarist to more freely chosen relations, from informal to formally organized contexts, from intimacy to public accessibility, bring with them significantly different liberties, responsibilities and constraints on the possibilities of caring. It is understanding these differences that has been the primary concern of the preceding three chapters which aim to display a range of orientations and responses that are frequently collapsed into a unitary conception of care. Thus, for example, recognition of differences in the dependencies of infants and patients can prevent nursing care from slipping towards dangerous 'infantilization' of mature patients.

Congruently, however, continuities between these distinctive relations provide possibilities for modification and enrichment of that range. Recognition of similarities in the vulnerability of infants and patients, for example, can transform mothers' and nurses' responses, and levels of engagement and detachment. Mothers may learn that caring involves acceptance of infants' independent identities; nurses may learn that emotional attachment can enhance their caring. Thus, although citizenship relations are conventionally characterized by their discontinuities with the more personal practices already examined, the present chapter – in contrast with the earlier chapters – is concerned predominantly with (relatively controversial) claims concerning connections between these distinctively determined relational practices. To this end I want to suggest that expressions of ethical caring come to be significant to citizen relations from several different perspectives. By approaching citizenship in terms of its practical and conceptual content, it is possible to see that there are strong continuities between these so-called impersonal relationships and the more immediately personal practices already investigated.

But here, as intimated above, the impulse of this enquiry runs in a contrasting direction to that of its earlier chapters. In the first three chapters, the established links between caring, and practices of mothering, friendship and nursing, allowed different descriptions of each kind of practice to illuminate the multiple possibilities of care. In the case of citizenship relations the lack of such connections creates something of a reversal. Instead, here descriptions of different aspects of caring practices throw light on the possibilities of citizenship; the insights of ethical caring inspire enriched conceptualization of the practices and values of public life.

Such a change in orientation may, of course, invite the charge of self-contradiction. Rather than displaying the ways in which yet another set of relational practices embeds distinctive possibilities for care, thereby contributing to the overall project of unsettling reified understandings of the 'ethic of care', in this section it may seem that I am exploiting unitary and hypostatized notions of 'care' to further my ends. Such an objection, I think, mistakes the complexity of comparing different caring practices for the reductive process of subsuming particulars under pre-articulated abstract concepts. The 'insights of ethical caring' do not float unified and free of their relational context to be applied at will to any given set of practices. The concept of caring is constituted within relations, and it is in the play of contrasts and similarities between different relational practices that its import unfolds, producing new possibilities for other overlapping and intersecting practices. The process of transformation relies upon these continuities and intersections, even as it modifies, enriches or limits understandings both of the concept and of the nature of the relational practices in which caring is expressed. Thus, while my investigation of caring relations between citizens may seem to take its principal impetus from some abstract, generalized conceptions of care, rather than from established concepts of citizenship, these 'generalizations' do not fix the possibilities of citizen caring. On the contrary, the overlapping but distinctive ground of interpersonal relations that connects citizenship practices with the more conventionally recognized practices of care examined in the course of this book, produces the space for renewed understanding of the ethical possibilities of citizen practices of care.

The work of rethinking conventional ethical distinctions between personal and public relations, and reconceptualizing the caring possibilities of citizenship is also, of course, intricately interwoven with issues of gender. Until recently, the realm of official citizenship in the West has been accessible only to men, while practices of caring have been largely assigned to the domestic responsibility of women.[7] As a result, both the possibilities of caring relations and the interests and responsibilities of women have been deemed to be outside the ambit of citizen practices. Where formal organization of caring has been required, for example in the practice of clinical nursing, its practitioners have predominantly been women.

These gendered patterns of inclusion and exclusion, cutting across practices of caring and practices of citizenship, are further complicated by recent changes in social organization that allow women formal access to the official arenas of state, paid employment and public discourse.[8] The formal opportunities for women to participate in these areas of citizenship relations, combined with the continuation of informal – cultural, social and psychological – constraints on their doing so, has frequently resulted in the transfer of women's well-being from dependency on men in the realm of private, family relations to direct dependency on publicly administered services.[9] The official incorporation of women in all spheres of public practice has produced new patterns of gender in citizen relations as women increasingly become the major clientele and employees of state welfare services. In the light of these developments, consideration of citizenship care is of pressing importance to gender-sensitive understanding of the ethics of caring.

Given the critical and exploratory nature of this project, with its aim of reorienting the possibilities of both citizenship and caring, my discussion in this chapter will follow a different pattern from that of earlier chapters. Ideas about the possibilities of caring in the public sphere emerge from consideration of different aspects of the function and nature of citizenship practices: questions concerning the proper content of citizenship, the appropriate orientation of the state to its citizenry and of citizens to each other, as well as ideals of community membership and organization. I will proceed, therefore, by looking at a number of these interconnected dimensions of citizenship in turn. First, I will reflect on the interdependence of public and personal practices of caring. Second, I will explore ways in which this interdependence may be acknowledged in the social organization of the public sphere and in the material content of citizenship. Finally, I will examine how citizen relations are understood with respect to the public ideals within which they are structured, and how those ideals may be transformed by caring values.

II

At least since the days of antiquity the private sphere of house-holding relationships has been recognized as imperative to the well-being of the public world of citizenship. Despite the sharp distinction between public and private in ancient Greece, and the systematic downgrading of the latter in favour of the former, the public space of freedom in the *polis* was 'conceptually and structurally parasitic' on the private sphere of necessity.[10] The practices of production and reproduction in the household provided the preconditions on which the functioning of the public realm of politics was dependent for its survival. Analogously, the values nurtured in the realm of necessity were conceived as imperative to those extolled in the world of freedom. The virtues of the private sphere: affection, tenderness, responsiveness and caring, as well as obligation and duty, provided the training ground for virtuous citizenship.

Throughout the history of the West, the content of the two realms and the definition of their differentiation have varied considerably. Shifts across the divide, and differing constructions of the division itself, have brought changing understandings of the activities and values associated with each sphere.[11] Currently the public incorporates many civic and economic relations along with traditional political activities, while the private includes the more personal, voluntary and kinship relations – now para- doxically associated with the realm of individual choice and freedom. Despite these changes, the conventions that distinguish these realms of human interests and values also characteristically link them in a relation of necessity: both public and private practices are crucial to the satisfaction of human ends.[12]

Recent feminist studies pointing to connections between these conventions and gender oppression, however, have questioned the nature and implications of this imperative. Insights concerning the gendered effects of the division have brought challenges to the categorical boundaries it has tended to impose on the organization and ordering of social practices and values, and the lives of those involved in them. Discussion of the necessary interdependence of public and private practices highlights their interpenetration and the limits of conceptions that insist on their inherent dis- tinctiveness.

By contrast with emphases on autonomous citizens' rights and responsibilities in reflections on public values, many feminist theorists have focused on the importance of virtues like nurture, responsivity and trust in sustaining the persons who participate in citizen practices. Annette Baier, for example, argues that 'persons essentially are *second* persons . . . heirs to other persons who formed and cared for them'.[13] Persons are formed through the nurture of child-rearing relationships, and they develop in response to both this genesis and the shifting configurations of their other interpersonal relations. As citizens they are, therefore, only conditionally autonomous and self-sufficient. Although we may think of them in abstraction from their interpersonal de- pendencies, our understanding of persons relates them to their histories and the biological conditions in which one generation nurtures the next in preparation for its succession.

The obvious though frequently overlooked point is that for any citizen interactions to take place at all – even 'a war of each against each' – every citizen must have been nurtured and cared for by others in order to survive her or his infancy.[14] Without appropriate responses to infants' survival demands, future citizens would simply die. But, as Ruddick notes, maternal relationships meet demands not only from the children themselves but also from the socio-political group in which those relations are integrated: demands that their children be raised in a manner congruent with the values of the group. This training function intrinsic to maternal caring is not simply an independent prerequisite to successful citizenship; its terms are necessarily carried into activities in the public sphere. As Baier explains, public justice must borrow from the relations of parental caring that develop a sense of the justice and moral obligations required of citizens if the just society is to last beyond the first generation.[15]

Thus, while the biological conditions of life necessitate personal caring relations on which public practices depend for the succession of their participants, the social conditions of life also create analogous interdependencies. Nurturing relations that are conducive to children's flourishing must foster the public values through which those children's social environments are ordered. Failure in one's intimate relations to learn the ethical orientations appropriate to one's social milieu, results in social maladjustment and ethical alienation. From the other side, public practices must express in their own values the virtues of personal practices of positive co-operation and training – as well as the more impersonally oriented ends of consistency, order and predictability – that are necessary to their maintenance. For even the apparently simple conduct entailed in formal respect of another person's rights, for example, involves a whole range of informal and formal support relations. Informal 'training' relations, practices that secure the commitment of 'trainers' and practices that reinforce those practices in turn, are all required to maintain the society-wide co-operation demanded by any public norms.[16]

In addition to these educative and support functions, personal caring practices provide the experience of continuous relations of being cared for, and of trusting in that care, that is presupposed by such dispositions as being fair to others and fulfilling contractual obligations. Baier points out that willingness to engage in impersonal trust relations, such as those contracted in the public sphere, is encouraged by one's sense of participation in a general climate of trust. Personal experience of the advantages of relations in which one is able to rely on other persons' commitment to care for one's own cares, and awareness of customary relations of trust, are central to the creation of this possibility.[17] Together with more formal conventions and punitive customs, these understandings produce a climate conducive to engaging in long-term exchanges and even choices such as to smile at, speak to, or shake hands with strangers. At the communal level too, willingness to adhere to the precepts of one's society is preconditioned by the climate of care and trust conducive to understanding that one's own good, and that of those one most cares for, is bound up with observance of its conception of justice.

Thus, though the virtues of citizen relations may appear to be quite independent of those that structure more personal caring relations, success in understanding and practice of citizenship depends on recognition of the crucial ways in which it is strengthened and supported by caring values. Once the social conditions for public contracts of trust, promises, rights and responsibilities are in place, it is easy to take this impersonal morality in its own terms and to ignore its all-important conditions. As a result, the ethics of citizen practices are seen as quite self-sufficient and independent of the ethics of informal interpersonal practices.

The isolation of public values is also reinforced through the stereotyping of citizen practices with the traits of those officially sanctioned activities characteristically performed by an elite group of men. The dominance of the ideals of this privileged elite in contemporary public life limits understanding of public practices. A remarkably circumscribed set of activities determines the scope of public values, and the different ethical orientations embedded in other currently unrecognized public activities is concealed. Among these hidden public practices are many informal caring practices that function in the construction and maintenance of the structure of society.

For example, Kathryn Pyne Addelson shows how the volunteer care work carried out by women raising funds for political candidates – conventionally seen as an adjunct to official relations – functions independently in fostering community solidarity. The myriad small gestures of hospitality – and attentiveness to the uniqueness of the individuals involved – that are vital to the formal success of this work, create an ambience in which personal loyalties and commitments to collective representations can be reaffirmed and solidified.[18] According to Addelson such caring practices are part of the hidden know-how essential to the maintenance of all successful institutions. The social relations that hold every group together – whether formal or informal, comprised of one or of both genders – have to be created through practices of care that preserve each member's identity while holding the group together. To the extent that caring relations are absent from social institutions, those institutions fail to fulfil their responsibilities to the collectivity. Without any caring relations those institutions would collapse.

The point here is not that an accurate account of citizen care would replace more formal, impersonal moral systems with non-hierarchical relations of loving care. Rather the call is to understand the multi-dimensional ethical processes that contribute to the maintenance of citizens and their societies and, in the light of the gendered division of social labour, to take women seriously as moral beings and citizens. Perhaps this call may be compatible with a conception of distinctive moral spheres or distinctive ethical dispositions appropriate to distinctive kinds of practices. Perhaps the interpenetration of these different realms can be held in tension with their significant discontinuities. But even if the practical and moral importance of the distinction between formal and informal relations warrants its current primacy, it is clear that the perspectives and values learnt in the vital practices of intimacy are as significant to the well-being of the collectivity, and of all the individual citizens who participate in its activities, as those employed in more formal interactions. Even by the criteria John Rawls uses to characterize basic institutions of society, as Claudia Card points out, informal and personal relationships of care are as fundamental as the impersonal institutions on which his discussion of social ethics is focused. Measured by their import-ance to persons' 'starting places' in life, their contribution to individuals' self-esteem and their creation of special respons-ibilities, these relations of intimacy are just as significant to social structure as the formal institutions that give rise to Rawls's concept of justice, and his claims for its moral primacy.[19]

Neither of these different sets of institutions with their different ethical priorities is reducible to the other; nor do the differences between the two frameworks imply incompatibility. There seems to be no logical reason why the concerns and orientations central to personal caring practices cannot be recognized in continuity with those operative in more formal practices of citizenship. But the weight of attention given to this possibility suggests otherwise. In reflections on public morality, the priority accorded to ideals of universalizability, impartiality, autonomy and rights that over-ride or neglect values of particularity, responsiveness to con-textual differences, and maintenance of relations of care and attachment, is a priority which encourages the perception that the former are the defining values of citizen relations. This emphasis is reinforced through its alignment with the status attributed in public undertakings to legal, political and economic power at the expense of concern for enabling the personal caring attachments imperative to individual and social well-being. The persistent patterns of inclusion and exclusion produced by these theoretical and practical emphases have solidified into an ideologically biased tradition. The public significance of the values and prac- tices of interpersonal relations of care is removed from the main stage of public affairs, thereby entrenching the perception that these relations are subordinate, irrelevant, intractable, or even antithetical to the concerns of citizenship.

Associating the ways of thinking and the activities that are included in citizen relations with males, and associating the orientations and involvements that are excluded from citizen relations with females, adds another layer to the bias. The per- vasive effect of this gender polarity is such that the hierarchical evaluation of the practices of males and females is frequently maintained irrespective of the actual content of those practices. Women's activities concerned with public projects, for example, may be viewed as peripheral, lacking in significant perspective, or trivial in relation to citizen affairs.[20] Male engagement with the same projects often confers public legitimacy on them – especially when the controlling judicial, legislative and executive positions are occupied predominantly by males. As well as diminishing the importance of personal and informal relations of care, then, the ideological bias in which the split between public and private spheres is cemented, tends to prevent women from realizing their full citizenship. Men, on the other hand, through their use of fundamental caring relations typically serviced by women, to- gether with their participation in the realm of citizen relations regarded as their birthright, may at least attain to the status of full citizenship, if not to the fullness of experience, perspectives and values that citizen relations might possibly include.

It is evident from these discussions that the ethical limitations of citizenship, produced by this public/private division, cannot be removed by a 'simple' revaluation of the perspectives and values acquired in personal practices of care (even if it were possible to imagine how this could be done).[21] Despite the equal status of public and private spheres, the gendered division of citizen possibilities remains to inhibit the comprehensiveness of citizenship. Nor can the problems be resolved 'simply' by extending formal entry to both realms to all members of both genders.[22] In the first place, the depth of the cultural associations of gender resists any easy annulment. It is a feminist commonplace that 'open access, participatory parity, and social equality' (to quote Nancy Fraser) are rarely achieved by the elimination of formal exclusions from citizenship based on gender.[23] Informal impediments due to inequalities in material resources, education, language use, protection against violence and concepts of merit, as well as those obstacles due to deeply internalized experiences of self, one's potentials and inadequacies, are perhaps more important than the presence or absence of formal exclusions.[24]

Second, the organization of practices within each side of the divide tends to set up conflicts between the two domains. For any individual person, full and direct participation in the whole range of practices is constrained by organizational structures that restrict successful engagement in both spheres. The public world of paid work tends to be organized as if participants have no significant or time-consuming desires and responsibilities within the private realm. Correspondingly, engagement in the practices of domesticity is inclined to isolate participants and to preclude effective participation in public relations (as the case of mothering discussed in Chapter 1 has shown). Location in either one of the separate spheres functions to preclude location in the other and, correlatively, preservation of the values of any one sphere is perceived to require the continuous dedication of individual persons to that single locale. Debates over the alleged demise of (white) 'family values', for example, frequently reduce to discussion of the problem of mothers' participation in the public world of paid labour instead of staying at home to care for their children.[25] Those persons who do attempt to participate fully in both spheres often report enormously stressful conflicts among the differently located needs, aspirations and values to which they are responsive.[26]

Third, it is obvious from this discussion that the boundaries of citizenship themselves are at issue. The division that effectively insulates public practices and values from the responses and ways of thinking typical of practices of care – diminishing and demeaning the possibilities of caring in the process – not only fails in terms of personal fairness to those whose lives are confined to the 'wrong' side of the divide, but also undermines the validity of those public values. Without input from the whole range of understandings of civic values, understandings that are acquired in the essential activities of nurturing children, friendship, and caring for the sick, for example, the inclusiveness of allegedly universal public values is fundamentally flawed. The social order that defines citizenship in opposition to relations of care distorts and truncates public practices of justice, equality, freedom, responsibility, nurture and community that claim to comprehend the full range of human needs and aspirations.

For these reasons, explorations of the ethical possibilities of citizenship care involve challenges to the boundaries of the public sphere that acknowledge the public implications of its imperative relationship with personal and informal practices of care. In the following sections of this chapter, I will consider some of these challenges in terms of the material content of citizenship and the nature of the ideals and values that emerge from and represent the claims for that content. I turn first to look at some aspects of social organization involved in the recognition of the significance of ethical practices of care in citizenship relations. In the final section I will explore ways in which the ethical insights of caring may be brought to bear in rethinking the values within which citizenship practices are organized.

III

Given the connections between women and caring, recognition of the significance of relations of care in citizenship practices requires social restructuring that enables both wider responsibility for nurture and participatory parity for women in public affairs. The social organization of citizenship that takes seriously both 'second-personhood', and the mutual responsibility of men, women and the state for sharing the joys and burdens of caring, is not just a matter of making needs for care itself a central public concern.[27] In addition, it necessarily entails challenging prescriptive practices of care that support the disempowerment and dependency of (predominantly female) carers. For the tendency to naturalize women's caring, and to ascribe subordinate value both to women and their practices, can only be abrogated by citizenship that includes and encourages active, egalitarian participation of women and men in all its possibilities.

It is important to note, however, that the intertwined issues of public responsibility for care and participatory parity for women in citizenship do not reduce to self-interested demands for the redistribution of public resources. To the extent that concerns about caring being made a part of everyone's lives are expressed in contexts that emphasize persons' needs and desires for connection, expression and mutuality in relationships, these concerns demand a reconceived citizen ethics that reaches beyond the confines of distributive justice. The caring focus on relationship, vulnerability, and nurture of others for their own sake, enjoins the restructuring of social and political institutions towards an inclusivity and equality in participatory possibilities that challenges the relations of dominance and dependency, as well as the distributive norms which those institutions conventionally sustain. With respect to the current focus on gender-sensitive citizen policies, this restructuring links the public significance of care for the vulnerable with attentiveness to the life possibilities of women.

In contemporary Western societies these interconnected issues have come to the fore as conjoined but contradictory demands. The pressures for reconsideration of public policies for the long-term care of the aged and the mentally and physically handicapped, and for child-care, are in part a response to increased enablement of women's participation in activities outside the private domain of conventional subordination. The brute fact that increasingly large numbers of women, and large numbers of mothers, currently work outside the home in order to support themselves and their families has resulted in enormous stresses on these women's traditional caretaking responsibilities.[28] The difficulties for women in combining their wage-earning and career activities with their personal and informal caring activities has focused attention both on the pivotal role of caring in keeping human enterprises going, and the need for public support for workers with these responsibilities.

In addition, demographic changes in culturally dominant groups – decreases in the birth rate and longer life expectancy – have resulted in a decline in the number of potential caregivers, and alterations in the shape of caregiving responsibilities. Helga Hernes reports that in Scandinavia, for example, 'during the last century and the first half of this century dependents in need of care were mainly children; today about half of all dependents in need of care are old people'.[29] Meanwhile, widespread attacks on public funding for human services, 'the spectre of uncontrollable

health and social service costs associated with an ageing popu-
lation', and dissatisfaction with depersonalized, disengaged nurture, has led to a search for alternatives to expensive institution-
based services.[30]

These structural pressures on practices of care, and on the
activities of women, raise questions concerning the locus of
responsibility for care, how caring can provide comfort and
protect personal values, and how it can be practised without
exploitation of the unpaid, or low-paid, labour of mainly female
caregivers. Orthodox answers to these questions, however, tend
to rely heavily on the very social divisions that have created both
the public diminishment of the significance of care and the
oppressive contradictions in women's lives. On the one hand
contemporary 'public' policies for long-term care explicitly presume the obligations and service of low-status, informal and
unpaid practices of care; on the other hand the organization of
both paid employment and political activities tends either to run
in direct conflict with practitioners' caregiving responsibilities, or
to exploit the low status of practices of care.

On the public care policy front, for example, so-called 'community care' programmes direct funding towards services that
'complement and sustain families and friends as caregivers' and
which increase the numbers of persons served in their own
homes.[31] In the name of expanded services, programmes focus on
encouraging self-help groups and informal helping networks or
using neighbours and volunteers. Informal and family caring
relations are seen as appropriate to all categories of dependency,
no matter what the needs and wishes of dependent persons or
their putative carers may be. The family itself is idealized as the
most appropriate location and unit for care: a conflict-free domain
of privacy, where the self-esteem and independence necessary to
human well-being is nurtured and sustained in an atmosphere of
harmony and consensus.

Evidence suggests, however, that family life is often far from
realizing these ideals. The discussion in Chapter 1, for example,
has shown how the patriarchal social structures in which mothering practices occur severely constrain their possibilities. Contrary
to the egalitarian, mutually beneficiary associations extolled by
community care advocates, families are more usually hierarchic-
ally ordered units that do not benefit all of their members equally.
The gendered division of labour on which they depend usually

results in care for dependents devolving upon the closest female members, with little choice for either party to the relationship. The burdens of this structure for women and dependent children are well-documented. Relations of domination and subordination prevail and are increasingly expressed in physical violence and abuse.[32] The naturalization and devaluation of women's caring in the domestic sphere is consolidated, thereby reducing women's public possibilities and entrenching their socio-economic dependency.

These inequalities within family life reverberate throughout the public dimensions of life as well. They are replicated in the hierarchical cleavage between the public and private that models the terms of paid employment and political activity on the presumption that care for the vulnerable, and even day-to-day practices of self-care and maintenance, can be delegated to someone else. Those (women) who take responsibility for caring practices are therefore only permitted marginal status in public and citizenship practices.[33] Within the activities of the public sphere itself, social relations follow the same pattern: female occupations are frequently based on servicing males' work and demand subordination to the authority of that work as, for example, in the case of clinical nursing. Where responsibility for caring practices is acknowledged in the public sphere, the great majority of service workers are women whose 'natural' caring activities are frequently defined as unskilled labour and paid accordingly.[34] Thus public policies that uphold and exploit the ideology of family-based practices of care simultaneously play into social structures that sustain multi-layered relations of dominance and subordination, and support women's dependency in citizenship.

The terms of activities in the public sphere – both paid employment in the market economy and political participation – reinforce these structures. The organization of labour and political activities which detaches participants from their social lives as parents, children and spouses remains largely intransigent with respect to accommodating their caring responsibilities. Where the significance of caring is recognized, the family-based model still shapes policy provisions. Take, for example, recent public acknowledgement in the United States – in the wake of women's increased participation in the paid workforce – of the significance of child care in terms of workers' needs for time away from their children.[35]

The programmatic translation of this need into either privatized provision of day care services or state supported tax subsidies without concern for the gendered subordination of caring practices, has itself played into the multi-level replication in the public sphere of family structures of inequality and dependency. Drenched in discourses of women's natural propensities, the work of care has little status or reward in the labour market. In addition, constraints on women's career possibilities ensure a large pool of potential care workers who have few choices for paid employment. Consequently, the provision of privatized day care merely enables wealthier consumers of those services to enhance their own possibilities in the public sphere at the expense of their poorer peers' low-paid labour. State policies reiterate this class-biased market dynamic. Tax subsidies in support of caring responsibilities give middle-class women financial aid at levels that assume low wages for day-care work while forcing poor women to take low-paying jobs, and excluding them from higher education.[36]

The important point here is that these contradictions between public acknowledgements of the importance of care and the exploitation of women's caring services are contradictions in social policy. There is no inherent necessity in the conflict between women's (or mothers') requirements for public support for their caring and the imperative needs for care of the elderly, the sick, the disabled and the young. Contrary to the accusations of popular culture and neo-conservative rhetoric, analyses of the inequities of family-based models of caring are not necessarily an attack on the importance of caring practices by proponents of the selfish pursuit of women's rights. While such discussions frequently emphasize the negative consequences of women's practices of care and the burdens women bear in order to ensure that their loved ones do not suffer, they also tend to show how important women think caring is for the well-being of themselves and others. The rethinking of the possibilities and constraints of caring, and the appropriate social organization that will encourage its values and benefits does not entail the abdication of caring responsibilities by women.[37]

Discussions of the imperatives of caring, and the congruent emergence of caring issues on the public agenda, are also not

simply developments aimed at transferring determinate responsibilities from one sphere of life to another. Nor are they motivated
by ambitions to elevate relations of care above all other relational
practices that contribute to the well-being of persons. The focus
that demonstrates the critical ethical and practical importance of
caring relations, and the ways in which their undervaluing is
detrimental both to those cared for and those who do most of the
caring, calls for a thoroughgoing collective acknowledgement of
caring responsibilities that forges connections between persons'
needs for care and their other relational requirements for flourishing lives. Insofar as the social organization of caring produces
many of the contradictions that women experience as they attempt
to combine their public lives in the paid workforce and communal
projects with their private lives in the domestic sphere, this
acknowledgement entails restructuring the relationships among
these domains. Thus, from the perspective of social policy, the
incorporation of the insights of ethical practices of care in citizen
relations involves challenging conventional assumptions about
the nature and structure of family life, as well as about labour
market activity and the state.

The specific issues through which these challenges are expressed include changes in social policies that allow carers and
mothers choice in the practice and timing of their caring and
mothering, adequate health care for aged, disabled, young and
pregnant persons, and shared responsibility for tending the personal needs and desires of those receiving care. These changes,
in turn, involve concerns with workplace accommodation of
domestic caring and parental responsibilities, maternity leave,
parental leave and day care facilities, as well as the compar-
able worth and affirmative action measures that will eliminate
women's citizen subordination and structural dependency on
men. The citizen relations of care expressed in these programmes
undermine the boundaries between the personal and public
spheres of life, and help liberate practices of care from the
destructive effects of their naturalization in and banishment to the
realm of domesticity.

But as the child care example mentioned above suggests,
contemporary moves in the West, towards the social reorganization that would rebuild the possibilities of citizenship in this
way, carry with them the disabling ideological effects of the very
structures under challenge. Policy initiatives seem to be inherently

limited by their primary affiliation with the worker/citizen side of the boundary between public and private. The focus on workplace reforms tends to prevent serious challenges to the devaluation of (women's) caring practices. Alternatively, policies aimed at revaluing caring responsibilities – that is, policies affil- iated with the caregiver side of the divide – while they ascribe intrinsic value to practices of care, tend to reaffirm the gendered division between worker citizen and caregiver.[38] Citizenship care remains characteristically tainted by incongruity.

For this reason many theorists are exceedingly cautious about views that promote the centrality of ethical practices of caring in conceptions of public life. Indeed, use of the language of care in discussions of the values of citizenship is frequently dismissed as reactionary – as damaging to the cause of women's equality, drawing on inappropriate relational models, and appealing to the whims of particularized compassion.[39] The important insight here is that calls for the rethinking of public values in terms that are sensitive to the ethical imperatives of practices of care are some- times naive in their abstraction from those social realities which rely on powerful, cultural perceptions of women's naturalized altruism.[40] Again, revaluations of caring frequently display in- appropriate idealism in their underestimation of the structural constraints on care and the dangers of its deformations.[41] From the other side, public invocations of care – for example from supermarket owners or from political leaders – often express the empty rhetoric of moral opportunism.

Further support for the dismissal of visions of society shaped by caring comes from evident deficiencies in those domains in which public provision of care does have established legitimacy. In the institutions of the welfare state, for example, the force of demands for economic efficiency, administrative control and predictability, obstructs and constrains the possibilities of caring. The case of nursing relations, discussed in the last chapter, provides an example of the limits and contradictions that the demands of institutional settings, and their self-confident under- standings of the links between care and authority – between needs and control – place on the ethical import of person-to-person practices of care. The divisive possibilities latent in the difference between professionals' diagnoses and patients' experiences, be- tween organizational routines and personal needs, between quan- tifiable tasks and affective work, between physicians' power and nurses' activities, can all be seen to erupt in conflicts that distort and deform the ethical import of nursing care. It is evident that this is not simply a matter of the conflict of interests inherent in caring services supplied by the market. That the alternative ethics of the 'bottom line', of professional expertise, and of bureaucratic process, frequently operate to the detriment of personal needs and attachments (and to the disadvantage of predominantly female caregivers) in state medical and social services, is amply documented in commentaries on the welfare state.[42]

More comprehensive analyses of the 'colonization of the [personal] lifeworld' of citizens by the (public) 'system', like that of Jürgen Habermas,[43] and descriptions of the proliferation of state apparatuses of 'general surveillance', such as those related by Michel Foucault,[44] concur with these observations. Their critiques of social organization are premised on understandings of deep antagonisms between the caring possibilities of personal life and the capacities of the state. Such accounts seem to indicate the intractability of the dominant divide and the impossibility of transformation that, by necessity, must originate within the public sphere. The interpenetration of insights from apparently discontinuous domains of life – the validation of women as full citizens and of citizenship as a field of caring responsibilities – remains illusory.

I want to suggest, however, that analyses along these lines capitulate too quickly to the persistent connections between caring, women and domesticity. Their resistance to the possibilities of citizen care runs the risk of oversimplifying and misunderstanding the complex and long-term trajectories of social change. In this respect recent developments in Scandinavia are instructive.[45] Acknowledgement that caring and reproductive labour are socially necessary practices has led to varying public measures that accept every citizen's right to publicly sponsored care, provided either formally to individuals or through support of informal, family relations. These initiatives recognize the social necessity of caring in terms of carers' status in the labour market rather than direct validation of caring itself.

But although the programme has been driven primarily by understandings of the significance of labour market activity, it has not functioned entirely at the cost of the gendered division of labour with respect to caring, or the revaluation of the caring work that women do. Its effect in enabling the increased involvement of women in the labour force has made the power imbalance within families much more visible and accessible to change.[46] In addition, women's increased participation in the public realm as both consumers and employees of state care-giving services has opened up more subtle and perhaps more significant transformative possibilities for their citizenship. Women's visibility is a constant reminder of the corresponding demands for recognition of their citizen status. At the same time, their public activities can provide a location for more directly political practices, and a training ground in the kind of know-how, thinking and decision-making that is crucial to empowering citizenship.[47] These possibilities are, of course, circumscribed by the different resources different women possess, as well as the particular institutional settings in which they are involved. Nevertheless, engagement in spheres beyond the confines of a single domestic abode offers opportunities for learning and exercising citizen roles and responsibilities. The collective force of this engagement constitutes what Helga Hernes has called the 'feminization from below' of the public sphere.[48]

From this perspective, the integration of caring practices in the public sphere – though it may be tied to definitions of worker status rather than direct revaluations of care – extends the content of citizenship, both in terms of the compass of its legitimate responsibilities and the terrain in which those responsibilities are contested and decided. Conventional understandings of the political as confined to the activities of elected officials and the workings of government are exploded by expressions of resistance and political mobilization produced through citizens' complicated involvements in the social institutions on which they depend. The ground of citizenship comes to include the wide range of activities and affiliations – 'below' the official hierarchies of government – that challenge the institutions through which the basic power relations of society are structured.[49]

Further, the activities and experiences of bringing new issues and insights connected with the significance of relations of care into the public arena are themselves part of the process of learning what it is to be a citizen, participating in collective, inclusive and generalized relations, and deliberating over issues of common concern. As Hanna Pitkin has suggested, through actual engagement in political action – motivated in the first place by personal need and private interests – we experience the relationship of our values and power to those of others. Deliberation and conflict with others teaches the 'long-range and large-scale' public meanings of our aspirations and forces the translation of special interests into a more broadly based citizen perspective.[50]

More specifically, Patricia Boling has described the ways in which a campaign for pregnancy leave inevitably involves engagement with the generalized standards of fairness to which employers and unions conventionally appeal. Far from being relevant only to personal relations, and thus discontinuous with genuine political practices of 'engaging with other citizens in determining and pursuing individual and common interests', this kind of campaign necessarily connects with wider issues.[51] Similarly, a potential mother's interest in protecting her infant becomes a concern with 'recognition of the principle of equality for women in the workplace' that 'broaden[s] the community's standards beyond the notion of economic rationality to a more inclusive and generous notion of fair play'.[52] Joan Tronto makes a similar point when she argues that responding to and assessing needs for care, calls on judgements and understandings of socio-political possibilities that extend beyond personal concerns.[53]

These possibilities for the transformation of allegedly personal interests into the broader concerns conventionally associated with citizenship are matched by opportunities to reconfigure the conventions of citizenship itself. While they are caught up within the dominant constructions of care-giving and citizenship, public participants also bring with them their personal experiences and aspirations of alternative practices. And it is with these understandings of the possibilities and choices, that different practices of care and different relations of citizenship allow, that they are able to 'work within-against'[54] – to contest, reconceive, and change conventional relations of citizen care from within their conventional positions of involvement.

These movements for change may not be swift: frequently, they entail humiliating compromise, tokenism and appropriation. But the sites of structural contradiction and conflict within the 'system' – the overlapping realms of both 'social services', and personal and informal caring – retain the potential for producing new norms, symbols and meanings for citizen care.[55] Commentaries, on the Scandinavian experience at least, indicate that 'conscious institutionalization' of connections between public and private, community and personal aspects of life, has enabled women to become important partners in citizenship.[56] Intersecting changes in the valuation and gendered segregation of practices of caring are proving more difficult to effect. But the treatment of responsibility for nurture as a public issue is facilitating the rethinking of public values that connect the marginalization of women and their practices of care, the injustices of gendered labour arrangements and the irresponsibility of most men with regard to our intrinsic vulnerabilities and interdependencies. In this respect, Jane Lewis and Gertrude Astrom report that 'attitude surveys show that all Swedish men between the ages of twenty-one and sixty at least feel that they *should* participate in unpaid [care] work'.[57]

However, in as much as this rethinking occurs through changes in social organization and claims for public recognition of caring responsibilities, it is also a question of reconceiving the shared values through which these changes are represented. The integration of caring practices in citizen relations is as much a matter of what issues appear on the public agenda as how public issues are conceptualized in general, what their guiding values are, and how those values can reflect the ethical insights of care. It is the exploration of this more theoretical project of citizen care that is the subject of the following section.

IV

The widespread difficulties and failures in practices of public responsibility for care that emerge from the experiences of liberal welfare states demonstrate the limitations of the concepts of care expressed by those states. To a large extent these limitations are due to the constitution of the values that guide practice in the public sphere. Support for individuals' needs for care in public policies tends to produce a double betrayal of the ethical possibilities of caring. First, the cumbersome organization of caregiving and its operational routines obstructs the flexibility and interpersonal responsiveness that is the hallmark of ethical caring. In particular, the affective dimension of nurture – the feeling of concern for the other for her or his own sake and the feeling of being cared for in one's own right – that is intrinsically resistant to impersonal, generalizing and quantifying processes, frequently falls foul of institutional forms.

The force of competing institutional demands for the order and predictability provided by determinate and universal norms, and by the rules that enable these to be applied repeatedly and exchangeably to all persons, this force overwhelms caring's promise of particularistic attentiveness. Care is transformed into what Margaret Walker has called 'administrative care'.[58] The specificity of the myriad relations and affections that constitute persons' particularity, and the crucial bonding and attachment that the care for that particularity generates, tend to be reduced to standardized conceptions of persons' requirements for independence and autonomy. The (apparent) practical limitations of attention, skill and access to full knowledge of the needs of persons at the institutional level, Walker explains, result in reliance primarily on highly general and selective schemata.[59]

Second, in the absence of responsive attentiveness to the particularities of persons and their attachments, professional practices of care build resistance to interactive and normative questioning. The categorical and selected uniformities on which professional practices are based tend to endorse a presumption of their own adequacy – or, at least, the understanding that they are the best that can be done. This presumption effectively erases the limitations of their constitution. The partiality of the formulas, the interests they include and exclude, are thereby insulated against reflexive questioning and the challenge to seek out different perspectives. The conjunction of this self-confidence with administrative concern for authority, stability, control and predictability, seriously undermines the relational mutuality of care.

Caring becomes an externally dictated activity – a predetermined gift, in respect to a 'generalized other'[60] – that fails to reflect on its own terms or on the relationships that confirm the dependency of the vulnerable and the authority of the carer. This 'mischievousness of power'[61] turns care into paternalism; often, even if unwittingly, reducing its recipients to submissive dependence and self-alienation. As Martin Heidegger suggests, the managerial orientation that colours this care parallels our engagement with things in the world in terms of their practical use to us, rather than their own intrinsic value.[62]

In earlier chapters I have discussed some of the different ways in which this difficulty is confronted in maternal, friendly and nursing care through the nurture of relational values of trust and mutuality. In contemporary liberal states, conventional responses to the relational complexity of persons' different aspirations, vulnerabilities and needs usually invoke collective values – like those of liberty, equality and justice – to address corruptions of power. Individual and group powers are defined with respect to these values in terms of rights, obligations and entitlements. The attenuation of relational possibilities, in a context where large numbers of differently constituted lives converge, provokes the articulation of these citizen values to cover for the lack of trust and agreement in the ordering and planning of each person's life with respect to the lives of all.[63] Ideally, implementation of such values enables all persons – including the subordinate, marginalized and dependent – to press for the collective's attention to their citizenship status and its grievances. They are also conducive to a measure of predictability and accountability in interactions between persons who have little opportunity or desire for the kind of engagement that builds personal trust.

Supported by a weighty tradition dating back to the seventeenth and eighteenth centuries, the ethical language of rights has enormous discursive and practical strength in this sphere. In the United States, for example, this strength is exemplified by the success of civil rights movements in the 1950s and 1960s. The recent addition of the Charter of Rights and Freedoms (1982) to the Canadian constitution, and recent proposals for an Australian 'bill of rights', provide further evidence for the contemporary significance of rights talk.[64] In view of this significance, my focus in the following discussion of the regulative values of citizenship will be the ethical possibilities of rights. Through reflection on this important example of the conception of public values, my aim is to show how the insights of caring may transform the ethical concepts under which citizenship is practised.

Despite its persuasive power, rights language is often impoverished and clumsy. For, like the language of public welfare, rights language characteristically relies on static and generalized conceptions of the 'normal' competences and purposes of autonomous individuals. Given the crucial connections between persons' choices and actions, and the important dimensions of self-understanding, identity, responsibility and well-being developed in their caring relations, these conceptions are insufficient to express the particularity, social interrelatedness and dynamics of specific person's identities and needs.[65] Determinations of who is included in rights-bearing groups reduce the rich and complex range of persons' different needs, relations and values to a common, administrative identity. In similarly reduced and stereotypical terms, they also specify – if only by default – who and which dimensions of personhood are to be excluded.

Attention to those dimensions of persons' needs and responsibilities that fall outside standardized accounts, then, is split off from the concerns of citizenship, and sequestered in the private realm. The claims of all those personal needs for social relations – that is, particularistic relations of trust, care, self-respect, mutually appreciated expression and shared enjoyment – together with the claims of all those persons whose class, race, age, sex, physical or mental condition excludes them from the community of rights bearers, are dismissed from the range of collective values. As a result, personal and informal relations, not citizenship, carry responsibility for all the enormous variety of human possibilities and vulnerabilities that lie beyond the limited entitlements of generalized, individual rights.

That there are indeed some personal needs that can be satisfied only in relations of intimacy – that the gestures, affections and connections that confer personal meaning and validation cannot be fully guaranteed by public legislation – may indeed be true.[66] That the movement from the realm of the personal to the citizen sphere – 'of relating *I* to *we*, in a context where many other selves have claims on that *we*' – necessarily involves standing back a little from oneself, and putting personal claims in perspective with claims to recognize the significance of what others have to say, is also true.[67] There is also no doubt that the order and accountability of relational responses encouraged by formally designated rights and responsibilities are important dimensions of the best kinds of lives. But the point here is one of more general orientation and ethos. The insulation of citizen values from considerations relating to the particularity of persons and their relational concerns denies the imperative connection between shared public values and the caring practices and values developed in intimate life. It forces a destructive split between necessarily interconnected aspects of life: on the one hand paring down the ethical opportunities of citizenship; on the other, deflecting public attention from abuses of intimacy.[68]

Further, the focus of citizenship practices on the categorization of the similarities of persons masks the power of those who determine the categories, and their authority to reject or respond to differing claims. While appeals to rights may avoid the shame frequently inhering in requests for public welfare, like these

requests, they require acquiescence in pre-determined community
norms and institutions. Conferrals of rights, like dispensations
of benevolence, tend to keep the existing power relations intact.
In this respect Martha Minow's discussion of legal strategies
designed to enable established public norms in the United States
to be responsive to marginalized groups is apposite. Minow
explains that although such strategies may be helpful, they still
maintain the pattern of relationships that gives some people the
power to make decisions about the needs of others 'without
having to encounter their own implication in the social patterns
that assign the problems to those others'.[69] For Minow, traditional
citizen values of justice, equality and liberty, embedded in the
languages of benevolence and rights, are impoverished by their
insensitivity to these marginalizing relations, and more generally,
to the kinds of relational values learned and developed in ethical
practices of care.[70] The task for citizenship, then, is to transform
the public norms; to develop a new conceptual language that is
capable of incorporating these relational insights within its terms.

It is important to re-emphasize that this process is not one of
supplanting traditional understandings of justice with those of
care,[71] of prioritizing caring values as either the fullest or primary
expressions of morality,[72] or of adding to or complementing the
range of possible orientations to citizen morality by acknowledging another, different ethical perspective.[73] The dynamic of
transformation involved in the project of reconceptualization is
more a question of working through established concepts from a
different point of view, than applying a new set of norms. The
point is to reinvigorate the language of the inherited tradition of
citizenship with that caring perspective on the relations between
selves and others that recognizes the imperative link between the
well-being of citizens and the quality of their social relations. And
while there are dangers that the use of conventional categories
may entail succumbing to them – and arguably the history of the
welfare state is an example of this hazard – the alternatives of
ignoring or setting them aside risk losing the space and power
they command, as well as the shared insights they provide.

Minow's work, in articulating what she calls a 'social-relations
approach' to the use of rights in the law, is an illuminating and
perceptive guide to this conceptual dimension of citizen care.
She sets out her theoretical position in the context of legal

problems arising from tensions between conceptions of equality and difference, arguing that conventional rights approaches to the correction of inequalities frequently entrench further social discrimination. Conventional rights analyses of problems involving the social significance of differences among persons are flawed, she claims, by their crude ascriptions and the limits they place on understanding the interconnectedness of persons. At the same time, however, she recognizes the practical value of rights in particular historical contexts for providing communally accepted strategies for challenging the boundaries created between people by differential ascriptions of status. Minow's response to this apparent conflict is to offer an example of legal practice in which rights language is transformed through the incorporation of values that develop from recognition of the ethical import of practices of care.[74]

In order to understand this process of transformation, I want to explore Minow's analysis in more detail. My hope is that the example she provides will help to show the way to the reconceptualizations of public values which gender-sensitive citizen care demands. But, by its nature, this project can only be exploratory and heuristic. The kind of conceptual changes involved cannot constitute any sort of ultimate language for ethical practices of citizenship, for public values, like the publics from which they emerge, are many and varied, historically situated and structured. No single language suffices to capture the complexity and ambiguity of any social setting, and all require flexibility and openness to the dynamic and contingent concatenation of relations they express.

Minow uses Carol Gilligan's work – on the implications of caring practices for moral development – to illustrate what she sees as four major, transformative themes that emerge from feminist reflections (MAD 195–8). In keeping with her focus on the ways that rights analyses produce obstructions to understanding the relations between persons, her accounts of these themes highlight their relational dimensions. The first, described as a concern with the 'relationship between the knower and the known' (MAD 194), arises in part from feminist understandings of the way women's perspectives are denigrated or excluded from epistemological enquiries. Care theorists, in particular, have shown how care perspectives have been overlooked or trivialized in mainstream moral theory. Minow cites Gilligan's exposure of the relations between Lawrence Kohlberg's scheme for moral development and the exclusionary assumptions he, as a (potential) knower, brought to this knowledge-making project, as evidence of this theme.

The epistemological status of Gilligan's research is by no means uncontroversial,[75] and discussions of the neglect of practices of care by no means present the only example of the perspectival character of knowledge.[76] However, feminist thinking about the intersection between practices of care and the exclusion of women's perspectives from the dominant fields of human enquiry, makes an important contribution to this theme. Not only does it point up subjective dimensions of knowing, but it provides a striking illustration of the connection between knowledge and power. The exclusion or devaluation of the significance of caring relations by philosophers, political theorists, historians, social scientists, economists, lawyers and physicians, imposes a dominating understanding of knowledge that masks its exploitation of those relations and the oppression of the (mostly female) persons whose lives are shaped by the obligations of care.[77] Seen in this light, practices of care foreground both the differences and distinctiveness of different persons' perspectives and the relations of power embedded in prevalent assertions of knowledge.

These insights concerning knowledge relations, that emerge from consideration of the socio-political contexts of caring, are also confirmed within caring practices themselves. The partiality of knowledge, or perhaps more appropriately the 'positionality'[78] of knowledge, has been a continuous thread running throughout the investigations of caring practices included in my enquiry. The experiential aspect of knowing has been highlighted in discussions of the cognitive dimensions of caring for children, friends and the sick. In each case of ethical caring, attentiveness involves the interaction of persons' experience with their current perceptions to reveal new understandings.

Partiality, in the sense of incompleteness and openness to correction and change, is also embedded in the approaches to knowledge shown in the practices of caring already surveyed. Partiality is particularly important in the intensely dynamic relations of mothering, where openness to change is a key structural condition, but it is a strong theme in practices of friendship and nursing as well. Importantly, partiality in these cases also implies and exacts an obligation on knowers, not only to engage self-critically with their knowledge, but to seek out actively the perspectives of others in order to extend the possibilities of knowing. Knowledge is, therefore, always provisional, always in process, rather than determinate and stable. In all these different ways the positionality of knowledge – or, in Minow's terms, the relationship between the knower and the known – appears as a central dimension of practices of care.

In addition, each set of practices surveyed illustrates the connections between knowledge and power. Sometimes this insight emerges from reflection on the subordination of the epistemological possibilities of caring to the authority of prevailing views. The example of the denigration of the experiential knowledge acquired in nursing practices with respect to medical science is a potent reminder of this dynamic. But at other times it is deformations within caring practices themselves that provide evidence of the connection. Thus, in the course of nursing itself, impositions of nursing knowledge that fail to take patients' perspectives into account demonstrate the relational distortions of power.

Two of Minow's other key, relational themes are also discernible in the epistemological commitments of caring: the concerns with 'wholes and relationships rather than simply separate parts', and with the 'significance of contexts and particularities' (MAD 194). Once again, Gilligan's analysis of caring is used to illustrate these orientations. In the first place, Gilligan's research style itself, according to Minow, demonstrates her endorsement of these orientations. Her mode of thinking is characterized by a search for large patterns in subjects' responses to questions, rather than their individual scores; and this holistic orientation utilizes experientially based intuitions, rather than mechanistic analysis of separate units of problems. In addition, Gilligan's investigations are presented in a deliberative, narrative style that connects the particularities of her subjects' responses with attentiveness to the details of the contexts of those answers: the gender and ages of the respondents, their sense of their own identities, needs and aspirations. Gilligan does not formulate determinate rules or principles of moral development, and deliberately eschews research procedures that separate subjects' answers from considerations relating to their identities and their connections in the world.[79]

These features of Gilligan's methodology are, however, not unique to research on caring. Arguably, a pattern-making, holistic orientation, is characteristic of creative thinking in general;[80] and certainly Gilligan's contextual, narrative method of presentation is not an inevitable characteristic of studies of caring. But, as Minow points out, Gilligan's discussion of the modes of thinking characteristic of caring itself, clearly indicates that these themes are critical to understanding the cognitive dimensions of caring relations. The current investigation of practices of care provides convincing support for this perception. In different contexts, and with different emphases, each practice considered shows how the knowledge characteristic of ethical caring is constituted through contextual, elaborative processes.

More specifically, caring relations with children require particularistic attention that is strongly conditioned by responsiveness to the interplay between children's extensive dependency, their rapidly changing sense of themselves, and the social norms within which particular mothering relations are structured. While friendships entail all these dimensions to some degree, interactive reciprocity and shared perspectives and interests are more significant dynamics in the epistemological approaches these practices of care express. Nursing practices on the other hand – with less continuous intimacy in which to hone attentiveness, but more specific focus in the realm of personal breakdowns – rely extensively on the acquisition of experiential knowledge of that realm in order to respond to the uniqueness of a particular patient's situation.

All of these practices demonstrate the crucial affective powers of knowing as well, and the involvement of knowers that requires engagement of them as whole persons, not simply the operationalization of a single faculty in an analytical task. But some practices, like nursing, are more task-oriented than others. As a consequence, they bring to light the necessity – and the constraints and possibilities – of integrated knowing. Friendships, in contrast, may entail more intense emotional engagement and the increased vulnerability of attention that is directed without well-structured institutional support. Finally, all these caring practices illustrate the ways in which their own brands of particularistic knowing require attentiveness to the overall context through which different particulars are determined. Knowing other persons' needs and interests involves attentiveness to the context of the relations and commitments that make those persons who they each are in their own right, rather than simply projecting what one would feel were one in their shoes.

The three epistemological concerns that Minow identifies are tied together with a fourth relational theme, namely: 'reflection upon relationships between people rather than treating people as autonomous, with identities existing prior to their social relationships' (MAD 129). And again, although she traces dimensions of this theme through many areas of feminist enquiry, her touchstone is Gilligan's articulation of the nature of the perspectives and values that are intrinsic to relations of care. Minow's description of this central concern of ethical caring includes several interconnected aspects. First, it entails the notion, familiar from the first section of this chapter, that persons are essentially persons-in-relation, or 'second persons', to use Baier's term. From the perspective of caring, this means that the intersubjective constitution of persons carries ethical significance since concern with relationships and attachments, and the continuing importance of interpersonal connections in persons' lives, become central values.[81] So, for example, where some moral positions embrace rights of non-interference as the focus of value, the priority accorded to maintenance of responsiveness to others in caring relations frequently shows up non-interference as oppressive neglect. Thus caring gives voice to the idea that personal relations are imperative to the identity and well-being of persons.

Second, an emphasis on interdependence and the quality of relations between persons brings with it concern for the significance of interpersonal communication. Dialogue and conversation, the ability to listen to and to hear the voices of different others become ethical resources. Conversation offers the possibility for activating relationships, for understanding differences among persons, for mediating and offering compensations, as well as claiming respect for one's separateness and expressing willingness to observe boundaries. In the chapter on mothering, for example, Ruddick's emphasis on the development of relational attentiveness through 'critical conversational challenge', has been noted. Correspondingly, sensitivity to breakdowns in communication, to silencing and the inability to speak is an important insight of care as demonstrated in the discussion of nursing practices.

In the third place, the valuing of connections between persons entails recognition that the orientations towards persons, expressed in ethical practices of care, are intrinsic to interactions that fully recognize the worth of those persons. In other words, commitment to particular persons in all their uniqueness – to their 'emotional states, individuating differences and whole particularity', to quote Friedman[82] – is a primary value. This insight shows a marked contrast with moral theories, like conventional rights-based views, which emphasize respect for persons insofar as they are members of a particular species, nation, or categorically identified group. Reasoning with abstract classifications and principles, rather than attending to the different realities of other persons, is the hallmark of these moral stances.

All these relational commitments are clearly evident as guiding ethical orientations in all the practices of care discussed so far. Recognition and respect for the richness and wholeness of the particularity of one's children, friends and patients for their own sake, is the distinctive commitment that runs centrally throughout practices of mothering, friendship and nursing. Each distinctive set of caring practices is created through its own specific context of concerns, historical, socio-political, material and emotional relations, bringing with them different limitations and possibilities for personal recognition and respect.

Mothering, for example, creates the possibility for sensitive and responsive recognition of shared intimacy, but is constrained, at least initially, by the inequalities of dependency and the constitutive social structures that confine mothers' abilities to integrate their mothering with their other life aspirations, needs, desires and responsibilities. Friendship relations may not be subject to the same sort of inequalities or institutional binds but, as a consequence, sensitivity and responsiveness frequently lack the intensity of engagement that emerges from intimacy formed in infancy. The freedoms of friendship also colour this responsivity with the risks of greater vulnerability. Like mothering practices, clinical nursing relations are characterized by inequalities of dependency and overt structural limits. But the critical nature of their more instrumentally centred activities, and the stability of the institutions in which they occur, offer acutely focused possibilities for personal respect and support when the precariousness of life outruns the capabilities of informal care. Despite these important distinctions, however, caring in each case strives towards that quality of respect and responsiveness that recognizes the worth of persons in their own distinctiveness.

Further, this recognition of other persons' individuated worth is a self-reflexive relational stance that is inherently tied up with understanding the significance of the attachment for all particip- ants. Frequently, the reflexive, interdependent quality of rela- tionships is expressed in a dynamic of domination and subordina- tion, appropriation and exclusion, possession and self-sacrifice. Mothering and nursing relations, for example, are often prey to these deformations of mutuality and reciprocity. Yet, these risks notwithstanding, the survey of caring relations presented here demonstrates that each set of practices carries the requirement and promise of the growth and validation of interdependent self- and other-understanding for all of their unique and different particip- ants. From the perspective of care, this possibility becomes an important reference point for understanding and transforming collective values.

These relational themes are brought together in Minow's 'social- relations approach' to understandings of difference and equality in the language of rights. She summarizes their force in the following way:

> The challenge is to maintain a steady inquiry into the inter- personal and political relationships between the knower and the known; a concern for the relations between wholes and parts; a suspicion of abstractions, which are likely to hide under claims of universality what is in fact the particular point of view and experience of those in power; and a respect for particularity, concreteness, reflection on experience and dialogue. (MAD 217)

Contemporary understandings of rights claims in law generally endorse the view that rights apply universally to all persons. Rights approaches thus inspire scepticism about the validity of assumptions and ascriptions of difference, especially when label- ling has often been flawed and a mask for prejudice and power. At the same time, however, this view coexists with the idea that there are certain differences that are, in some sense, 'real' and 'natural'. Women, children and disabled persons, for example, frequently seem to bear differences that involve treating them differently or which entitle them to special rights. In this sense, attributions of sameness and difference are frequently determin- ant for citizen possibilities, and, thereby, for the constituency of public values of justice and equality.

As Minow explains, there is a central instability in the premise of equal rights that admits the possibility that some special rights may be necessary, either to address some special characteristics of persons, or to remove the effects of past exclusion. The attempt to justify equal and special treatment itself 'offers no answer to the question it poses: when are historical attributions of difference acceptable and when are they false?' (MAD 109). Nor does this approach specify when a violation of rights can be remedied by imposing equality, or when special treatment is justified. By vesting the courts with the task of enquiring into and deciding these issues, however, it sustains the perception that despite mistaken definitions in the past, the judiciary has access to reliable sources of knowledge relating to the nature and significance of differences among persons.

Aided by insights concerning the perspectival nature of knowing, and the connections between persons and their particularity, the 'social-relations approach' to rights challenges the determinant attributions of difference that are used to define and describe persons in conventional approaches. From this perspective, Minow claims, 'assertions of difference may be understood as statements of relationships' (MAD 111). The relational focus highlights the point that the notion of difference takes its meaning from the relation of comparison it draws between two entities.

'As a relational notion, difference is reciprocal: I am no [more] different from you than you are from me' (MAD 111). As features of the intrinsic connectedness among persons, 'differences' are therefore written into the centre of the 'social-relations approach'. Comparisons that draw distinctions from and similarities to what is already known are seen as one of the most important ways in which people get to know and understand each other. Far from distinguishing aberrant traits of individuals, ascriptions of differences confirm the relationships between persons. Conceptually they rely on the connection between the two sides that are distinguished by the ascription; more practically, they depend on the connections among the persons who recognize and affirm that distinction (MAD 10).

Combined with the epistemological insights of care, this understanding of the logic of differences as relational comparisons exposes the ways in which statements of difference are used to distribute public power and status. On the conventional rights view, differences are assigned as distinctions that determine the boundaries between the aberrant and the normal rather than drawing comparisons between them. Knowledge and ascriptions of differences seem unproblematic because they are widely confirmed in other public practices and institutions. However, this naming of boundaries, Minow notes, 'disguises the power of the namers, who simultaneously assign names and deny their relationships with and power over the named' (MAD 111). The 'social-relations' position that knowledge is rooted in specific perspectives, and that 'prevailing views' express the perspectives of those in positions to enforce their points of view, inspires new strategies for dealing with statements of difference.

One strategy enjoins those responsible for naming to seek out other perspectives, especially the perspectives of those assigned the label of difference, recognizing that 'knowing' the perspective of another is an open-ended process that incorporates experiential, emotional, rational and imaginative dimensions. This strategy cautions against understanding labels as immutable and unresponsive to changing social realities; it questions ascriptions that are distant from the concrete and dynamic context of persons' lives. The labelling of family relations as inherently different from citizen relations – with respect to the legitimacy of public intervention, for example – is questioned for its failure to respond to the violence that frequently occurs within those relations. Warnings are also issued against group labels that obscure the range of differences within those groups. Considerations of women's rights to abortion, for example, look very different when the relations between 'racial ethnic' and middle-class, white women are taken into account. Then the important issue is seen as the broader one of reproductive rights, rather than the narrower question of a right to abortion.[83]

A related strategy entails exploring the social and normative meanings that ascriptions of difference and sameness carry in the community. At one level judges are asked to question their own implication in their judgements of difference: to recognize how their perspectives contribute to sustaining their power with respect to those named as different. More generally, the demand that differences be considered in terms of the relationships through which they are constructed compels investigation of those constructions in the light of the norms and patterns of institutional relationships that make some traits prescriptive for the possibilities of those who bear them. The relational approach questions the effects of labelling on the social relations of those labelled. It asks how labels affect ongoing relations and whether such categorization inhibits mutual respect between persons.

To illustrate this approach, Minow discusses the case of pregnancy and employment conditions (MAD 86–90). She explains how conventional analyses of this problem construe it in the either/or terms of equality versus difference. From the equality side, workers' conditions and rights are determined as applying universally to all persons, irrespective of whether they may become pregnant or not. If pregnancy and child-care duties interfere with the responsibilities of paid work, the costs are therefore assigned entirely to the mother. From the difference side, the allocation of special rights to mothers shifts the burden to the employer, or perhaps indirectly to other workers or consumers. The 'social-relations approach' contests the ways both these analyses set up associations of sameness with equality, and difference with disability that turn a condition as normal, common and important as pregnancy into something negative.

More equitable analyses may take the perspective of women workers into consideration by extending the relevant grounds of sameness to include home and work responsibilities. The old norm of workers without family responsibilities might be replaced with a new norm of workers with family duties. While this attempt to include other perspectives is clearly in line with the kind of relational outlook inspired by reflection on practices of care, it too holds to the same basic framework, simply 'enshrin[ing] a new and better norm against which to judge difference' (MAD 89). In contrast, the 'social-relations approach' enquires into the wider set of social arrangements through which the significance of pregnancy and child rearing is given meaning. From this perspective pregnancy is a concern not just for pregnant women, but for men who have family responsibilities, for employers who will benefit from the talents of women and men, and for the whole community which has an interest in the reproduction of the species as well as production in the workplace. Seeing pregnant women in their particularity and through their relationships within the community acknowledges the protection of these broader interests and relationships as a shared responsibility and benefit for employers, public officials, workers and family members.

This transformed conception of social possibilities, however, is not without its own difficulties. In moving away from the problems of abstract ascriptions of sameness and difference that obstruct connections between persons and reinforce relations of power, the relational approach raises other concerns. Perhaps foremost among these is the charge that it condones a form of relativism. The notions that identities and knowledge are relationally constituted, that meaning is social rather than natural, invite the objection that adjudication between different perspectives is completely arbitrary. In the case of pregnancy, for example, the 'social-relations approach' does not resolve conflicts concerning which particular interests and relationships require collective protection. For some citizens, the community-wide interest in reproduction may mean protecting gendered labour relations rather than integrating women in the workplace.

The response from the relational approach, Minow remarks, 'will not satisfy objectors, because it calls for shifting the frame of reference, the very criterion for judging normative judgements' (MAD 222). Her point is that abstract criteria, in themselves, do not provide their own means of application to any particular context. Their alleged answers come only from their implicit affirmation or neglect of unstated features of that context. A judgement that responsibility for coping with pregnancy should remain with the pregnant is only an appropriate answer if it can presume, for example, the network of support relations that creates this possibility, or if it overlooks women's career aspirations and their needs to participate fully in the public sphere. Denying the multiplicity of perspectives, as such criteria do, does not dissolve that diversity, but rather entrenches rigid constructions that constrain social possibilities. The commitment of the 'social-relations approach' to caring attentiveness to particulars and their relational contexts, on the other hand, does not eschew normative judgements or claim that any value is as good as another. Instead, as the preceding chapters have shown, it reveals the ethical dimensions of attending to the details of the relationships between particular contexts and particular values.

In its turn, this commitment, however, produces the further problem of apparently limitless epistemological and normative responsibilities. The relational focus on caring connections between persons, and the critical, reflexive requirement to search out new perspectives, threatens to overwhelm persons with endless responsibilities to others. The complexity, diversity and multiplicity of interpersonal relationships, and the partiality and

open-endedness of knowledge, suggest that there are no limits to
ethical culpability. And indeed, for many women caught in the
endless labours of informal practices of care, for example, the
relational approach may seem to endorse a life of perpetual self-
sacrifice.[84] Precisely this sort of difficulty may be a motivation
for conventional understandings of rights and the limits they
place on citizens' obligations to each other: a protection against
the excesses of internally imposed exploitation as well as external
interference. Here the relational approach itself seems to require
some kind of determinate limits.

Such a view, however, is party to at least two misunder-
standings. In the first place, the relatedness between persons
embedded in the care perspective does not encourage some kind
of global identification with other persons' needs and interests
that submerges the separate identities of participants. On the
contrary, each of the practices of care I have surveyed points to
the reflexive nature of caring: the ways in which ethical caring
requires and creates the possibility for the development of both
self and other. Responsibilities to other persons with whom one
is connected, even in the relatively uni-directional contexts of
mothering and nursing, always take their reference point from this
understanding of mutuality.

Second, it is precisely the distortions of limits and certainty
imposed by rights positions that the 'social-relations approach'
exposes and challenges. The equation of sameness with equality,
defined from the perspective of those who have the power to
shape prevailing views, does provide a measure of certainty and
predictability, it does set constraints on obligations. And these are
not values to be dismissed out of hand. Difficulties arise, however,
because these limits are not unconditional. Certainty and predictability are themselves intrinsically limited by their appeal to the
dominant perspective, and are used to justify the curtailment of
some persons' citizenship possibilities in virtue of the perspectives
associated with their gender, race, class, mental or physical
abilities. The relational insights of care do not provide a blueprint
for social justice that erases these problems but they offer a
framework for redressing those collective practices and values
that deny the mutual dependence of citizens.

Perhaps the significance of this approach warrants the abandonment of rights language altogether. The point is not indisputable.[85] But for Minow and other legal theorists working towards

the transformation of collective values,[86] there is something too valuable in the contemporary resonances of rights with aspirations of inclusivity and challenges to the hierarchies of power, to risk relinquishing their force. In a social context that is grounded so deeply on assumptions that shift the burdens of all citizens' vulnerability and need to some, different others, the rhetoric of rights provides a space for the burdened to raise claims to citizen respect. Infused with the insights of care, rights can be understood more as the language of a continuing process of relational responses, rather than as fixed rules. In this sense, assertions of particular rights may be determinative in particular contexts, says Minow:

> but their origins and their future viability depend upon a continuing, communal process of communication ... The language of rights thus draws each claimant into the community and grants each a basic opportunity to participate in the process of communal debate. (MAD 296)

When rights are understood in this way, formulaic definitions of sameness and difference that give content to the notions of equality and freedom, that substantialize the meaning of citizenship, are dissolved in a quality of mutual attentiveness: listening and hearing, looking at and seeing. Thus, Minow explains that 'the equality embodied by rights claims is an equality of *attention*' (MAD 297). Rights give forms for the protection of interests and freedoms but the values they express are given meaning and substance by the qualities of attentiveness and conduct directed towards the persons they protect. The structure of the communal debate, its capacity to attend to and hear the voices of those who are least powerful, to reflect on and to challenge its own reference points, shapes the value that particular rights protect.

As Minow is only too aware, there are, of course, still difficulties with the different possibilities that different voices are able to sustain. Some claims will be recognized as more persuasive than others and some points of view may be less adaptable than others to the vocabulary of pre-existing claims. Other claimants may feel so alienated from the rights discourse that its use may seem nonsensical, and still others may find speaking itself risks too much of the limited control they have over their lives (MAD 298). The language of rights will always be constrained by the limits of its own linguisticality; it is always vulnerable to neglect of its own assumptions, and at risk of succumbing to its own seductive power. But the language of rights, oriented by the relational perspectives and values of care, can reconfirm collective values even as it expresses conflicts and divisions.

I have dwelt at length on Minow's work, for it shows in a context of immediate significance to citizenship, some of the ways in which the values of public life can be transformed through the incorporation of ethical perspectives developed in practices of care. Legal judgments, in their explicit processes of relating theoretical justifications to practical decisions, provide instructive examples of the complex interrelation of conceptual values and social practices, and explicit illustrations of the possibilities for changes in the relations of citizenship.

But Minow's discussion of legal rights is presented here in an exploratory and heuristic context: a tentative suggestion as to how the process of transformation might proceed. Her work does not stand alone. Other theorists have also taken up the task of showing the importance of ethical insights from practices of care and their intersection with women's citizen possibilities, for the formulation of inclusive understandings of collective values. Among others, Carole Pateman has studied the notion of consent and Nancy Hirschman has begun 'rethinking obligation'.[87] Anna Jonasdottir has enquired into the inclusiveness of the concept of interest, while Nancy Fraser talks about the contextual relations of needs.[88] Iris Young has brought relational insights to bear on understandings of justice, and Anne Phillips has described a process of engendering democracy.[89] Virginia Held and Kathleen Jones have tapped the ethical resources of caring relations to reconceptualize liberty, equality and authority.[90] Together these investigations create the space for renewed understanding of the ethical possibilites of citizen practices of care.

Epilogue

> Caring is pivotal to keeping the human enterprise going, yet its
> function is invisible in the organization of our daily lives.
>   – Sheila M. Neysmith[1]

This investigation does not argue for any definitive or comprehensive conclusions. My point has not been to produce a
consensus, or to catch the essence of care, nor yet to unearth some
hidden truth that shows that there has been implicit agreement all
along about the meaning of caring. For it is my claim that it is
precisely these kinds of aims that tend to lead understanding
astray, and to cause us to overlook the complexity and diversity
of the ethical possibilities of care. Accordingly, the idea of reaching
a conclusion has always been an obstacle to understanding,
encouraging the universalization of necessarily partial perspectives that neglect their own contextual origins and the multiplicity
of different perspectives that lie outside the range of their vision.

But, as I explained in the Introduction, this insight does not
reduce understanding and knowledge to disarray. The inability to
define the ethic of care, or to determine its boundaries with
precision, does not signal the impossibility of knowledge, or the
chaos of relativism. Rather, following the lead of Wittgenstein –
and his specific discussion of the practical concept, 'game' – it
suggests that understanding can be expressed by describing
examples of various kinds of caring; showing how all sorts of other
practices of care can be constructed on the analogy of these;
indicating that some practices can scarcely be included among
examples of caring; and so on (PI 75). This approach to understanding has propelled my investigation. By juxtaposing descriptions of different practices of care, and by crossing back and

forth many times through their overlapping domains, I have aimed to show what can be known but cannot be defined. If the survey has been successful the reader will now be in a position to appreciate its implications: the illusions of definitive approaches to understanding and attempts to pin down the ethical significance of care will have been dispelled.

My purpose, however, has not been simply therapeutic. While the labyrinth of uses of care described here has shown that ethical practices of caring cannot be understood comprehensively or with exactness, it has brought into focus an ethos of relatedness among persons that is frequently overlooked. For, as Neysmith remarks, 'the function of caring is invisible in the organization of our daily lives'. Her comment is directed specifically to the social organization of caring work. Invisibility in this context refers to the way caring tends to be transparent to the public domain (and to the contemporary bent of Canadian policy-makers to see caring for others as a private responsibility). It also refers to the difficulty in specifying or prescribing the complex of emotional and material concerns that caring entails, and the subsequent tendencies to reduce care to its visible objective tasks, and to deny the value inherent in its complexity.[2] Philosophical reflection, as both a product and producer of this socio-political order, largely affirms its visions and its oversights. A primary intent of my investigation, therefore, has been to unmask the conceptual ascription of the ethical significance of caring to 'private responsibility', as it were, by placing a range of personal caring practices at the centre of philosophical concern.

This end has been shaped by my understanding of the intrinsic complexity of ethical practices of care: their integration of cognitive and emotional dimensions, their contextual and particularistic constitution in relation to socio-historical conditions, their diversity, ambiguity and contingency. In light of this understanding I have approached the project of bringing care into view by refusing to accept analyses based on any one set of caring relations or any one account of the ethical implications of care. By surveying a variety of specific examples of caring relations between persons, I have shown that practices of care display a range of ethical priorities, commitments, attitudes and beliefs that are central to the well-being of persons.

At the same time, the examples of caring examined here have highlighted the ways in which the 'invisibility' and devaluing of the ethical significance of these practices is intimately connected with the failure of allegedly impartialist theories to take into account their gendered structures. The selection of examples itself, and the process of investigating the ethical import of each of these 'objects of comparison', have brought to the fore the ways in which gender is deeply implicated in practices of care, and understandings of their ethical significance. The survey has shown how the subordination – and frequent neglect – of caring in the discourses of conventional moral philosophy is continuous with and provides support for the exclusion of experiences, interests, needs and desires, characteristically associated with women. The discussions of mothering, nursing and citizenship practices, for example, have shown how gendered social structures systematically and explicitly ascribe distinctive roles and concerns to women that limit and devalue their ethical possibilities. And from the discussion of friendship relations in Chapter 2, it has become evident that even relational practices that appear to be equally accessible to both women and men have gendered ethical implications. By placing these different examples of caring practices beside each other, the focal importance of gender sensitivity for ethics is revealed in vivid relief.

Thus it is too, that while one of my major purposes has been to unsettle fixed and unitary understandings of caring by displaying the contexts in which ethical values arise, the juxtaposition of practices with different contexts has also revealed common themes. From the exploration of different examples of care a cluster of common epistemological orientations relating to the perspectival nature of knowing and the links between knowledge and power has emerged. Reflection on the intersection between practices of caring, and the exclusion of women's perspectives from authoritative fields of enquiry, has confirmed both the intrinsic partiality of knowledge and the imposition of a dominating perspective that conceals the exploitation of caring relations and those persons who are identified with them. The investigation has also shown how caring practices embed approaches to knowledge that emphasize the significance of contexts and particularities, and the importance of the relationships between them.

In addition, each set of practices surveyed has demonstrated an emphasis on the interdependence of persons and the quality of their relationships. From the perspective of caring, the intersubjective constitution of persons carries an ethical significance that makes concern with relationships and attachments – and the continuing importance of interpersonal connections in persons' lives – central values. And these commitments to the values of personal relations bring with them an insistence on the ethical importance of particularistic appreciations of persons: a valuing of persons for whom they uniquely are in all their individuating differences.

In the final chapter on citizenship relations these continuities of perspective – illustrated in the earlier accounts of different but conventionally established practices of care – are shown to provide possibilities for moving through the theoretical and practical distinction constructed between personal caring relations and the more formal relations of the public domain. The exploration of citizenship practices has brought to light ways in which ethical expressions of caring come to be important at both the practical and conceptual levels of these publicly constituted relations. Identification of this overlapping, but distinctive territory of interpersonal relations, opens up the space for a transformed understanding of the ethical possibilities of citizen practices of care. In Minow's work on legal rights, for example, conventional understandings of these public values are transformed by bringing the different ethical perspectives and insights developed in informal caring practices to bear on their meaning. By unmasking traditional restrictions on the moral constitution of citizenship relations, the investigation has pointed towards more comprehensive conceptions of collective values that recognize a whole range of understandings of human needs acquired in informal caring practices.

But while it has been the aim of this work to foreground the ethical values of caring and their implications for gender-sensitive enquiry, conventional requirements for fixed definitions and determinate solutions to problems identified in both traditional and feminist ethics have been rejected. I have proceeded by providing illustrations of possibilities, not precise formulations or conclusive analyses. In this respect, it is my hope that this conclusion will be a beginning, not an ending: that it will create openings for further investigations of other examples of caring that will enrich understanding and visibility of their ethical significance in the organization of our daily lives.

Notes

INTRODUCTION

1 L. Wittgenstein, *Philosophical Investigations*, 2nd edn, trans. G. Anscombe, Oxford, Basil Blackwell, 1958, section 90 (hereafter PI followed by relevant section number).

2 J. Tronto, 'Care as a basis for radical political judgements', *Hypatia*, 1995, vol. 10, pp. 141–9.

3 U. Narayan, 'Colonialism and its others: consideration on rights and care discourses', *Hypatia*, 1995, vol. 10, pp. 133–40.

4 J. Dancy, 'Caring about justice', *Philosophy*, 1992, vol. 67, pp. 447–66.

5 See J. Tronto, *Moral Boundaries: A Political Argument for an Ethic of Care*, New York, Routledge, 1993, for a recent example of this neglect. L. Shrage, *Moral Dilemmas of Feminism: Prostitution, Adultery, and Abortion*, New York, Routledge, 1994, pp. 18–22, and C. Mouffe, 'Feminism, citizenship and radical democratic politics', in *The Return of the Political*, London, Verso, 1993, pp. 74–89, provide examples of the way critics of care overlook this challenge.

6 For example A. Baier, *Moral Prejudices: Essays on Ethics*, Boston, Harvard University Press, 1994; M. Walker, 'Moral understandings: alternative "epistemology" for a feminist ethics', *Hypatia*, 1989, vol. 4, pp. 15–28; 'Partial consideration', *Ethics*, 1991, vol. 101, pp. 758–74; 'Feminism, ethics and the question of theory', *Hypatia*, 1992. vol. 7, pp. 23–38.

7 H. Sidgwick, *The Methods of Ethics*, 7th edn, London, Macmillan, 1907. See also A. Jonsen and S. Toulmin, *The Abuse of Casuistry: A History of Moral Reasoning*, Berkeley, University of California Press, 1988, p. 12 and Walker, 'Moral understandings'.

8 Further evidence for the pervasiveness of this tradition is provided by contemporary public debates of moral issues in Western societies, where the rhetoric of conflicts over abortion, euthanasia, capital punishment, affirmative action, pornography, etc., very frequently turns on 'matters of principle'. See Jonsen and Toulmin, *The Abuse of Casuistry*, p. 4.

9 Famous contenders include appeals to *a priori* reflection, and claims to the effect that any rational agent will arrive at the same

methodology, intent and conclusions as any other when she or he deliberates about moral life.

10 B. Williams, 'Saint-Just's illusion', in B. Williams, *Making Sense of Humanity and Other Philosophical Papers*, Cambridge, Cambridge University Press, 1995, p. 139.

11 *Ibid.*, p. 149.

12 The literature here is enormous. J. Grimshaw, *Philosophy and Feminist Thinking*, Minneapolis, University of Minnesota Press, 1986, pp. 36–74, gives a useful review of different understandings of the '"maleness" of philosophy'.

13 See C. Calhoun, 'Justice, care, gender bias', *Journal of Philosophy*, 1988, vol. 85, pp. 451–63, for an insightful discussion of the gendered ideological entailments created by the patterns of themes conventionally included in and excluded from moral philosophy.

14 This intent is important to many feminist projects. For a recent example, see V. Held, *Feminist Morality: Transforming Culture, Society and Politics*, Chicago, University of Chicago Press, 1993.

15 C. Gilligan, *In a Different Voice: Psychological Theory and Women's Development*, Cambridge, Massachusetts, Harvard University Press, 1982.

16 See, for example, L. Walker, 'Sex differences in the development of moral reasoning: a critical review', *Child Development*, 1984, vol. 55, pp. 667–91.

17 See, for example, N. Noddings, *Caring: A Feminine Approach to Ethics and Moral Education*, Berkeley, University of California Press, 1984; S. Mullett, 'Shifting perspective: a new approach to ethics', in L. Code, S. Mullett and C. Overall (eds), *Feminist Perspectives: Philosophical Essays On Method and Morals*, Toronto, University of Toronto Press, 1988, pp. 109–26; R. Manning, *Speaking From the Heart: A Feminist Perspective on Ethics*, Lanham, Maryland, Rowman & Littlefield, 1992; Held, *Feminist Morality*.

18 See, for example, M. Friedman, 'Beyond caring: the de-moralization of gender', in M. Hanen and K. Nielsen (eds), *Science, Morality & Feminist Theory*, Calgary, Alberta, University of Calgary Press, 1987, pp. 87–110; S. Ruddick, *Maternal Thinking: Toward a Politics of Peace*, Boston, Beacon Press, 1989; C. Card, 'Gender and moral luck', in O. Flanagan and A. Rorty (eds), *Identity, Character and Morality: Essays in Moral Psychology*, Cambridge, Massachusetts, MIT Press, 1990, pp. 199–218; K. Addelson, 'What do women do? Some radical implications of Carol Gilligan's ethics', in *Impure Thoughts: Essays on Philosophy, Feminism and Ethics*, Philadelphia, Temple University Press, 1991, pp. 188–211.

19 See, for example, S. Okin, 'Reason and feeling in thinking about justice', *Ethics*, 1989, vol. 99, pp. 229–49; R. Dillon, 'Care and respect', in E. Cole and S. McQuin (eds), *Explorations in Feminist Ethics: Theory and Practice*, Bloomington, Indiana University Press, 1992, pp. 69–81; M. Friedman, *What Are Friends For? Feminist Perspectives on Personal Relationships and Moral Theory*, Ithaca, New York, Cornell University Press, 1993; Held, *Feminist Morality*.

20 See, for example, A. Baier, 'What do women want in a moral theory?' *Nous*, 1985, vol. 19, pp. 53–64; O. Flanagan and K. Jackson, 'Justice, care, and gender: the Kohlberg–Gilligan debate revisted', *Ethics*, 1987, vol. 97, pp. 622–37; M. Moody-Adams, 'Gender and the complexity of moral voices', in C. Card (ed.), *Feminist Ethics*, Lawrence, Kansas, University Press of Kansas, 1991, pp. 195–212.

21 See, for example, L. Kohlberg *et al.*, 'Moral stages: a current statement. Response to critics. Appendix A, in L. Kohlberg, *Essays in Moral Development*, vol 2: *The Psychology of Moral Development*, New York, Harper & Row, 1984, p. 232; J. Habermas, *Moral Consciousness and Communicative Action*, Cambridge, Massachusetts, MIT Press, 1990, pp. 175–81, and *Justification and Application*, Cambridge, Massachusetts, MIT Press, 1993, pp. 153–4; W. Kymlicka, *Contemporary Political Philosophy: An Introduction*, Oxford, Oxford University Press, 1990, pp. 262–86.

22 See, for example, G. Nunner-Winkler, 'Two moralities? A critical discussion of an ethic of care and responsibility versus an ethic of right and justice', in W. Kutines and J. Gewirtz (eds), *Morality, Moral Behaviour and Moral Development*, New York, Wiley, 1984, pp. 348–61; B. Williams, *Ethics and the Limits of Philosophy*, Cambridge, Massachusetts, Harvard University Press, 1985; T. Nagel, *The View From Nowhere*, New York, Oxford University Press, 1986.

23 See L. Blum, 'Gilligan and Kohlberg: implications for moral theory', *Ethics*, 1988, vol. 98, pp. 472–91, for a review of these positions. A significant contribution here is J. Blustein, *Care and Commitment: Taking the Personal Point of View*, New York, Oxford University Press, 1991. Blustein argues that the morality of care depends on the possibility that the justification for its regulating ideals can be specified impartially.

24 B. Houston, 'Rescuing womanly virtues: some dangers of moral reclamation', in Hanen and Nielsen, *Science, Morality & Feminist Theory*, pp. 237–62.

25 K. Ferguson, *The Feminist Case Against Bureaucracy*, Philadelphia, Temple University Press, 1984; Grimshaw, *Philosophy and Feminist Thinking*; S. Hoagland, *Lesbian Ethics: Toward New Value*, Palo Alto, California, Institute of Lesbian Studies, 1988; Card, 'Gender and moral luck'; E. Spelman, 'The virtue of feeling and the feeling of virtue', in Card, *Feminist Ethics*, pp. 213–32.

26 Ferguson, *The Feminist Case*; Grimshaw, *Philosophy and Feminist Thinking*; L. Code, *What Can She Know? Feminist Theory and the Constitution of Knowledge*, Ithaca, New York, Cornell University Press, 1991, pp. 87–109.

27 See, for example, 'care' in *The Oxford English Dictionary*, 2nd edn, prepared by J. Simpson and E. Weiner, Oxford, Clarendon Press, 1989, vol. 2, pp. 893–4.

28 The terms 'modernism' and 'postmodernism' have given rise to an enormous variety of interpretations. I use 'modernism' very loosely here to indicate theoretical approaches that embrace universalist discourses of objectivity, truth and reason. 'Postmodernism' refers to

allegedly non-universalist approaches that stress the demands of the local and particular. D. Patterson, 'Postmodernism/feminism/law', *Cornell Law Review*, 1992, vol. 77, pp. 254–317, has perceptive discussions of these two orientations.

29 Houston, 'Rescuing womanly virtues', p. 257. This point is also suggested by L. Blum, 'Vocation, friendship and community: limitations of the personal–impersonal framework', in Flanagan and Rorty, *Identity, Character and Morality*, pp. 173–98.

30 See, for example, Noddings, *Caring*; Baier, 'What do women want in a moral theory?'; S.T. Fry, 'The role of caring in a theory of nursing ethics', *Hypatia*, 1989, vol. 4, pp. 88–103; Tronto, *Moral Boundaries*. Importantly, this difficulty often arises despite the best intentions of care theorists. Not surprisingly critics of the 'ethic of care' frequently interpret caring in reductionist terms: for example, Hoagland, *Lesbian Ethics*; Kymlicka, *Contemporary Political Philosophy*; H.J. Curzer, 'Is care a virtue for health care professionals?' *Journal of Medicine and Philosophy*, 1993, vol. 18, pp. 51–69. Shrage, *Moral Dilemmas*, is a recent discussion that is critical of accounts of the 'ethic of care' for their failure to provide a foundational moral concept.

31 On mothering, see: Ruddick, *Maternal Thinking*; C. Whitbeck, 'A different reality: feminist ontology', in C. Gould (ed.), *Beyond Domination: New Perspectives on Women and Philosophy*, Totowa, New Jersey, Rowman & Allanfield, 1984, pp. 64–88; M. Dietz, 'Citizenship with a feminist face: the problem of maternal thinking', *Political Theory*, 1985, vol. 13, pp. 19–37; Mouffe, 'Feminism, citizenship'. On friendship, see: J. Raymond, *A Passion for Friends: Toward a Philosophy of Female Affection*, Boston, Beacon Press, 1986; Code, *What Can She Know?*

32 b. hooks, 'Revolutionary parenting', in *Feminist Theory: From Margin to Center*, Boston, South End Press, 1984, pp. 133–46, and 'Violence in intimate relationships: a feminist perspective', in *Talking Back: Thinking Feminist, Thinking Black*, Boston, South End Press, 1989, pp. 84–91; A. Lorde, 'Man child: a black lesbian feminist's response', in *Sister Outsider*, Freedom, California, Crossing Press, 1984, pp. 72–80; L. Maracle, 'Normal vs. natural', in *I Am Woman*, North Vancouver, British Columbia, Write-On Press Publishers, 1988, pp. 165–79; P. Collins, *Black Feminist Thought: Knowledge, Consciousness and the Politics of Empowerment*, Boston, Unwin Hyman, 1990; M. Lugones, 'On the logic of pluralist feminism', in Card, *Feminist Ethics*, pp. 35–44.

33 This is a common theme in recent feminist theory. See, for example, J. Butler and J. Scott (eds), *Feminists Theorize the Political*, New York, Routledge, 1992.

34 Referring to this productive possibility, Wittgenstein says: 'concepts lead us to make investigations; are the expression of our interest, and direct our interest' (PI 570).

35 G. Baker, '*Philosophical Investigations* section 122: neglected aspects', in R. Arrington and H. Glock (eds), *Wittgenstein's Philosophical Investigations: Text and Context*, London, Routledge, 1991, p. 62. My interpretation of Wittgenstein is heavily indebted to discussions with Jim Tully and Natalie Brender, as well as J. Tully, 'Rights in abilities',

Annals of Scholarship, 1988, vol. 5, pp. 363–81, and 'Ludwig Wittgenstein and political philosophy: understanding practices of critical reflection', *Political Theory*, 1989, vol. 17, pp. 172–204; and N. Brender, 'Redescribing *Middlemarch*: literature as ethical practice', unpublished manuscript, 1989. Many of the ideas that emerged in those discussions have been crystallized and confirmed by Baker's essay, cited above.

36 Though he makes no direct reference to Wittgenstein on this point, my understanding of it owes much to Patterson, 'Postmodernism/feminism/law'.

37 L. Wittgenstein, *The Blue and Brown Books: Preliminary Studies for the 'Philosophical Investigations'*, New York, Harper & Row, 1958, pp. 19–20, cites Socrates' dismissal of the relevance of concrete cases to understanding the usage of the concept 'knowledge' as evidence of this deeply entrenched orientation.

38 For perceptive examples of work using this approach see Tully, 'Rights in abilities', and 'Ludwig Wittgenstein and political philosophy'.

39 This move is analogous to the extension of the range of justice into the realm of intimacy as proposed, for example, by S. Okin, *Justice, Gender and the Family*, New York, Basic Books, 1989.

40 See, for example, P. DiQuinzio, 'Exclusion and essentialism in feminist theory: the problem of mothering', *Hypatia*, 1993, vol. 8, pp. 1–19; P. Collins, 'Shifting the center: race, class and feminist theorizing about motherhood', in E. N. Glenn, G. Chang and L. R. Forcey (eds), *Mothering: Ideology, Experience and Agency*, New York, Routledge, 1994, pp. 45–64, A. Bailey, 'Mothering, diversity and peace politics', *Hypatia*, 1994, vol. 9, pp. 188–98, on mothering. E. Badinter, *Mother Love, Myth and Reality: Motherhood in Modern History*, New York, Macmillan, 1980, argues that no generalizations can be made about motherhood because our notion of mother-centred infant care is a product of the eighteenth-century development of the bourgeois family in Europe.

41 J. Ringelheim, 'Women and the holocaust: a reconsideration of research', *Signs*, 1985, vol. 10, pp. 741–61.

42 R. Ross, *Dancing with a Ghost: Exploring Indian Reality*, Markham, Ontario, Octopus Publishing Group, 1992, p. 42. I am grateful to Jim Tully for bringing this work to my notice.

43 Baker, '*Philosophical Investigations*, section 122', pp. 58–63.

CHAPTER 1: MOTHERING

1 N. Noddings, *Caring: A Feminine Approach to Ethics and Moral Education*, Berkeley, University of California Press, 1984, pp. 79–80, argues that our memories of being cared for and caring contribute a powerful motivation for our caring practices.

2 *Ibid.*, *passim*.

3 V. Held, 'Feminism and moral theory', in E.F. Kittay and D.T. Meyers

(eds), *Women and Moral Theory,* Totowa, New Jersey, Rowman
Littlefield, 1987, pp. 111–28. See also V. Held, 'Non-contractual
society: a feminist view', in M. Hanen and K. Nielsen (eds), *Science,
Morality & Feminist Theory,* Calgary, Alberta, University of Calgary
Press, 1987, pp. 111–37, in which she compares mothering relations
with contractual relations. The ethical significance of mothering
relations is further developed in V. Held, *Feminist Morality: Transforming Culture, Society and Politics,* Chicago, University of Chicago
Press, 1993.

4 W. Ruddick, 'Parents and life prospects', in O. O'Neill and W.
Ruddick (eds), *Having Children: Philosophical and Legal Reflections on
Parenthood,* New York, Oxford University Press, 1979, pp. 124–37.

5 K.A. Rabuzzi, *Motherself: A Mythic Analysis of Motherhood,* Bloomington, Indiana University Press, 1988, p. 11.

6 A classic reference point for this tradition in its most extreme form is
Hobbes' 'mushroom' metaphor that considers 'men [*sic*] ... as if
but even now sprung out of the earth, and suddenly, like mushrooms,
come to full maturity, without any kind of engagement with each
other.' Quoted by S. Benhabib, 'The generalized and the concrete
other: the Kohlberg–Gilligan controversy and moral theory', in Kittay
and Meyers, *Women and Moral Theory,* p. 161.

7 See P.L. Bowden, 'Relationships with others: insights from the work
of Martin Heidegger for feminism, ethics and care', MA thesis, McGill
University, Montreal, 1987, especially Chs 2 and 3, for a discussion of
these different kinds of connections among persons. See also J.
Nedelsky, 'Reconceiving autonomy: sources, thoughts and possibilities', *Yale Journal of Law and Feminism,* 1989, vol. 1, pp. 7–36; Held,
Feminist Morality, pp. 60–2.

8 See, for example, Rabuzzi, *Motherself,* especially pp. 48–53; J. Lazarre,
The Mother Knot, New York, McGraw-Hill, 1976, *passim.*

9 S. de Beauvoir, *The Second Sex,* trans. H.M. Parshley, New York, Alfred
A. Knopf, 1953. Notable book-length contributions to this discussion
include: J. Bernard, *The Future of Motherhood,* New York, Penguin,
1974; A. Rich, *Of Woman Born: Motherhood as Experience and Institution,*
New York, W.W. Norton, 1976; D. Dinnerstein, *The Mermaid and the
Minotaur: Sexual Arrangements and Human Malaise,* New York, Harper
& Row, 1976; Lazarre, *Mother Knot;* N. Chodorow, *The Reproduction
of Mothering,* Berkeley, University of California Press, 1978; E. Badinter,
Mother Love, Myth and Reality: Motherhood in Modern History, New
York, Macmillan, 1980; A. Rossiter, *From Private to Public: A Feminist
Exploration of Early Mothering,* Toronto, The Women's Press, 1988; S.
Ruddick, *Maternal Thinking: Toward a Politics of Peace,* Boston, Beacon
Press, 1989, 1995; B.K. Rothman, *Recreating Motherhood: Ideology and
Technology in a Patriarchal Society,* New York, W.W. Norton, 1989; C.
Everingham, *Mothering and Modernity,* St Leonards, Allen & Unwin,
1994. The anthologies, J. Treblicot (ed.), *Mothering: Essays in Feminist
Theory,* Totowa, New Jersey, Rowman & Allanfield, 1984; J.P. Knowles
and E. Cole (eds), *Woman-Defined Motherhood,* New York, Harrington
Park Press, 1990; J.F. O'Barr, D. Pope and M. Wyer (eds), *Ties that*

Bind: Essays on Mothering and Patriarchy, Chicago, University of Chicago Press, 1990; D. Bassin, M. Honey and M. Kaplan (eds), *Representations of Motherhood,* New Haven, Connecticut, Yale University Press, 1994; E.N. Glenn, G. Chang and L.R. Forcey (eds), *Mothering: Ideology, Experience and Agency,* New York, Routledge, 1994 provide a useful spectrum of issues and analyses. For a detailed bibliography see P. Dixon, *Mothers and Mothering: An Annotated Feminist Bibliography,* New York, Garland Publishing, 1991.

10 Ruddick, *Maternal Thinking,* 1989, p. 11 (hereafter MT followed by page numbers). The Western philosophical canon from Plato through to the twentieth-century has largely ignored mothering, except as it bears upon education of the young. Other disciplines have produced reams of guidance and analyses. See, for example, the penetrating social history by B. Ehrenreich and D. English, *For Her Own Good: 150 Years of the Experts' Advice to Women,* New York, Anchor Books, 1979, in which the authors track the recent course of the extensive medical and psychological 'thinking about mothers and their children'.

11 Ruddick's first essay on 'maternal thinking' appeared as 'Maternal thinking' in *Feminist Studies,* 1980, vol. 6, pp. 342–67. Ruddick, *Maternal Thinking,* 1989 (republished with a new preface, 1995) is her most detailed examination of these themes. Her essay 'Thinking mothers/conceiving birth', in D. Bassin, M. Honey and M.M. Kaplan (eds), *Representations of Motherhood,* New Haven, Connecticut, Yale University Press, 1994, pp. 29–45, reflects on responses to *Maternal Thinking.*

12 Patricia Hill Collins argues that the dangers for racial ethnic children are more fundamental than those Ruddick mentions. High infant mortality rates, poverty, drugs, crime and industrial pollutants are characteristic vulnerabilities which require their mothers' attention. P. Collins, 'Shifting the center: race, class and feminist theorizing about motherhood', in E. N. Glenn, G. Chang and L. R. Forcey (eds), *Mothering: Ideology, Experience and Agency,* New York, Routledge, 1994 pp. 49–52.

13 See J. Benjamin, *The Bonds of Love: Psychoanalysis, Feminism and the Problem of Domination,* New York, Pantheon, 1988, pp. 126–8. Benjamin's analysis draws on D.W. Winnicott's notion of a 'transitional space' between children and their mothers.

14 J. Lazarre, *The Mother Knot,* New York, McGraw-Hill, 1976, p. ix.

15 S.L. Hoagland, *Lesbian Ethics: Toward New Value,* Palo Alto, California, Institute of Lesbian Studies, 1988, pp. 69ff.

16 See also S. Mullett, 'Moral talk', *Resources for Feminist Research,* 1987, vol. 16, pp. 32–5; N. Noddings, 'Conversation as moral education', *Journal of Moral Education,* 1994, vol. 23, pp. 107–18; J. Sabini and M. Silver, 'A plea for gossip', in J. Sabini and M. Silver, *Moralities of Everyday Life,* Oxford, Oxford University Press, 1982, pp. 89–106; M. Walker, 'Moral understandings: alternative "epistemology" for a feminist ethics', *Hypatia,* 1989, vol. 4, pp. 15–28; M. Walker, 'Feminism, ethics and the question of theory', *Hypatia,* 1992, vol. 7, pp. 23–38;

194 Notes

M. Walker, 'Keeping moral space open: new images of ethics consulting', *Hastings Center Report*, 1994, vol. 23, pp. 33–40.
17 Ruddick acknowledges and addresses this difficulty in 'Thinking mothers/conceiving birth'. Again, though, rather than considering continuities between birthgiving and mothering – where this is appropriate – she reflects on birthing and mothering as distinctive practices.
18 C. Whitbeck, 'The maternal instinct', in Treblicot, *Mothering*.
19 See, for example, Dinnerstein, *The Mermaid*; Chodorow, *Reproduction of Mothering*; J. Flax, 'The conflict between nurture and autonomy in mother–daughter relationships and within feminism', *Feminist Studies*, 1978, vol. 4, pp. 171–89; L. Irigaray, 'And the one doesn't stir without the other', trans. H. Wenzel, *Signs*, 1981, vol. 7, pp. 60–7; Benjamin, *Bonds of Love*.
20 Lazarre, *Mother Knot*, passim.
21 Bernard, *Future of Motherhood*, p. 81.
22 Collins, 'Shifting the center', p. 57.
23 Women of ethnic minorities report with dismay how frequently they express their own powerlessness by abusing their children. See, for example, L. Maracle, 'Normal v. natural', in *I Am Woman*, North Vancouver, British Columbia, Write-on Press, 1988, pp. 165–6.
24 C. Gudorf, 'Parenting, mutual love and sacrifice', in B. Andolsen, C. Gudorf and M. Pellauer (eds), *Women's Consciousness, Women's Conscience: A Reader in Feminist Ethics*, Minneapolis, Minnesota, Winston Press, 1985, p. 178.
25 *Ibid.*, p. 179.
26 *Ibid.*, p. 190. See also Irigaray, 'And the one doesn't stir '.
27 Noddings, *Caring*, p. 52.
28 See, for example, Hoagland, *Lesbian Ethics*; B. Houston, 'Caring and exploitation', *Hypatia*, 1989, vol. 5, pp. 115–19: B. Houston, 'Prolegomena to future caring', in D. Shogan (ed.), *A Reader in Feminist Ethics*, Toronto, Canadian Scholars' Press, 1992, pp. 109–27.
29 See also R. Schmitt, 'Nurturing fathers: some reflections about caring', *Journal of Social Philosophy*, 1993, vol. 24, pp. 138–51. This theme will be developed in the discussion of other caring relationships in later chapters.
30 A. Lorde, 'Man child: a black lesbian feminist's response', in A. Lorde, *Sister Outsider*, Freedom, California, Crossing Press, 1984, p. 76. Quoted in MT, p. 106.
31 The phrase comes from I. Murdoch, 'The idea of perfection', in I. Murdoch, *The Sovereignty of Good*, London, Routledge & Kegan Paul, 1970, pp. 1–45.
32 See Held, 'Non-contractual society' and *Feminist Morality*, pp. 192–214, for an elaboration of the ethically significant distinctions between contractual and maternal relations.
33 I am grateful to an anonymous reader for Routledge for this point.
34 See also, L. Code, *What Can She Know? Feminist Theory and the Constitution of Knowledge*, Ithaca, New York, Cornell University Press, 1991, pp. 92–3.

35 N. Chodorow and S. Contratto, 'The fantasy of the perfect mother', in B. Thorne and M. Yalom (eds), *Rethinking the Family: Some Feminist Questions*, New York, Longman, 1982, pp. 54–75, suggest historical, psychic and cultural origins for the blame and idealization of mothering. See also, Benjamin, *Bonds of Love*, pp. 206ff.

36 A. Klein, 'Finding a self: Buddhist and feminist perspectives', in C. Atkinson, C. Buchanan and M. Mills (eds), *Shaping New Vision: Gender and Values in American Culture*, Ann Arbor, Michigan, UMI Research Press, 1987, pp. 191–218.

37 The work of ethnic racial theory is relevant here. The difficulties facing many mothers in social contexts of inequality and poverty point to the flaws of this conception of individual mothers' ethical possibilities. See, for example, Collins, 'Shifting the center'.

38 Lazarre, *Mother Knot*, p. 27.

39 Code, 'Second persons', pp. 367–8.

40 J. Attanucci, 'In whose terms: a new perspective on self, role and relationship', in C. Gilligan, J. Ward and J. Taylor (eds), *Mapping the Moral Domain: A Contribution of Women's Thinking to Psychological Theory and Education*, Cambridge, Massachusetts, Center for the Study of Gender, Education and Human Development, 1988, pp. 201–23, discusses the problems that role socialization creates for mothers in distinguishing their first and third person perspectives. Everingham, *Mothering and Modernity*, makes the additional point that the needs themselves are not given.

41 I owe this phrasing to Jim Tully.

42 Chodorow and Contratto, 'Fantasy of the perfect mother', pp. 70–1, claim that this kind of model is common to much of mothering theory.

43 *Ibid.*, p. 71. To this end Chodorow and Contratto point to feminist uses of psychoanalytic object-relations theory, and cognitive developmental psychology in the Piagetian tradition, as fruitful lines of enquiry.

44 Rossiter, *From Private to Public*, p. 279 (hereafter FPP followed by page numbers).

45 This sensitivity is endorsed by the recent anthology Glenn, Chang and Forcey, *Mothering*.

46 See P. Lauritzen, 'A feminist ethic and the new romanticism – mothering as a model of moral relations', *Hypatia*, 1989, vol. 4, pp. 29–44 for a criticism of biological maternalism.

47 See Held, *Feminist Morality*, pp. 80–4, for a discussion of the possible significance of the personal and biological aspects of birthing for ethical experience.

48 Women's disempowerment through the medicalization of childbirth is a common theme in feminist writing. See, for example, Rich, *Of Woman Born*, pp. 149–82; Rothman, *Recreating Motherhood*, pp. 152–84.

49 One mother, Tina, recalled childbirth as a joyful discovery of her bodily potential, but the overwhelming force of contradictory practices of bodily restriction and objectification rendered this experience idiosyncratic and unacceptable to her self-understanding (FPP 226–32).

50 See, for example, Bernard, *Future of Motherhood*; Lazarre, *Mother Knot*.
Rossiter cites D. Hobson, 'Housewives: isolation as oppression', in
Women's Studies Group, Centre For Contemporary Cultural Studies
(eds), *Woman Take Issue*, London, Hutchinson, 1978 (FPP 285).
51 See also N. Fraser, 'What's critical about critical theory? The case of
Habermas and gender', in Nancy Fraser (ed.), *Unruly Practices: Power,
Discourse and Gender in Contemporary Social Theory*, Minneapolis,
University of Minnesota Press, 1989.
52 A more extended treatment of this theme is given in Z. Eistenstein,
The Radical Future of Liberal Feminism, New York, Longmans, 1981.
53 These difficulties are further compounded by the demands of other
life activities, like caring for partners or paid employment, which fail
to recognize the limits and possibilities of mothering.

CHAPTER 2: FRIENDSHIP

1 N. Badhwar (ed.), *Friendship: A Philosophical Reader*, Ithaca, New York,
Cornell University Press, 1993, is a notable exception.
2 D. Bolotin, *Plato's Dialogue on Friendship: An Interpretation of the 'Lysis'
with a New Translation*, Ithaca, New York, Cornell University Press,
1979; Aristotle, *Nicomachean Ethics*, trans. W.D. Ross, Oxford, Oxford
University Press, 1925 (hereafter NE followed by page and line
number).
3 Cicero, *Laelius De Amicitia*, trans. W.A. Falconer, London, Heinemann,
1964; M. de Montaigne, 'Of friendship' in *The Complete Essays of
Montaigne*, trans. D. Frame, Stanford, Stanford University Press, 1958;
F. Bacon, 'Of friendship', in F. Bacon, *Essays*, London, J.M. Dent, 1906;
H.Thoreau, 'Friendship', in *A Week on the Concord and Merrimack Rivers*,
Boston, Walden, 1906; R. Emerson, 'Friendship', in *The Complete Essays
and Other Writings*, New York, Random House, 1940.
4 C. Card, 'Virtues and moral luck', in *Institute for Legal Studies, Working
Paper*, Series 1, Madison, University of Wisconsin–Madison Law
School, 1985, p. 11, notes that Nietzsche observed this blurring of the
distinction between good enemies and good friends.
5 This revaluation is not, of course, solely a product of feminist theory.
A notable account of concern, in ethics, for the attachments and
commitments of persons has been given in L. Blum, *Friendship,
Altruism and Morality*, London, Routledge & Kegan Paul, 1980
(hereafter FAM followed by page numbers). See also B. Williams,
'Persons, character and morality', in *Moral Luck*, New York, Cambridge University Press, 1981, pp. 1–19; B. Williams, *Ethics and the
Limits of Philosophy*, Cambridge, Massachusetts, Harvard University
Press, 1985.
6 V. Held, 'Feminism and moral theory', in E. Kittay and D. Meyers
(eds), *Women and Moral Theory*, Totowa, New Jersey, Rowman
Littlefield, 1987, p. 117; V. Held, *Feminist Morality: Transforming
Culture, Society and Politics*, Chicago, University of Chicago Press,
1993, briefly alludes to this move. More emphatic appeals are made

by L. Code, 'Second persons', in M. Hanen and K. Nielsen (eds), *Science, Morality & Feminist Theory*, Calgary, Alberta, University of Calgary Press, 1987, pp. 369–71, and L. Code, *What Can She Know? Feminist Theory and the Constitution of Knowledge*, Ithaca, New York, Cornell University Press, 1991, pp. 95–105. See also M. Friedman, 'Feminism and modern friendship: dislocating the community', *Ethics*, 1989, vol. 99, pp. 275–90; M. Friedman, *What Are Friends For? Feminist Perspectives on Personal Relationships and Moral Theory*, Ithaca, New York, Cornell University Press, 1993.

7 For example, C. Smith-Rosenberg, 'The female world of love and ritual: relations between women in nineteenth-century America', *Signs*, 1975, vol. 1, pp. 1–29; L. Faderman, *Surpassing the Love of Men: Romantic Friendship and Love Between Women from the Renaissance to the Present*, New York, William Morrow, 1981; J. Raymond, *A Passion for Friends: Toward a Philosophy of Female Affection*, Boston, Beacon Press, 1986; S. Myers, *The Bluestocking Circle: Women, Friendship and the Life of Mind*, New York, Oxford University Press, 1990.

8 In her discussion of nineteenth-century attitudes to female friendships, P. Nestor, *Female Friendships and Communities: Charlotte Brontë, George Eliot, Elizabeth Gaskell*, Oxford, Clarendon Press, 1985, pp. 7–27, identifies at least five different ploys that contribute to this process of devaluation.

9 I am thinking here specifically of Card, 'Virtues and moral luck'; Friedman, 'Feminism and modern friendship'; S. Bartky, 'Feeding egos and tending wounds: deference and disaffection in women's emotional labor', in S. Bartky, *Femininity and Domination: Studies in the Phenomenology of Oppression*, New York, Routledge, 1990, pp. 99–119.

10 See, for example, N. Sherman, 'Aristotle on friendship and the shared life', *Philosophy and Phenomenological Research*, 1987, vol. 47, p. 593; M. Nussbaum, *The Fragility of Goodness: Luck and Ethics in Greek Tragedy and Philosophy*, Cambridge, Cambridge University Press, 1986, pp. 371, 499.

11 J. Raymond, 'Female friendship and feminist ethics', in B. Andolsen, C. Gudorf and M. Pellauer (eds), *Women's Consciousness: Women's Conscience*, Minneapolis, Minnesota, Winston Press, 1985, pp. 161–74, for example, connects Aristotle's conception of friendship with dependence on battlefield camaraderie.

12 It is difficult to hold to this position with accuracy, however, since Aristotle's inclusion of maternal relationships in *philia* allows women access to the attachment. At the same time the highest ethical possibilities of *philia* are accessible only to men. Little guidance is given as to precisely where on this scale generic terms may convert to gendered.

13 Sherman, 'Aristotle on friendship', pp. 594–5.

14 Aristotle, *Rhetorica*, 1380b35–1381a1, cited by Nussbaum, *Fragility*, p. 355, and J. Cooper, 'Aristotle on friendship', in A. Rorty (ed.), *Essays on Aristotle's Ethics*, Berkeley, University of California Press, 1980, p. 302. Much of the following discussion also owes a considerable debt to these two sources.

15 Cooper, 'Aristotle on friendship', pp. 313–14, explains that this 'concern' will be limited to the extent that it is compatible with the existence and continuation of the special properties of pleasantness and advantageousness on which the friendships are grounded.
16 See also *ibid.*, pp. 314–15.
17 Nussbaum, *Fragility,* p. 356.
18 The problem has some resemblance to, and perhaps is connected with, that famous conundrum of the *Nicomachean Ethics*: the apparent confusion between 'the good for man' and 'the good man'. For an exploration of the latter see, for example, K. Wilkes, 'The good man and the good for man in Aristotle's ethics', in Rorty, *Essays*, pp. 341–57.
19 This phrase is taken from F. Schoeman, 'Aristotle on the good of friendship', *Australasian Journal of Philosophy,* 1985, vol. 63, pp. 269–82, in which he suggests that Aristotle conflates the distinction between a person's good qualities and his good for his own sake (p. 275). See also J. Annas, 'Plato and Aristotle on friendship and altruism', *Mind*, 1977, vol. 86, pp. 548–50, for a similar argument.
20 Nussbaum interprets Aristotle in this light when she claims that, far from overriding their particularity, the 'alikeness' of virtue in each *philosi* reminds us what important constituents of individuality can be shared (*Fragility,* p. 357).
21 Compare, for example, Schoeman, 'Aristotle on the good of friendship'.
22 Sherman, 'Aristotle on friendship', p. 597.
23 See also J. Annas, 'Self-love in Aristotle', *The Southern Journal of Philosophy,* 1988, vol. 27, pp. 1–18.
24 Cooper, 'Aristotle on friendship', p. 322. See also Nussbaum, *Fragility,* p. 364.
25 Compare Cooper, 'Aristotle on friendship', p. 339, note 23.
26 See *ibid.*, pp. 324–30 for an insightful discussion of this theme.
27 'Friendship [*philia*] is said to be equality' (NE 1157b36). 'But there is *another* kind of friendship [*philia*], viz., that which involves an inequality between the parties, e.g., that of father to son and in general elder to younger, that of man to wife and in general that of ruler to subject' (NE 1158b12–15) (my emphasis).
28 See also H. Hutter, *Politics as Friendship: The Origins of Classical Notions of Politics in the Theory and Practice of Friendship*, Waterloo, Ontario, Wilfred Laurier University Press, 1978, especially pp. 102–16, 184–5.
29 See Schoeman, 'Aristotle on the good of friendship', for a discussion of the ethical significance of the conflict and vulnerability at the heart of respect for the independence of the other.
30 Some commentators are more generous to Aristotle on this point. Perhaps his reference to the 'sharing of conversation and thought' (NE 1170b) allows for this kind of intimacy. See L. May and R. Strikwerda, 'Male friendship and intimacy', *Hypatia*, 1992, vol. 7, pp. 110–25.
31 L. Blum, 'Particularity and responsiveness', in J. Kagan and S. Lamb (eds), *The Emergence of Morality in Young Children*, Chicago, University of Chicago Press, 1987, pp. 306–37 (reprinted in L. Blum, *Moral*

Perception and Particularity, Cambridge, Cambridge University Press, 1994, pp. 183–214).

32 *Ibid.*, p. 330.

33 *Ibid.*

34 See also M. Friedman, 'Beyond caring: the de-moralization of gender', in Hanen and Nielsen, *Science*, pp. 106–7; 'Friendship and moral growth', *Journal of Value Inquiry*, 1989, vol. 23, pp. 3–6 (reprinted, with revisions, in *What Are Friends For?*, pp. 135–6, 188–95).

35 L. Blum, 'Iris Murdoch and the domain of the moral', *Philosophical Studies*, 1986, vol. 50, pp. 343–67 (reprinted in Blum, *Moral Perception*, pp. 12–29).

36 The discussion originates with C. Gilligan, *In a Different Voice: Psychological Theory and Women's Development*, Cambridge, Massachusetts, Harvard University Press, 1982, and N. Noddings, *Caring: A Feminine Approach to Ethics and Moral Education*, Berkeley, University of California Press, 1984. Other important contributions include: S. Benhabib, 'The generalized and the concrete other: the Kohlberg–Gilligan controversy and moral theory', in Kittay and Meyers, *Women and Moral Theory*, pp. 154–77; M. Walker, 'What does the different voice say? Gilligan's women and moral philosophy', *The Journal of Value Inquiry*, vol. 23, 1989, pp. 123–34; R. Manning, *Speaking from the Heart: A Feminist Perspective on Ethics*, Lanham, Maryland, Rowman & Littlefield, 1992; Friedman, *What Are Friends For?*; V. Held, *Feminist Morality: Transforming Culture, Society, and Politics*, Chicago, University of Chicago Press, 1993.

37 M. Stocker, 'Values and purposes: the limits of teleology and the ends of friendship', *Journal of Philosophy*, vol. 78, 1981, pp. 747–65, discusses this quality as the 'arche' of friendship.

38 Similarly N. Badhwar, 'Introduction: the nature and significance of friendship', in Badhwar, *Friendship*, pp. 26–7, argues that our legitimate expectations of justice from friends must be satisfied 'out of friendship' and not out of compliance with impersonal obligation.

39 L. Rubin, *Just Friends: The Role of Friendship in Our Lives*, New York, Harper & Row, 1985, p. 40.

40 *Ibid.*, pp. 40–1.

41 *Ibid.*, p. 186.

42 *Ibid.*, p. 41ff.

43 *Ibid.*, p. 49.

44 Friedman, 'Friendship and moral growth'.

45 *Ibid.*, p. 7.

46 Compare Bacon, 'Of friendship', p. 83: 'this communicating of a man's self to his friend'.

47 Rubin, *Just Friends*, p. 74.

48 *Ibid.*

49 I owe this formulation of the nature of the relationship to Dick Ounsworth.

50 Other ordering structures, for example race, ethnicity, class and age, are doubtless also significant. See L. Verbrugge, 'The structure of

adult friendship choices', *Social Forces*, vol. 56, 1977, pp. 576–97, for an analysis of cultural constraints on friendship.

51 S. Miller, *Men and Friendship*, Boston: Houghton Mifflin Company, 1983 (hereafter MF followed by page numbers).

52 See also May and Strikwerda, 'Male friendship and intimacy'.

53 Compare L. Thomas, 'Friendship', *Synthese*, 1987, vol. 72, p. 218: 'One does not shop for a friend in the way that one shops for an article of clothing.'

54 Primary sources include N. Chodorow, *The Reproduction of Mothering*, Berkeley, University of California Press, 1978 and Gilligan, *In a Different Voice*. See also L. Rubin, *Just Friends*; *Intimate Strangers: Men and Women Together*, New York, Harper & Row, 1987; L. Pogrebin, *Among Friends*, New York, McGraw-Hill, 1987.

55 G. Little, 'Freud, friendship and politics', in R. Porter and S. Tomaselli (eds), *The Dialectics of Friendship*, London, Routledge, 1989, pp. 143–58, typifies this kind of account of friendship. See also Rubin, *Just Friends*; May and Strikwerda, 'Male friendship and intimacy'.

56 J. Richards, '"Passing the love of women": manly love and Victorian society', in J. Mangan and J. Walvin (eds), *Manliness and Morality: Middle-class Masculinity in Britain and America, 1800–1940*, Manchester, Manchester University Press, 1987, p. 100. See also J. Sattel, 'The inexpressive male: tragedy or sexual politics?', *Social Problems*, 1976, vol. 23, pp. 469–77.

57 Sattel, 'The inexpressive male'.

58 Card, 'Virtues and moral luck'. See also Card, 'Gratitude and obligation', *American Philosophical Quarterly*, 1988, vol. 25, pp. 115–27.

59 Card, 'Virtues and moral luck', pp. 13–15.

60 *Ibid.*, p. 23. M. Shanley, 'Marital slavery and friendship: John Stuart Mill's "The Subjection of Women"', in Badhwar, *Friendship*, pp. 267–84, argues that recognition of the defects of inequalities in marital relations is an impetus for John Stuart Mill's promotion of women's equality. On this point, see also N. Urbinati, 'John Stuart Mill on androgyny and ideal marriage', *Political Theory*, 1991, vol. 19, pp. 626–48.

61 Bartky, 'Feeding egos and tending wounds', especially pp. 111–13.

62 Card, 'Virtues and moral luck', p. 12.

63 *Ibid.*, p. 11.

64 This term is adapted from Bartky's suggestion that unreciprocated emotional support produces epistemic and ethical 'leans'. See Bartky, 'Feeding egos and tending wounds', pp. 111–13.

65 Feminist psychologists such as D. Dinnerstein, *The Mermaid and the Minotaur: Sexual Arrangements and Human Malaise*, New York, Harper & Row, 1976, Chodorow, *Reproduction of Mothering*, and J. Benjamin, *The Bonds of Love: Psychoanalysis, Feminism and the Problem of Domination*, New York, Pantheon, 1988, attribute women's tendencies to merge their identities with those of their intimates to the fact that little girls, unlike little boys, are not required to sever their original identification with their mothers.

66 Raymond, *A Passion For Friends*, pp. 6, 222 (hereafter PF followed by page numbers).
67 Montaigne, 'Of friendship', p. 138.
68 Other feminist writers have, of course, also noted the relative invisibility of women's same-sex relations. See, for example, C. Heilbrun, *Writing a Woman's Life*, New York, Ballantine Books, 1988, pp. 96–108; R. Auchmuty, 'By their friends we shall know them: the lives and networks of some women in North Lambeth, 1880–1940', in *Not a Passing Phase: Reclaiming Lesbians in History, 1840–1985*, Lesbian History Group (eds), London, The Women's Press, 1989, pp. 77–98. See also notes 7, 8 above.
69 This is a common theme in feminist writing. See, for example, E. Freedman, 'Separation as strategy: female institution building and American feminism 1870–1930', *Feminist Studies*, 1979, vol. 5, pp. 512–29; E. Du Bois *et al.*, 'Politics and culture in women's history: a symposium', *Feminist Studies*, 1980, vol. 6, pp. 26–64; B. Solomon, *In the Company of Educated Women*, New Haven, Connecticut, Yale University Press, 1985. Friedman, *What Are Friends For?* discusses the politically subversive potential of friendship. J. Mansbridge, 'The limits of friendship', in J. Pennock and J. Chapman (eds), *Participation in Politics*, New York, Lieber-Atherton, 1975, p. 246–75 and A. Phillips, *Engendering Democracy*, University Park, Pennsylvania, Pennsylvania State University Press, 1991, pp. 120–46, discuss the limits of friendship with respect to political participation.

CHAPTER 3: NURSING

1 I use 'private' here and throughout this work to distinguish relations marked by their informality in contrast to those regarded centrally as formal. This usage is not to be confused with that other common use of 'private' to designate relations regulated primarily by the market in contrast to those occurring within governments and their instrumentalities.
2 Here again I am collapsing an enormous variety of relations into a singular type. Doubtless there are as many relations of nursing care as there are individual nurses and patients and institutional arrangements within which they are situated. In defence of this reduction I can only ask that before judging its employment the reader read on, reflecting on the understanding it permits in the current context of its application.
3 See also S. Gadow, 'Body and self: a dialectic', *Journal of Medicine and Philosophy*, 1980, vol. 5, pp. 172–85.
4 H. Engelhardt, 'Physicians, patients, health care institutions – and the people in between: nurses', in A. Bishop and J. Scudder (eds), *Caring, Curing, Coping: Nurse, Physician, Patient Relationships*. University, Alabama, University of Alabama Press, 1985, pp. 62–79.
5 J. Ashley, *Hospitals, Paternalism and the Role of the Nurse*, New York, Teachers' College Press, 1976; C. Davis, *Gender and the Professional Predicament in Nursing*, Buckingham, Open University Press, 1995.

6 Davis, *Gender and the Professional Predicament*, reports that about 10 per cent of nurses in the United Kingdom are males. Census data for 1986 and 1991 from the Australian Bureau of Statistics indicate that about 7 per cent of nurses in Australia are males (personal communication, 1995). Studies indicate that male nurses accede to authority positions at a disproportionate rate compared with their female colleagues. See L. Hardy, 'Career politics: the case of career histories of selected leading female and male nurses in England and Scotland', in R. White (ed.), *Political Issues in Nursing*, Volume II Chichester, John Wiley, 1986, pp. 69–82.

7 The most detailed treatments of nursing care are given in P. Benner, *From Novice to Expert: Excellence and Power in Clinical Nursing Practice*, Menlo Park, California, Addison-Wesley, 1984, and P. Benner and J. Wrubel, *The Primacy of Caring: Stress and Coping in Health and Illness*, Menlo Park, California, Addison-Wesley, 1989 (hereafter FNE and PC respectively, followed by page numbers). P. Benner and C. Tanner, 'Clinical judgement: how expert nurses use intuition', *American Journal of Nursing*, 1987, vol. 87, pp. 23–31, and P. Benner, 'The role of articulation in understanding practice and experience as sources of knowledge in clinical nursing', in J. Tully (ed.), *Philosophy in an Age of Pluralism: The Philosophy of Charles Taylor in Question*, Cambridge, Cambridge University Press, 1994, pp. 136–55, provide succinct accounts of the practical expertise displayed by nurses. Specifically ethical questions are discussed in P. Benner, 'The moral dimensions of caring', in J. Stevenson and T. Tripp-Reimer (eds), *Knowledge About Care and Caring: State of the Art and Future Developments*, Kansas City, Missouri, American Academy of Nursing, 1990, pp. 5–17.

8 H. Dreyfus and S. Dreyfus, *Mind Over Machine: The Power of Human Intuition and Expertise in the Era of the Computer*, New York, Free Press, 1985.

9 Benner and Tanner, 'Clinical judgement', pp. 23–31.

10 For example, Benner and Tanner, 'Clinical judgement', p. 24, quote an expert's comments on how textbooks cannot provide the experiential knowledge required to read Swan–Ganz wave forms accurately.

11 Benner and Wrubel specifically cite Maurice Merleau-Ponty, Hubert Dreyfus and Michael Polanyi as sources for their phenomenology. It is worth noting that these male philosophers are not known for their gender sensitivity. For feminist critiques of the phenomenological tradition see J. Butler, 'Sexual ideology and phenomenological description: a feminist critique of Merleau-Ponty's phenomenology', in J. Allen and I. Young (eds), *The Thinking Muse: Feminism and Modern French Philosophy*, Bloomington, Indiana University Press, 1989, pp. 85–100; I. Young, 'Pregnant embodiment: subjectivity and alienation', in *Throwing Like a Girl and Other Essays in Feminist Philosophy and Social Theory*, Bloomington, Indiana University Press, 1990, pp. 160–76, and 'Throwing like a girl: a phenomenology of feminine body comportment, motility, and spatiality', in *Throwing Like a Girl*, pp. 141–59.

12 H. Curzer, 'Fry's concept of care in nursing ethics', *Hypatia*, 1993, vol.

8, pp. 174–83, American Nurses' Association, *Educational Preparation for Nurse Practitioners and Assistants to Nurses*, New York, American Nurses' Association, 1965. See J. Liashenko and A. Davis, 'Nurses and physicians on nutritional support: a comparison', *Journal of Medicine and Philosophy*, 1991, vol. 16, pp. 259–83, for an account of the breakdown of this distinction in the case of nutritional care.

13 P. Benner and C. Tanner, 'Clinical judgement', pp. 25–6.

14 I. Murdoch, 'The idea of perfection', in *The Sovereignty of Good*, London, Routledge & Kegan Paul, 1970, pp. 1–45.

15 See also H.L. Nelson, 'Against caring', *Journal of Clinical Ethics*, 1992, vol. 3, pp. 12–14, for another account of this kind of attentiveness – though Nelson distinguishes her analysis from what she construes as the damaging sentimentality of the ethics of caring.

16 See H. Curzer, 'Is care a virtue for health care professionals?', *Journal of Medicine and Philosophy*, 1993, vol. 18, pp. 51–69, for a recent critique of this perspective.

17 L. Blum, 'Vocation, friendship and community: limitations of the personal–impersonal framework', in *Moral Perception and Particularity*, Cambridge, Cambridge University Press, 1994, pp. 98–123, uses the example of teaching relationships to describe his understanding of vocational care.

18 Benner and Wrubel use this term to express the global background of concern characteristic of relationships with 'significant others' (PC 391).

19 S. Gadow, 'Existential advocacy: philosophical foundation of nursing', in S. Spicker and S. Gadow (eds), *Nursing: Images and Ideals: Opening Dialogue with the Humanities*, New York, Springer, 1980, pp. 79–101.

20 *Ibid.*, pp. 91–2.

21 S. Tisdale, *The Sorcerer's Apprentice: Tales of the Modern Hospital*, New York, McGraw-Hill, 1986, pp. 129–30.

22 R. Zaner, 'Chance and morality: the dialysis phenomenon', in V. Kestenbaum (ed.), *The Humanity of the Ill: Phenomenological Perspectives*, Knoxville, University of Tennessee Press, 1982, p. 53.

23 See also M. Rawlinson, 'Medicine's discourse and the practice of medicine', in Kestenbaum, *Humanity of the Ill*, pp. 74–8.

24 Gadow, 'Existential advocacy'. See also Zaner, '"How the hell did I get here?" Reflections on being a patient', in Bishop and Scudder, *Caring, Curing, Coping*, pp. 80–105.

25 S. Gadow, 'Nurse and patient: the caring relationship', in Bishop and Scudder, *Caring, Curing, Coping*, pp. 34–7. See also S. Gadow, 'Touch and technology: two paradigms of patient care', *Journal of Religion and Health*, 1984, vol. 23, pp. 63–6. Gadow makes the point that far from being the cause of alienation, technology brings into view the violation, often overlooked in its less perceptible forms, of reducing the body to a machine.

26 S. Gadow, 'The advocacy covenant: care as clinical subjectivity', in Stevenson and Tripp-Reimer, *Knowledge About Care*, pp. 33–40.

27 S. Gadow, 'Covenant without cure: letting go and holding on in

chronic illness', in J. Watson and M. Ray (eds), *The Ethics of Care and the Ethics of Cure: Synthesis in Chronicity,* New York, National League for Nursing, 1988, p. 14.

28 Gadow, 'The advocacy covenant'.

29 See P. Roth and J. Harrison, 'Orchestrating social change: an imperative in care of the chronically ill', *The Journal of Medicine and Philosophy,* 1991, vol. 16, pp. 343–59, for a critique of these 'autonomy' models which are common in the field of bio-ethics.

30 A. Griffin, 'A philosophical analysis of caring in nursing', *Journal of Advanced Nursing,* 1983, vol. 6, p. 293.

31 In Benner's subdued words, 'Getting appropriate and timely responses from physicians' (PC 140–4).

32 A. Bishop and J. Scudder, *The Practical, Moral and Personal Sense of Nursing: A Phenomenological Philosophy of Practice,* Albany, New York, State University of New York Press, 1990.

33 *Ibid.,* pp. 18–20.

34 A. Kitson, 'An analysis of lay-caring and professional [nursing] caring relationships', *International Journal of Nursing Studies,* 1987, vol. 24, pp. 160–1. S. Swider, B. McElmurry and R. Yarling, 'Ethical decision making in a bureaucratic context by senior nursing students', *Nursing Research,* 1985, vol. 34, pp. 108–12 report that 60 per cent of nurses questioned about a case depicting an ethical dilemma opted for institutional-centred allegiance, rather than patient-centred (9 per cent), or physician-centred (20 per cent).

35 Bishop and Scudder, *Practical, Moral and Personal,* p. 117.

36 *Ibid.,* p. 140.

37 See also K. Pagana, 'Let's stop calling ourselves "patient advocates"', in T. Pence and J. Cantrall (eds), *Ethics in Nursing: An Anthology,* New York, National League of Nursing, 1990, pp. 64–5.

38 Bishop and Scudder, *Practical, Moral and Personal,* pp. 137–44.

39 For examples of the rights and autonomy emphasis see M. Benjamin and J. Curtis, *Ethics in Nursing,* 3rd edn, New York, Oxford University Press, 1992; R. Veatch and S. Fry, *Case Studies in Nursing Ethics,* Philadelphia, J.B. Lippincott, 1987; J. Thompson and H. Thompson, *Bioethical Decision Making for Nurses,* Norwalk, Connecticut, Appleton-Century-Crofts, 1985; A. Jameton, *Nursing Practice: The Ethical Issues,* Englewood Cliffs, New Jersey, Prentice-Hall, 1984.

40 Bishop and Scudder, *Practical, Moral and Personal,* pp. 127–37. The particular protest under attack is that of R. Yarling and B. McElmurry, 'The moral foundation of nursing', *Advances in Nursing Science,* 1986, vol. 8, pp. 63–73.

41 See also C. Gunning, 'The profession itself as a source of stress', in S. Jacobsen and H. McGrath (eds), *Nurses under Stress,* New York, Wiley, 1976, pp. 113–26; M. McClure and M. Nelson, 'Trends in hospital nursing', in L. Aiken (ed.), *Nursing in the 1980s: Crisis, Opportunities, Challenges,* Philadelphia, J.B. Lippincott, 1982, pp. 59–73; A. Cox, 'Role restructuring in hospital nursing', in Aiken, *Nursing in the 1980s,* pp. 75–99; V. Cleland, 'Nursing economics and the control of nursing practice', in Aiken, *Nursing in the 1980s,* pp. 383–97; S. Growe, *Who*

Cares? The Crisis in Canadian Nursing, Toronto, McClelland & Stewart, 1991.

42 Growe, *Who Cares?*. See also A. Davis and M. Aroskar, *Ethical Dilemmas and Nursing Practice*, New York, Appleton-Century-Crofts, 1978.

43 This is a frequently articulated theme. See, for example, S. Reverby, *Ordered to Care: The Dilemma of American Nursing, 1850–1945*, Cambridge, Cambridge University Press, 1987; K. Sacks, 'Does it pay to care?' in E. Abel and M. Nelson (eds), *Circles of Care: Work and Identity in Women's Lives*, Albany, New York, State University of New York Press, 1990, pp. 188–206; L. Mackay, *Nursing a Problem*, Milton Keynes, Open University Press, 1989; S. Tisdale, *Harvest Moon: Portrait of a Nursing Home*, New York, Henry Holt, 1987; J. Salvage, *The Politics of Nursing*, London, Heinemann, 1985; J. Muff, 'Origins of stress in nursing', in E. Smythe (ed.), *Surviving Nursing*, Menlo Park, California, Addison-Wesley, 1984, pp. 13–37; S. Harding, 'Value-laden technologies and the politics of nursing', in S. Spicker and S. Gadow (eds), *Nursing: Images and Ideals: Opening Dialogue with the Humanities*, New York, Springer, 1980, pp. 49–75.

44 Bishop and Scudder, *Practical, Moral and Personal*, p. 132.

45 *Ibid.*, p. 128.

46 *Ibid.*, p. 130.

47 See J. Tully, 'Rights in abilities', *Annals of Scholarship*, 1988, vol. 5, pp. 363–81, for a survey of different historical constructions of the connection between labour obligations and workers' rights in their abilities.

48 S. Reverby, 'A caring dilemma: womanhood and nursing in historical perspective', *Nursing Research*, 1987, vol. 36, pp. 5–11, and *Ordered to Care*.

49 Reverby, 'A caring dilemma', p. 8.

50 Reverby, *Ordered to Care*, pp. 41–3.

51 Reverby, 'Health: women's work', in D. Kotelchuck (ed.), *Prognosis Negative: Crisis in the Health Care System*, New York, Vintage Books, 1976, pp. 176–7.

52 See also M. Lovell, 'Silent but perfect "partners": medicine's use and abuse of women', *Advances in Nursing Science*, 1981, vol. 3, pp. 25–40.

53 Reverby, 'A caring dilemma'.

54 Ashley, *Hospitals, Paternalism*, pp. 49ff.

55 Reverby, 'A caring dilemma', p. 8.

56 Reverby, *Ordered to Care*, p. 200.

57 This discussion draws on the insightful analysis given by Harding, 'Value-laden technologies'.

58 Tisdale, *Harvest Moon*, pp. 103–4.

59 Harding, 'Value-laden technologies', p. 66. See also note 34 above.

60 Growe, *Who Cares?*, pp. 100–1.

61 Harding, 'Value-laden technologies', p. 62. See also J. Ehrenreich and B. Ehrenreich, 'Hospital workers: a case study in the "new working class"', in Kotelchuck, *Prognosis Negative*, pp. 191–2.

62 Late nineteenth-century clashes are described in Reverby, *Ordered to Care*, pp. 122–42, especially pp. 131–6.
63 Growe, *Who Cares?*, pp. 98ff.; M. Campbell, 'Accounting for care: a framework for analysing change in Canadian nursing', in R. White (ed.), *Political Issues in Nursing: Past, Present and Future, Volume III*, Chichester, John Wiley & Sons Ltd, 1988, pp. 53–5.
64 Ehrenreich and Ehrenreich, 'Hospital workers', p. 192.
65 Growe, *Who Cares?*, pp. 132–54.
66 D. Kotelchuck, 'The health-care delivery system', in *Prognosis Negative*, pp. 5–30.
67 S. Hewa and R. Hetherington, 'Specialists without spirit: crisis in the nursing profession', *Journal of Medical Ethics*, 1990, vol. 16, pp. 179–84.
68 Growe, *Who Cares?*, pp. 120–1
69 See L. Code, *What Can She Know? Feminist Theory and the Constitution of Knowledge*, Ithaca, New York, Cornell University Press, 1991, pp. 222–50, for a perceptive discussion relating the devaluation of nurses' knowledge to the use of the knowledge/experience distinction.
70 See, for example, T. Sheard, 'The structure of conflict in nurse–physician relations', *Supervisor Nurse*, 1980, vol. 11, pp. 14–15, 17–18; B. Kalisch and P. Kalisch, 'An analysis of the sources of physician–nurse conflict', in J. Muff (ed.), *Socialization, Sexism and Stereotyping: Women's Issues in Nursing*, St Louis, Missouri, C.V. Mosby Co., 1982, pp. 221–33; Lovell, 'Silent but perfect "partners"', and 'Daddy's little girl: the lethal effects of paternalism in nursing', in Muff, *Socialization, Sexism and Stereotyping*, pp. 210–20; A. Baumgart, 'Women, nursing and feminism: an interview with Alice J. Baumgart by Margaret Allen', *Canadian Nurse*, 1985, vol. 1, pp. 20–2; M. Aroskar, 'Ethical relationships between nurses and physicians: goals and realities – a nursing perspective', in Bishop and Scudder, *Caring, Curing, Coping*, pp. 44–61; H. Engelhardt, 'Physicians, patients, health care'; Growe, *Who Cares?*, pp. 113–31. Many of Benner's exemplars include accounts of difficult nurse–physician relations. Nurse–physician relations are discussed explicitly in FNE, pp. 140–4.
71 L. Stein, 'The doctor–nurse game', *American Journal of Nursing*, 1968, vol. 68, pp. 101–5.
72 *Ibid.*, p. 75.
73 M. Campbell, 'Accounting for care', p. 65.
74 This term is taken from Dorothy Smith's Foucaultian influenced work on the social organization of knowledge. It refers to the loosely co-ordinated 'sites of governing, management, administration, discursive relations, professional associations, etc.'. Campbell, 'Accounting for care', p. 46.
75 *Ibid.*, pp. 49–51.
76 *Ibid.*, pp. 52–3.

CHAPTER 4: CITIZENSHIP

1 For a review of recent discussions of citizenship from the perspective of identity and civic virtue see W. Kymlicka and W. Norman, 'Return

of the citizen: a survey of recent work on citizenship theory', *Ethics*, 1994, vol. 104, pp. 352–81.

2 See H. Pitkin, 'Justice: on relating private and public', *Political Theory*, 1981, vol. 9, pp. 328–31, for a discussion of 'the public' that incorporates similar themes.

3 Rawls and Kohlberg are leading, contemporary proponents of this kind of characterization of the norms formed in what they call, respectively, 'social institutions' and 'the public sphere'. See J. Rawls, *A Theory of Justice*, Cambridge, Massachusetts, Harvard University Press, 1971; L. Kohlberg, *Collected Papers on Moral Development and Moral Education*, Cambridge, Massachusetts, Harvard University, Moral Education Research Foundation, 1971.

4 This theme is developed in C. Card, 'Gender and moral luck', in O. Flanagan and A. Rorty (eds), *Identity, Character and Morality: Essays in Moral Psychology*, Cambridge, Massachusetts, MIT Press, 1990, pp. 199–218.

5 The problem of clustered oppositions is a common theme in feminist discussions. In particular the alignment of the opposition between masculine and feminine with oppositions between (for example) active and passive, reason and emotion, principled and sensitive, has come under intense scrutiny for its tendency to encourage illegitimate stereotypes. See J. Grimshaw, *Philosophy and Feminist Thinking*, Minneapolis, University of Minnesota Press, 1986, pp. 42–7, for a discussion of this problem in the context of Kantian ethics.

6 This is the kind of move that is attributed to so-called 'maternalists', Sara Ruddick and Jean Elshtain, by M. Dietz, 'Citizenship with a feminist face: the problem of maternal thinking', *Political Theory*, 1985, vol. 13, pp. 19–37 and C. Mouffe, 'Feminism, citizenship and radical democratic politics', in *The Return of the Political*, London, Verso, 1993, pp. 74–89.

7 Recent analyses of these gendered distinctions in political thought and practice include S. Okin, *Women in Western Political Thought*, Princeton, New Jersey, Princeton University Press, 1979; J. Elshtain, *Public Man, Private Woman: Women in Social and Political Thought*, Princeton, New Jersey, Princeton University Press, 1981; A. Saxonhouse, *Women in the History of Political Thought*, New York, Praeger, 1985; K. Jones and A. Jonasdottir (eds), *The Political Interests of Gender: Developing Theory and Research with a Feminist Face*, London, Sage, 1988; C. Pateman, *The Disorder of Women: Democracy, Feminism and Political Theory*, Stanford, Stanford University Press, 1989.

8 N. Fraser, 'Rethinking the public sphere: a contribution to the critique of actually existing democracy', *Social Text*, 1990, vol. 25/26, p. 57.

9 E. Boris and P. Bardaglio, 'The transformation of patriarchy: the historic role of the state', in I. Diamond (ed.), *Families, Politics, and Public Policy*, New York, Longman, 1983, pp. 70–93; H. Hernes, 'The transition from private to public dependence', in *Welfare State and Woman Power: Essays in State Feminism*, Oslo, Norwegian University Press, 1987, pp. 31–49; N. Fraser, 'Talking about needs: interpretive contests as political conflicts in welfare-state societies', *Ethics*, 1989,

vol. 99, pp. 291–313; C. Pateman, 'The patriarchal welfare state', in *The Disorder of Women: Democracy, Feminism and Political Theory*, Stanford, Stanford University Press, 1989, pp. 179–209; A. Bullock, 'Community care: ideology and lived experience', in R. Ng, G. Walker and J. Muller (eds), *Community Organization and the Canadian State*, Toronto, Garamond Press, 1990, pp. 65–82; P. Evans, 'The sexual division of poverty: consequences of gendered caring', in C. Baines, P. Evans and S. Neysmith (eds), *Women's Caring: Feminist Perspectives on Social Welfare*, Toronto, McLelland & Stewart, 1991, pp. 169–203.

10 Elshtain, *Public Man, Private Woman*, p. 12.

11 Many feminist theorists have been active in tracing the historical dynamics of the categories 'public' and 'private'. See note 7, above; L. Nicholson, 'Feminist theory: the private and the public', in C. Gould (ed.), *Beyond Domination: New Perspectives on Women and Philosophy*, Totowa, New Jersey, Rowman & Allanfield, 1983, pp. 221–30, and *Gender and History: The Limits of Social Theory in the Age of the Family*, New York, Columbia University Press, 1986; C. Pateman, *The Sexual Contract*, Stanford, Stanford University Press, 1988, and 'Feminist critiques of the public/private dichotomy', in *The Disorder of Women*, pp. 118–40; M. Shanley and C. Pateman (eds), *Feminist Interpretations and Political Theory*, University Park, Pennsylvania, Pennsylvania State University Press, 1991.

12 One of the most famous statements of this theme in recent times is given by C. Lasch, *Haven in a Heartless World: The Family Besieged*, New York, Basic Books, 1977. Another version seems to be flourishing in contemporary debates concerning the links between public disharmony and an alleged decline in 'family values'. See J. Klein *et al.*, 'Whose family? who makes the choices? whose values?', *Newsweek*, 8 June 1992, pp. 18–27; W. Gairdner, *The War Against the Family: A Parent Speaks Out*, Toronto, Stoddart, 1992.

13 A. Baier, 'Cartesian persons', in *Postures of the Mind: Essays on Mind and Morals*, Minneapolis, University of Minnesota Press, 1985, pp. 84–6. See also L. Code, *What Can She Know? Feminist Theory and the Constitution of Knowledge*, Ithaca, New York, Cornell University Press, 1991, pp. 82–7, for a discussion of Baier's understanding of 'second persons'.

14 O. Flanagan and K. Jackson, 'Justice, care, and gender: the Kohlberg–Gilligan debate revisited', *Ethics*, 1987, vol. 97, p. 631.

15 Unpublished section of A. Baier, 'What do women want in a moral theory?', *Nous*, 1985, vol. 19, pp. 53–64, quoted by Flanagan and Jackson, 'Justice, care, and gender', p. 630.

16 A. Baier, 'Poisoning the wells', in *Postures of the Mind*, pp. 271–2.

17 A. Baier, 'Trust and antitrust', *Ethics*, 1986, vol. 96, p. 245.

18 K. Addelson, 'What do women do? Some radical implications of Carol Gilligan's ethics', in K. Addelson, *Impure Thoughts: Essays on Philosophy, Feminism and Ethics*, Philadelphia, Temple University Press, 1991, pp. 204–5.

19 Card, 'Gender and moral luck', pp. 211–14.

20   The application of the term 'social housekeeping' to women's public activities in the Progressivist era is an example of the practice of trivialization of citizen practices in which women engage.

21   Feminist projects directed towards this end are often designated 'cultural feminist' in virtue of their alleged tendency to promote women's interests in terms of their culturally ascribed roles and attributes. See L. Alcoff, 'Cultural feminism versus post-structuralism: the identity crisis in feminist theory', *Signs*, 1988, vol. 13, pp. 405–36. Apart from discontinuities between roles and attributes actually exercised and those culturally ascribed, it is difficult to imagine how any such reversal that attained evaluative parity with attributes culturally ascribed to men would hold its own ascriptions intact. Not only inferior value, but dependency, subordination and lack of decision-making power are also intrinsic to these culturally ascribed feminine traits.

22   Feminist projects directed towards this end are often designated 'liberal feminist' in virtue of their alleged tendency to promote women's interests by increasing their access to citizenship activites as defined within the Western liberal tradition. See A. Jaggar, *Feminist Politics and Human Nature*, Totowa, New Jersey, Rowman & Allanfield, 1983, pp. 173–206. In contrast, projects that promote more active engagement of men in the private sphere are more commonly included in 'cultural feminist' congeries for their focus on the significance of practices culturally ascribed to women.

23   Fraser, 'Rethinking the public sphere', pp. 63–5.

24   See V. Held, *Feminist Morality: Transforming Culture, Society and Politics*, Chicago, University of Chicago Press, 1993, pp. 175–82.

25   E. Cameron, 'Woman-think '92', *Chatelaine*, September 1992, pp. 88ff; Klein *et al.*, 'Whose family?'; Gairdner, *The War Against the Family*. Exclusive mothering by women has many defenders, for example: J. Bowlby, *Maternal Care and Mental Health*, New York, Schocken, 1966; S. Fraiberg, *Every Child's Birthright: In Defence of Mothering*, New York, Basic Books, 1977; Lasch, *Haven in a Heartless World*; Elshtain, *Public Man, Private Woman*; B. Berger and P. Berger, *The War Over the Family: Capturing the Middle Ground*, Garden City, New York, Anchor Books, 1983.

26   A. Hochschild, *The Second Shift: Inside the Two-job Marriage*, New York, Viking, 1989.

27   See J. Tronto, *Moral Boundaries: A Political Argument for an Ethic of Care*, New York, Routledge, 1993, for a political argument for care in these terms.

28   According to Hochschild, *The Second Shift*, the number of mothers with children under the age of 6 in the paid workforce increased from 23 per cent to 54 per cent in the United States between 1950 and 1986.

29   H. Hernes, *Welfare State and Woman Power: Essays in State Feminism*, Oslo, Norwegian University Press, 1987, p. 124.

30   S. Neysmith, 'From community care to a social model of care', in C. Baines, P. Evans and S. Neysmith (eds), *Women's Caring: Feminist*

Perspectives on Social Welfare, Toronto, McLelland & Stewart, 1991, pp. 275ff. See also C. Ungerson, *Policy is Personal: Sex, Gender and Informal Care*, London, Tavistock, 1987; G. Dalley, *Ideologies of Caring: Rethinking Community and Collectivism*, London, Macmillan, 1988; N. Glazer, 'Overlooked, overworked: women's unpaid and paid work in the health services' "cost crisis",' *International Journal of Health Services*, 1988, vol. 18, pp. 119–37.

31 Neysmith, 'From community care', p. 275. See also Dalley, *Ideologies of Caring*.

32 E. Pleck, *Domestic Tyranny: The Making of Social Policy Against Family Violence from Colonial Times to the Present*, New York, Oxford University Press, 1987; L. Gordon, *Heroes of their Own Lives: The Politics and History of Family Violence, Boston, 1880–1960*, New York, Viking Press, 1988.

33 See A. Phillips, *Engendering Democracy*, University Park, Pennsylvania, Pennsylvania State University Press, 1991, pp. 126ff. and *Democracy and Difference*, University Park, Pennsylvania, Pennsylvania State University Press, 1993, pp. 110ff., for discussion of the clash between the participatory demands of political activities and caring responsibilities.

34 Dalley, *Ideologies of Caring*, pp. 21–5 discusses the reproduction of the social organization of family life in the public sphere. See also Neysmith, 'From community care'.

35 See Fraser, 'Talking about needs'.

36 *Ibid.* pp. 291–4, for a general discussion of the problems of this kind of 'thin' needs recognition.

37 I owe some of my phrasing of this point to Neysmith, 'From community care', pp. 273–4, who notes that none of the essays published in the anthology of feminist perspectives on social welfare in which her article is included, give 'even a hint that women were trying to abdicate their caring roles'. For a selection of other feminist research providing evidence for this conclusion see J. Finch and D. Groves, *A Labour of Love: Women, Work and Caring*, London, Routledge & Kegan Paul, 1983; S. Stephens and J. Christianson, *Informal Care of the Elderly*, Lexington, Massachusetts, Lexington Books, 1986; A. Kahn and S. Kamerman, *Child Care: Facing the Hard Choices*, Dover, Massachusetts, Auburn House, 1987; Hernes, *Welfare State and Woman Power*; Reverby, *Ordered to Care: The Dilemma of American Nursing, 1850–1945*, Cambridge, Cambridge University Press, 1987; Ungerson, *Policy is Personal*; E. Abel and M. Nelson, *Circles of Care: Work and Identity in Women's Lives*, Albany, New York, State University of New York Press, 1990.

38 N. Fraser, 'After the family wage: gender equity and the welfare state', *Political Theory*, 1994, vol. 22, pp. 591–618, provides an insightful analysis of the relative merits of these alternative strategies.

39 Critics of the public value of the so-called 'ethic of care' abound. For 'mainstream' views see M. Ignatieff, 'Citizenship and moral narcissism', *Political Quarterly*, 1989, vol. 60, pp. 63–74; W. Kymlicka, *Contemporary Political Philosophy: An Introduction*, Oxford, Oxford

University Press, 1990. Feminist critics include Dietz, 'Citizenship with a feminist face'; D. Rhode, *Justice and Gender: Sex Discrimination and the Law,* Cambridge, MA, Harvard University Press, 1989; Card, 'Gender and moral luck'; E. Spelman, 'The virtue of feeling and the feeling of virtue', in C. Card (ed.), *Feminist Ethics,* Kansas, University Press of Kansas, 1991, pp. 213–32; C. Mouffe, 'Feminism, citizenship and radical democratic politics', in *The Return of the Political,* London, Verso, 1993, pp. 74–89.

40 This complaint is frequently levelled at C. Gilligan, *In a Different Voice: Psychological Theory and Women's Development,* Cambridge, Harvard University Press,1982 and N. Noddings, *Caring: A Feminine Approach to Ethics and Moral Education,* Berkeley, California, University of California Press, 1984.

41 See, for example, the earlier discussions of the work of Ruddick in Chapter 1, Raymond in Chapter 2 and Benner in Chapter 3.

42 For general discussions of welfare provisions in the United States see, for example, R. Cloward and F. Piven, *Regulating the Poor: The Functions of Public Welfare,* New York, Pantheon, 1971; I. Glasser, 'Prisoners of benevolence: power versus liberty in the welfare state', in W. Gaylin *et al.* (eds), *Doing Good: The Limits of Benevolence,* New York, Pantheon, 1978, pp. 99–186; W. Graebner, *The Engineering of Consent and Authority in Twentieth-century America,* Madison, Wisconsin, University of Wisconsin Press, 1987. The discussion of Progressivism in M. Minow, *Making All the Difference: Inclusion, Exclusion and American Law,* Ithaca, New York, Cornell University Press, 1990, pp. 239–66, provides a useful guide to developments during the early twentieth century. For accounts of deformations of authority see P. Wilding, *Professional Power and Social Welfare,* London, Routledge & Kegan Paul, 1982; R. Sartorius, *Paternalism,* Minneapolis, Minnesota, University of Minnesota Press, 1983. For feminist perspectives see H. Holter, *Patriarchy in a Welfare Society,* Oslo, Universitetsforlaget, 1984; J. Dale and P. Foster, 'Welfare professionals and the control of women', in *Feminists and State Welfare,* London, Routledge & Kegan Paul, 1986, pp. 81–104; G. Pascall, *Social Policy: A Feminist Analysis,* London, Tavistock, 1986. In the Canadian context see C. Baines, 'The professions and an ethic of care', in Baines, Evans and Neysmith, *Women's Caring,* pp. 36–72, and the analysis of Canadian hospital services under Medicare in S. Growe, *Who Cares? The Crisis in Canadian Nursing,* Toronto, McClelland & Stewart, 1991.

43 J. Habermas, *Theory of Communicative Action. Vol. 2: Lifeworld and System: A Critique of Functionalist Reason,* trans. T. McCarthy, Boston, Beacon Press, 1987.

44 M. Foucault, *Discipline and Punish: The Birth of the Prison,* trans. A. Sheridan, New York, Vintage Books, 1979.

45 The following summary draws on Hernes, *Welfare State and Woman Power;* A. Sassoon (ed.), *Women and the State: The Shifting Boundaries of Public and Private,* London, Hutchinson, 1987; B. Siim, 'Towards a feminist rethinking of the welfare state', in Jones and Jonasdottir, *Political Interests of Gender,* pp. 160–86; J. Lewis and G. Astrom,

'Equality, difference and state welfare: labor market and family policies in Sweden', *Feminist Studies*, 1992, vol. 18, pp. 59–87. See also G. Bock and P. Thane (eds), *Maternity and Gender Policies: Women and the Rise of the European Welfare States, 1880–1950*, London, Routledge, 1991; S. Koven and S. Michel (eds), *Mothers of a New World: Maternalist Politics and the Origins of Welfare States*, New York, Routledge, 1993, for discussions of the complex and often contradictory effects on citizenship of the varying histories of 'maternalist politics' in different Western states.

46 In explanation of the focus on worker status, Lewis and Astrom, in 'Equality, difference and state welfare', observe that redefinitions of caring have 'little purchase' in 'liberal welfare regimes [where] the boundaries between primary and secondary labor markets and between paid and unpaid work have been more tightly drawn during the last decade' (p. 80). For a discussion of the differential benefits for labourers and mothers in the United States, see N. Fraser, 'Women, welfare and the politics of need interpretation', in *Unruly Practices: Power, Discourse and Gender in Contemporary Social Theory*, Minneapolis, Minnesota, University of Minnesota Press, 1989, pp. 144–60. See also Pateman, 'The patriarchal welfare state', in which the analysis of differential benefits is extended to Britain and Australia.

47 F. Piven, 'Ideology and the state: women, power and the welfare state', in L. Gordon (ed.), *Women, the State and Welfare*, Madison, Wisconsin, University of Wisconsin Press, 1990, pp. 250–64, discusses similar opportunities for citizen empowerment in the context of women's involvement in welfare services in the United States.

48 Hernes, *Welfare State and Woman Power*, p. 162.

49 This theme recurs frequently in feminist discussions of the boundaries of the political. See, for example, A. Bookman and S. Morgen (eds), *Women and the Politics of Empowerment*, Philadelphia, Temple University Press, 1988; G. West and R. Blumberg (eds), *Women and Social Protest*, New York, Oxford University Press, 1990. It derives considerable support from the work of Foucault: see, for example, M. Foucault, *Power/Knowledge: Selected Interviews and Other Writings, 1972–1977*, C. Gordon (ed.), trans. C. Gordon *et al.*, New York, Pantheon Books, 1980.

50 Pitkin, 'Justice', p. 347.

51 P. Boling, 'The democratic potential of mothering', *Political Theory*, 1991, vol. 19, p. 611. Boling quotes Dietz, 'Citizenship with a feminist face' as an example of this sort of criticism.

52 *Ibid.*, p. 616. For other, specific historical accounts of this process, see T. Kaplan, 'Female consciousness and collective action: the case of Barcelona, 1910–1918', in N. Keohane, M. Rosaldo and B. Gelpi (eds), *Feminist Theory: A Critique of Ideology*, Chicago, University of Chicago Press, 1982, pp. 55–76; M. Navarro, 'The personal is political: las madres de Plazo de Mayo', in S. Eckstein (ed.), *Power and Popular Protest: Latin American Social Movements*, Berkeley, California, University of California Press, 1989, pp. 241–58.

53 Tronto, *Moral Boundaries*, pp. 137, 167–70.

54 Jim Tully suggested this concept and helped me to understand its implications.

55 See Hernes, *Welfare State and Woman Power*, p. 158. See also N. Fraser, 'What's critical about critical theory? The case of Habermas and gender', in *Unruly Practices*, pp. 113–43.

56 Hernes, *Welfare State and Woman Power*, especially pp. 161–3. See also M. Ruggie, *The State and Working Women: A Comparative Study of Britain and Sweden*, Princeton, New Jersey, Princeton University Press, 1984; Siim, 'Towards a feminist rethinking'.

57 Lewis and Astrom, 'Equality, difference and state welfare', p. 81.

58 M. Walker, 'What does the different voice say? Gilligan's women and moral philosophy', *The Journal of Value Inquiry*, 1989, vol. 23, p. 127.

59 M. Walker, 'Partial consideration', *Ethics*, 1991, vol. 101, pp. 758–74.

60 See S. Benhabib, 'The generalized and the concrete other: the Kohlberg–Gilligan controversy and moral theory', in E. Kittay and D. Meyers (eds), *Women and Moral Theory*, Totowa, New Jersey, Rowman & Littlefield, 1987, pp. 154–77.

61 Glasser, 'Prisoners of benevolence', p. 123.

62 M. Heidegger, *Being and Time*, trans. J. Macquarrie and E. Robinson, New York, Harper & Row, 1962, p. 158. Habermas, *Theory of Communicative Action* and Foucault, *Discipline and Punish*, also foreground ways in which institutional practices tend to render citizens compliant with managerial requirements.

63 Card, 'Gender and moral luck', p. 210.

64 See D. Rothman, 'The state as parent: social policy in the Progressive era', in Gaylin, *Doing Good*, pp. 69–95, for a sketch of the proliferation of rights-based social reform movements on the 'civil rights' model. See also the discussion of the 'rights-analysis approach' in US law relating to mentally handicapped persons in Minow, *Making All the Difference*, pp. 107–14, 131–45.

65 M. Ignatieff, *The Needs of Strangers*, New York, Penguin, 1984, p. 13; Benhabib, 'The generalized and the concrete other', pp. 163–7; I. Young, *Justice and the Politics of Difference*, Princeton, New Jersey, Princeton University Press, 1990, pp. 96–7. See also the critique of the impoverished language of individualism and the liberal rights tradition in R. Bellah *et al.*, *Habits of the Heart: Individualism and Commitment in American Life*, Berkeley, California, University of California Press, 1985.

66 Ignatieff, *Needs of Strangers*, pp. 12–14.

67 Pitkin, 'Justice', p. 345. See also Phillips, *Engendering Democracy*, pp. 160–1.

68 S. Okin, *Justice, Gender and the Family*, New York, Basic Books, 1989.

69 Minow, *Making All the Difference*, p. 219 (hereafter MAD followed by page numbers). See also E. Schneider, 'The dialectic of rights and politics: perspectives from the women's movement', *New York University Law Review*, 1986, vol. 61, pp. 589–651 and H. Lessard, 'Relationship, particularity, and change: reflections on R. v. Morgentaler and feminist approaches to liberty', *McGill Law Journal*, 1991, vol. 36, pp. 263–307, who argue that reconceptions of rights cannot achieve

social change without the transformation of the forms that define and enforce them.

70 Minow discusses this tradition through an analysis of three different forms it has taken, viz: 'abnormal-persons approach', 'rights-analysis approach' and the 'benevolence' approach adopted in the social reform of the Progressivist era (MAD 105–10, 239–66).

71 This kind of position is adopted by Noddings, *Caring*.

72 See, for example, Walker, 'What does the different voice say?'

73 Gilligan, *In a Different Voice*, and 'Moral orientation and moral development', in Kittay and Meyers, *Women and Moral Theory*, pp. 19–33, and with A. Rogers and L. Brown, 'Epilogue: soundings into development', in C. Gilligan, N. Lyons and T. Hammer (eds), *Making Connections: The Relational Worlds of Adolescent Girls at Emma Willard School*, Cambridge, Massachusetts, Harvard University Press, 1990, pp. 314–34, are sometimes read in this light. Tronto, *Moral Boundaries*, with its more instrumental conception of care, can also be seen as contributing to this project.

74 More precisely, Minow argues that the relational perspectives that have emerged from feminist discussions, specifically discussions of caring, are 'most accessible and congenial' to her project (MAD 192–4), though she draws from a much wider set of practices ranging through sociology, physics, philosophy, anthropology and literary theory.

75 For a range of reviews of Gilligan's work see the essays in *Social Research*, 1983, vol. 50 and *Signs*, 1986, vol. 11, pp. 304–33.

76 Minow notes the corroboration of this theme in the work of feminist historians, scientist Barbara McClintock, and feminist literary theorists (MAD 198–205).

77 The discussion of nursing in Chapter 3 has shown how this dynamic operates in medical science.

78 K. Bartlett, 'Feminist legal methods', *Harvard Law Review*, 1990, vol. 103, pp. 880–7.

79 Not surprisingly this refusal has been the focus of attack by critics who deny the epistemological validity of her engaged, contextual presentation of research. See, for example, L. Walker, 'Sex differences in the development of moral reasoning: a critical review', *Child Development*, 1984, vol. 55, pp. 667–91; C. Greeno and E. Macoby, 'How different is the "different voice"?', *Signs*, 1986, vol. 11, pp. 310–16.

80 H. Boxenbaum, 'Scientific creativity: a review', *Drug Metabolism Reviews*, 1991, vol. 23, pp. 473–92.

81 As Walker notes in 'What does the different voice say?', pp. 128–9, the centrality of the value of caring attachments may be interpreted in different ways. Noddings, *Caring*, for example, argues that the creation and maintenance of caring relations is intrinsically good. Walker suggests that Gilligan's subjects affirm caring for its extrinsic values – that is, for creating the necessary conditions for varied human goods to emerge and flourish.

82 M. Friedman, 'Beyond caring: the de-moralization of gender', in M. Hanen and K. Nielsen (eds), *Science, Morality & Feminist Theory*, Calgary, Alberta, University of Calgary Press, 1987, p. 106.

83 P. Collins, 'Shifting the center: race, class, and feminist theorizing about motherhood', in E. N. Glenn, G. Chang and L. R. Forcey (eds), *Mothering: Ideology, Experience and Agency*, New York, Routledge, 1994, pp. 45–64. See also B. Houston, 'Are children's rights wrong rights?', *Proceedings of the Philosophy of Education Society*, 1992, vol. 48, pp. 145–55, for a discussion of the ways in which considerations of children's rights are affected by taking a 'relational' perspective.

84 Houston, 'Rescuing womanly virtues: some dangers of moral reclamation', in Hanen and Nielsen, *Science, Morality & Feminist Theory*, pp. 237–62; S. Hoagland, *Lesbian Ethics: Toward New Value*, Palo Alto, California, Institute of Lesbian Studies, 1988, pp. 82–6.

85 Mary Daly and Luce Irigaray, for example, have argued that the use of the 'language of the fathers' inevitably capitulates to patriarchal norms. See M. Daly, *Gyn/Ecology: The Meta-ethics of Radical Feminism*, Boston, Beacon Press, 1978; L. Irigaray, *This Sex Which is not One*, trans. C. Porter with C. Burke, Ithaca, New York, Cornell University Press, 1985.

86 See, for example, Schneider, 'The dialectic of rights and politics'; M. Matsuda, 'Looking to the bottom: critical legal studies and reparations', *Harvard Civil Rights–Civil Liberties Law Review*, 1987, vol. 22, pp. 323–99; P. Williams, 'Alchemical notes: reconstructing ideals from deconstructed rights', *Harvard Civil Rights–Civil Liberties Law Review*, 1987, vol. 22, pp. 401–33; Bartlett, 'Feminist legal methods'; Lessard, 'Relationship, particularity and change'.

87 Pateman, *Sexual Contract*; N. Hirschman, *Rethinking Obligation: A Feminist Method For Political Theory*, Ithaca, New York, Cornell University Press, 1992.

88 A. Jonasdottir, 'On the concept of interest, women's interests, and the limitations of interest theory', in Jones and Jonasdottir, *The Political Interests of Gender*, pp. 33–65; N. Fraser, 'Struggle over needs: outline of a socialist feminist critical theory of late capitalist political culture', in *Unruly Practices*, pp. 161–87, and 'Talking about needs'.

89 Young, *Justice and the Politics of Difference*; Phillips, *Engendering Democracy* and *Democracy and Difference*.

90 Held, *Feminist Morality*; K. Jones, *Compassionate Authority: Democracy and the Representation of Women*, New York, Routledge, 1993.

EPILOGUE

1 S. M. Neysmith, 'From community care to a social model of care', in C.T. Baines, P.M. Evans and S.M. Neysmith (eds), *Women's Caring: Feminist Perspectives on Social Welfare*, Toronto, McLelland & Stewart, 1991, p. 281.

2 Neysmith, 'From community care', pp. 282–3.

Index

relations: citizenship 141–5, 150,
152, 164, 177, 182, 186;
friendship 60–3, 65–7, 70–4, 78,
80, 85, 88, 90–2, 94–5, 98–100;
mothering 21–6, 28, 30–2,
34–40, 42–9, 51–8; nursing
101–9, 112, 114–17, 119–28, 135,
137–8
relativism 179, 183
replication 22
reproduction 21, 31, 147, 161,
177–9
respect 17
responsibility: care and 6, 10;
citizenship and 144, 146, 148,
150–1, 154–7, 159–60, 162, 164,
166–7, 178–80; friendship and
60, 78, 97; mothering and 25,
34–9, 45–6, 51–2, 54, 56–8;
nursing and 101, 104, 115, 127,
135, 138
responsiveness 6, 8, 17, 21, 28,
31–2, 33–5, 58, 78–9, 84, 87,
90–1, 101, 109, 140, 147, 164,
172–4
responsivity 69, 75, 83, 87, 98,
142–3, 148, 151
Reverby, Susan 128–31, 133, 139
Richards, Jeffrey 88
rights: care 6, 186; citizenship
142–3, 148–51, 158, 161, 166–9,
174–8, 180–2; friendship 61, 73,
78, 91; mothering 22; nursing
119, 126, 133
risk 26–7, 52, 84, 86–7, 88, 95
role: ascription 185; of caring 155;
of citizen 162; of friend 60, 81;
gender 23, 57, 104, 125, 129,
131–2, 136; of mother 21, 24,
42–3; of nurse 110–11; of self
79; social 5, 8, 88
Ross, Rupert 19
Rossiter, Amy 24, 45–58, 139
Rubin, Lillian 80–1, 83, 99, 114
Ruddick, Sara: comparison with
Rossiter 45–51, 55–6, 58; on
mothering 24–45; mothering
and citizenship 148, 173;
mothering and friendship 69,

74, 82; mothering and nursing
109–10, 116, 121–2, 139

Scudder, John 125–8, 138–9
seeing 181
self, concept of 42–3, 96, 113
self-affirmation 80–1, 83–4, 86, 88,
90–2, 94–5
self-definition 90, 92, 97, 99
self-disclosure 75, 77, 81, 83, 84, 86
self-esteem 39, 56, 72, 76, 83, 90,
116, 119, 123, 151, 156
self-help groups 156
self-interest 65, 71, 77, 80, 98
self-knowledge 32, 34, 39, 71–2,
76, 80–3, 88
self-loss 30, 39, 43, 50, 55, 57, 84,
92, 102
self-love 70–1, 98
self-objectification 103–4
self-questioning 35
self-reflection 119–20
self-respect 40, 122, 167
self-sacrifice 1, 8, 35–6, 43, 55, 58,
123, 124, 130–1, 134, 175, 180
self-sufficiency 41, 86, 88, 148, 150
self-understanding 11, 17, 166
self-validation 72, 80, 81–2, 91, 93,
95, 120
self-worth 56, 94–5, 120
Shakespeare, W. 88
sharing 29–30, 61, 64, 67–9, 72,
74–6, 80, 82–3, 86, 92, 94–5, 111,
172, 174
Sherman, Nancy 64, 69
Sidgwick, Henry 3
similarity 62, 66, 71–2, 74–6, 82,
99, 167, 175–81
social context 4, 38, 46–8, 52, 57,
121, 155, 162
social organization: citizenship
and 141, 146–8, 150–1, 153–4,
156–9, 161, 164, 168, 174;
friendship and 63, 73–4, 76–7,
84, 89, 91, 93, 98; mothering
and 45, 49, 53–6, 58–9; nursing
and 108, 115, 124, 184
social relations: citizenship and
143, 150, 157, 167–9, 172–3,